Interactions 1
Reading

Interactions 1

Reading

4th Edition

Elaine Kirn
West Los Angeles College

Pamela Hartmann
Los Angeles Unified School District

McGraw-Hill Contemporary

McGraw-Hill/Contemporary

*A Division of The **McGraw-Hill** Companies*

Interactions 1 Reading, 4th Edition

Published by McGraw-Hill/Contemporary, a business unit of The McGraw-Hill Companies, Inc., 1221 Avenue of the Americas, New York, NY 10020. Copyright © 2002, 1996, 1990, 1985 by The McGraw-Hill Companies, Inc. All rights reserved. No part of this publication may be reproduced or distributed in any form or by any means, or stored in a database or retrieval system, without the prior written consent of The McGraw-Hill Companies, Inc., including, but not limited to, in any network or other electronic storage or transmission, or broadcast for distance learning.

Some ancillaries, including electronic and print components, may not be available to customers outside the United States.

 This book is printed on recycled, acid-free paper containing 10% postconsumer waste.

7 8 9 0 QPD/QPD 0 9 8 7
13 14 15 QPD/QPD 0 9 8 7 6

ISBN-13: 978-0-07-233068-7
ISBN-10: 0-07-233068-6

ISBN-13: 978-0-07-118012-2 (ISE)
ISBN-10: 0-07-118012-5 (ISE)

Editorial director: *Tina B. Carver*
Series editor: *Annie Sullivan*
Developmental editor: *Louis Carrillo*
Director of marketing and sales: *Thomas P. Dare*
Project manager: *Sheila M Frank*
Production supervisor: *Laura Fuller*
Coordinator of freelance design: *David W. Hash*
Interior designer: *Michael Warrell, Design Solutions*
Photo research coordinator: *John C. Leland*
Photo researcher: *Amelia Ames Hill Associates/Amy Bethea*
Supplement coordinator: *Genevieve Kelley*
Compositor: *David Corona Design*
Typeface: *10.5/12 Times Roman*
Printer: *Quebecor World Dubuque, IA*

The credits section for this book begins on page 273 and is considered an extension of the copyright page.

INTERNATIONAL EDITION ISBN 0-07-118012-5
Copyright © 2002. Exclusive rights by The McGraw-Hill Companies, Inc., for manufacture and export. This book cannot be re-exported from the country to which it is sold by McGraw-Hill. The International Edition is not available in North America.

www.mhcontemporary.com/interactionsmosaic

Interactions 1

Reading

Interactions 1 **Reading**

Boost your students' academic success!

Interactions Mosaic, 4th edition is the newly revised five-level, four-skill comprehensive ESL/EFL series designed to prepare students for academic content. The themes are integrated across proficiency levels and the levels are articulated across skill strands. The series combines communicative activities with skill-building exercises to boost students' academic success.

Interactions Mosaic, 4th edition features

- updated content
- five videos of authentic news broadcasts
- expansion opportunities through the Website
- new audio programs for the listening/speaking and reading books
- an appealing fresh design
- user-friendly instructor's manuals with placement tests and chapter quizzes

In This Chapter gives students a preview of the upcoming material.

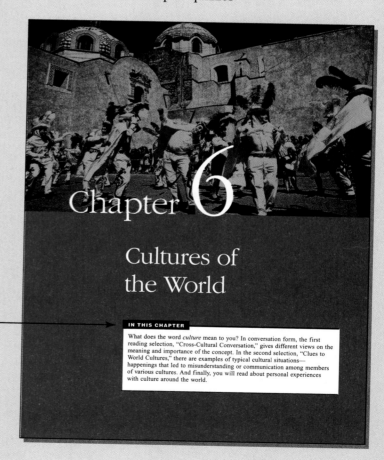

Chapter **6**

Cultures of the World

IN THIS CHAPTER

What does the word *culture* mean to you? In conversation form, the first reading selection, "Cross-Cultural Conversation," gives different views on the meaning and importance of the concept. In the second selection, "Clues to World Cultures," there are examples of typical cultural situations— happenings that led to misunderstanding or communication among members of various cultures. And finally, you will read about personal experiences with culture around the world.

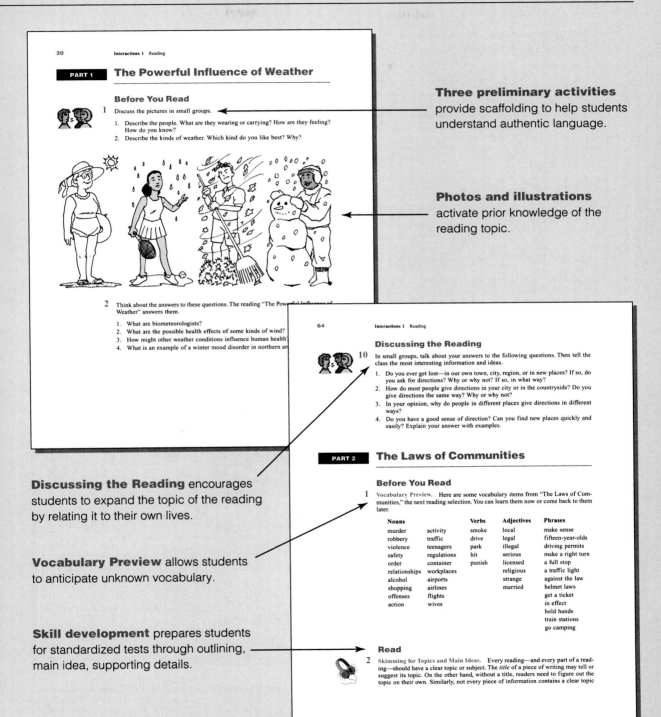

Three preliminary activities provide scaffolding to help students understand authentic language.

Photos and illustrations activate prior knowledge of the reading topic.

Discussing the Reading encourages students to expand the topic of the reading by relating it to their own lives.

Vocabulary Preview allows students to anticipate unknown vocabulary.

Skill development prepares students for standardized tests through outlining, main idea, supporting details.

PART 3 ## Vocabulary and Language Learning Skills

1 Recognizing Similar Meanings and Meaning Categories. Here are two good ways to learn new vocabulary quickly: look at the words and phrases with similar meanings together and learn items in meaning categories at the same time. With both methods, the words should be of the same *part of speech.* (The major examples of "parts of speech" are nouns, verbs, adjectives, and adverbs.)

In each of the following groups of words, do the vocabulary items belong together because they have the same or similar meanings? If so, write S for *similar* on the line. Or are the vocabulary items members of the same meaning category or classification? If so, write C on the line and name the possible category. Two items are done as examples.

1. __C__ walking / riding a bicycle / taking the bus / driving

2. _____ Oslo, Norway / Tokyo, Japan / Mexico City, Mexico / Valencia, Spain

3. __S__ rules / laws / regulations

4. _____ not often / seldom / rarely / infrequently

5. _____ make sense / seem reasonable / have a purpose / be understandable

6. _____ helmet laws / driving permits / fines for jaywalking / the legal driving age

7. _____ northeast / southwest / northwest / southeast

8. _____ move / motion / gesture / use body / language

9. _____ a colon / a semicolon / a comma / a period

For more practice, tell or write more items with similar meanings to the words in some of the groups. And you can tell or list more vocabulary items like the members of the categories.

2 Recognizing Nouns and Verbs. A very useful vocabula recognizing parts of speech. Some words can be more than examples, in the first sentence that follows, the words *motions* nouns; in the second sentence, the same words are verbs.

Two examples of body language are *motions* and *gest motions* or *gestures* with the hands, arms, or other body par On the other hand, some words in noun and verb pairs endings. Here are some examples of related words from Ch

Noun	Verb	Noun
movement	move	direction
expression	express	illustration

Vocabulary and language-learning strategies for synonyms, antonyms, context clues, and word families give students comprehension and self-assessment tools.

Real-life reading connects the classroom to real life through ads, application forms, brochures, and other realia.

Video news broadcasts immerse students in authentic language, complete with scaffolding and follow-up activities to reinforce reading skills.

Video Activities: Sight for the Blind

Before You Watch. Discuss the following questions with your class or in a small group.

1. How can technology help physically challenged people? Give examples.
2. As a child, did you ever try to "pretend" you were blind (unable to see)? How did it feel?

Watch. Write answers to these questions.

1. Who is Jerry, and who is Craig? _____
2. How does the new technology help Jerry? _____
3. Jerry is _____ years old. He became blind _____ years ago.
4. Craig has been blind for _____ year(s).

Watch Again. Circle the correct answers.

1. Craig became blind
   a. at birth   b. in an accident   c. because of a disease
2. According to Craig, when people pretend to be blind, they always cheat. He means:
   a. They ask someone to help them.
   b. They never really close their eyes.
   c. They open their eyes just a little.
3. The new device that helps Jerry to see uses a
   a. camera   b. computer   c. transistor
4. Craig's biggest dream is to _____ again.
5. How does Craig feel about the future?
   a. sad   b. hopeful   c. worried

After You Watch. The underlined words and phrases on the left are from the video segment. Use the context to match them with their definitions on the right.

1. _____ George lost his <u>sight</u> four years ago.	a. quickly
2. _____ You can become blind if you have a <u>disease</u> in your eye.	b. safe
	c. connected
3. _____ It is hard to feel <u>secure</u> if you cannot see.	d. a machine
4. _____ Doctors <u>hooked</u> the patient <u>up</u> to a machine.	e. the ability to see
5. _____ A new <u>device</u> can help blind people to see.	f. sickness
6. _____ Technology is advancing <u>at a torrid pace</u>. There are new inventions every day.	

Don't forget to check out the new *Interactions Mosaic* Website at www.mhcontemporary.com/interactionsmosaic.

- Traditional practice and interactive activities
- Links to student and teacher resources
- Cultural activities
- Focus on Testing
- Activities from the Website are also provided on CD-ROM

Interactions 1 Reading

Reading Skills/Strategies	Language	Real-Life Reading	Video Topics
■ Main idea ■ Finding details ■ Recognizing topic sentences	■ Recognizing book structure	■ College catalogs	■ Exchange Students
■ Recognizing paragraph topics ■ Main idea	■ Summarizing paragraphs	■ Physical and political maps	■ Winter Storm
■ Recognizing paragraph topics ■ Main idea ■ Supporting details ■ Paragraph titles and topics	■ Summarizing paragraphs	■ Menus and food labels	■ Treat Yourself Well Campaign
■ General and specific topics ■ Main idea ■ Skimming	■ Using colons, commas, semi-colons, quotation marks ■ Summarizing and paraphrasing ■ Recognizing nouns and verbs	■ Community services and signs	■ A Homeless Shelter
■ Paragraphs in time order ■ Main idea ■ Time details ■ Skimming for time and place	■ Time expressions ■ Summarizing historical information ■ Recognizing nouns and adjectives	■ Classified ads	■ Asthma and Dust Mites
■ Recognizing details of opinions	■ Conversation in paragraph form ■ Summarizing narratives ■ Recognizing nouns, verbs, and adjectives ■ Adverbs of manner	■ Calendar notices and announcements	■ Chinese New Year

(continued on next page)

Reading Skills/Strategies	Language	Real-Life Reading	Video Topics
■ Recognizing outline form ■ Main idea	■ Connecting words and phrases ■ Summarizing ■ Finding supporting reasons	■ Instruction for health emergencies	■ Marathon Man
■ Main idea	■ Comparison and contrast ■ Sequence of plot events ■ Summarizing a plot	■ Entertainment ads	■ Quiz Shows
■ Main idea ■ Making inferences	■ Conversation in paragraph form ■ Ellipsis ■ Summarizing	■ Personal ads	■ Online Love Story
■ Main idea ■ Using context to supply reference ■ Making inferences	■ Summarizing	■ Announcement and greeting cards	■ Puerto Rican Day Parade
■ Reviewing outline form ■ Main idea ■ Making inferences	■ Italics and quotation marks ■ Summarizing	■ Technology instructions	■ Sight for the Blind
■ Completing an outline ■ Recognizing exaggeration ■ Main idea ■ Recognizing point of view ■ Making inferences	■ Summarizing	■ Surveys and questionnaires	■ Spoiled Kids

Chapter 1

School Life Around the World

IN THIS CHAPTER

You will read about international students in higher education around the world. You will look at experiences and opinions of college life in different places.

PART 1

International Students

Before You Read

1 Discuss the pictures in small groups.

1. Name the places, things, and people.
2. Describe the pictures. Where is the place? What kind of place is it? Where are the people from? What do they do?
3. How is this place like your school? How is it different?

2   Think about the answers to these questions. The reading answers them.

1. What are international students? What are institutions of higher learning?
2. Where do most international students go to school?
3. Why do students want to attend colleges and universities far from home?
4. Why do institutions of higher learning want students from other countries?

3   **Vocabulary Preview.**   Here are some vocabulary items from the first reading. You can learn them now or come back to them later.

Nouns	Verbs	Adjectives	Adverb	Phrases
meaning	mean	international	abroad	attend college
a phrase	leave	foreign		by far
culture	attend	abroad		college degrees
nations	need	available		real life
a level		expensive		charge tuition
industrialization		private		pay fees
technology		legal		away from home
experience		full		spend money
business		various		save money
engineering				
subjects				
governments				
companies				
workers				
knowledge				
skills				
internationalism				
a campus				
ideas				
opinions				
a state				
recreation				

Read

4   Read the following material quickly. Then read the explanation and do the exercises after the reading.

International Students

[A]   All around the world, there are international students at institutions of higher learning. The definition of an international student is "a postsecondary student from another country." The meaning of postsecondary is "after high school." Another phrase for international students is "foreign students." The word *foreign* means "of a different country or culture." Even so, some people don't like the word *foreign,* so they use the phrase "international students." For institution of higher learning, they usually say "university," "college," or "school."

[B]   International students leave their home countries and go to school abroad. One meaning of the word abroad is "in a foreign place." By far, the country with the most students from abroad is the United States. Canada, Great Britain, and some European countries also have a lot of students from other countries. But more and more, students from around the world attend colleges and universities in the developing nations of Latin America, Asia, and Africa. Developing nations don't yet have a high level of industrialization or technology.

[C]   Why do high school and college graduates go to colleges and universities far from their homes? Undergraduates are postsecondary students without college degrees. Often, undergraduates want the experience of life in new cultures. Maybe they want to learn another language well, in school and in real life. Many older students want degrees in business, engineering, or technology. These subjects are not always available in their home countries. Some governments and companies send their best graduate students and workers to other countries for new knowledge and skills. And some students from expensive private schools at home save money through study abroad, especially in developing nations.

[D]   Why do institutions of higher learning want international students? Of course, students from other countries and cultures bring internationalism to the classroom or campus. They bring different languages, customs, ideas, and opinions from many places around the world. Usually, they study hard. Also, educational institutions need money. Tuition is the fee or charge for instruction, and private schools everywhere charge high tuition. One definition of citizens and immigrants is "legal members of a nation or country." International students are not citizens or immigrants, so they pay full tuition and fees to state or government schools. And all students away from home spend money for housing, food, recreation, and other things. For these reasons, many schools and groups of schools want students from other countries.

[E]   For various reasons, many high school and college graduates want or need to study abroad. For other reasons, many nations want or need students from other countries and cultures on their college and university campuses.

After You Read

5 **Recognizing Reading Structure: Readings, Chapters, and Paragraphs.** Most reading material has structure. The word structure means "organization or form." This book contains twelve chapters. Chapters are the largest divisions of the book. The title of Chapter 1 is "School Life Around the World." Each chapter of this book contains readings. The title of the first reading in Chapter 1 is "International Students." The information of the reading comes in paragraphs. A paragraph is a division or part about one idea or one kind of information. In the reading, there is a capital letter next to each of the five paragraphs. The information in each paragraph of the reading material answers a different question.

Which question does each paragraph answer? Write the letter A, B, C, D, or E on the line. The first one is done as an example.

1. ___C___ Why do international students go to school abroad?

2. ___B___ In what countries do international students attend colleges and universities?

3. ___A___ What are some definitions of words and phrases in international higher education?

4. ___D___ Why do institutions of higher learning want foreign students?

5. ___E___ What is the conclusion of this reading material?

6 **Understanding the Main Idea.** Often, the information in each paragraph of reading material answers a different question. A one- or two-sentence answer to this question can tell the point or "message" of the paragraph. It is the main idea. Each paragraph in the reading "International Students" has a point. Here are some possible statements of these main ideas. Write T (true) or F (false) on the lines. The first one is done as an example.

1. ___T___ International students in institutions of higher learning are foreign students at colleges and universities around the world.

2. ___F___ The United States and European countries have equal numbers of students from abroad. Foreigners don't study in developing countries.

3. ___F___ High school and college graduates go to school in foreign countries for only one reason. They want to leave home.

4. ___T___ Colleges and universities around the world want international students for several reasons, so they advertise and try to get students in other ways.

5. ___F___ Students don't like to go to school abroad. Colleges and universities don't want learners from other countries.

Now change the untrue sentences to true statements of the point of each paragraph. Here is an example of a correction for No. 2: The United States and some European countries have the most students from abroad. Foreigners also study in developing countries.

7   **Finding Definitions in Context.**   You do not need to look up the meanings of all new words and phrases in a dictionary. You can often find their meanings in the context. The context is the other words in the sentence or paragraph. A definition often comes in a sentence after the verbs *be* or *mean.* Here are some examples of definition sentences. The defined words are in italics. The definitions are in quotation marks.

The definition of a *university* is "an institution of higher learning with one or more undergraduate colleges and graduate schools." The word *college* means "a school of higher learning." And one meaning of the word *school* is "an institution for teaching and learning." What is a *graduate student?* The phrase means "a college student with a bachelor's degree or higher." The word *undergraduate* is for "a college student without a bachelor's degree."

For Nos. 1–4, find definitions in Exercise 7 Finding Definitions in Context. The definitions for Nos. 5–9 are in "International Students" on page 4. (The letters in parentheses are the letters of the paragraphs.)

1. the context _The other words in the sentence or paragraph._

2. a definition _The meaning of word._

3. a university _an institution of higher learning with the one or more_

4. a graduate student _____

5. an international student (A) _____

6. an institution of higher learning (A) _____

7. abroad (B) _____

8. developing nations (B) _____

9. citizens and immigrants (D) _____

For more practice, you can find definitions of more words and phrases. Look for these vocabulary items and others: *college, school, undergraduate, foreign, tuition, structure, chapters, paragraph.*

8   **Answering Paragraph Questions with Details.**   The information in each paragraph of a reading can answer a different question. An answer of one or two sentences can tell the point or main idea of the material. Also, most paragraphs give details of the main idea. The definition of *details* is "single or specific pieces of information." Some kinds of details are examples, facts, and reasons.

Here are five different questions about the information in the reading "International Students." Three details correctly answer each question. The other sentence is untrue or unrelated to the main idea. Cross out the untrue or unrelated detail. The first one is done as an example.

1. What are some definitions of words and phrases in international higher education?

a. The definition of an *international student* is "a postsecondary student from another country."

b. The meaning of *postsecondary* is "after high school."

c. ~~The word *school* usually means "a large group of fish."~~

d. Another phrase for *international students* is "foreign students."

2. Where do international students attend college and universities? (Give three facts.)
   a. The United States has the most students from other countries.
   b. Developing nations have a high level of industrialization or technology.
   c. Many foreign students attend school in Canada, Great Britain, and some European nations.
   d. More and more students from abroad attend school in Latin America, Asia, and Africa.

3. Why do international students go to school abroad? (Give three reasons.)
   a. They want the experience of life and language in another country and culture.
   b. They need technological information and skills not available in their home countries.
   c. They can't pay full tuition to state or government colleges and universities.
   d. In developing nations, they can save money through lower tuition and living costs.

4. Why do institutions of higher learning want international students? (Give three reasons.)
   a. They don't want to send their students to universities in other countries.
   b. International students bring internationalism to the classroom and campus.
   c. People from other countries are usually very good students.
   d. Foreign students pay high tuition and fees and put money into the economy.

For more practice, you can turn back to the Before You Read section on page 2 and answer the questions. Give definitions in your answer to No. 1. Give facts in your answer to No. 2. Give reasons in your answers to Nos. 3 and 4.

Discussing the Reading

9   In small groups, talk about your answers to the following questions. Then tell the class the most interesting information.

1. On the subject of higher education, what are some important vocabulary items? (Some possible examples are degree, visa, program, enrollment, registration, assignment, and sponsor.) What are some definitions of these words and phrases? Why are the items important to you?

2. Are you an international student, a citizen, or an immigrant? Are you studying at a secondary or a postsecondary school? Are you an undergraduate or a graduate student? Give details for your answers.

3. If you are an international student, do you like attending school abroad? If you are not an international student, do you want to study in another country? Give reasons for your answer.

4. Does your school want or need international students on campus? Give facts and reasons for your answer.

PART 2

College Life Around the World

Before You Read

1   **Vocabulary Preview.**   Here are some vocabulary items from the "College Life Around the World" reading. You can learn them now or come back to them later.

Nouns	Verbs	Adjectives	Adverb	Phrases
housing	differ	similar	casually	private homes
apartments	choose	different		public transportation
a subway	use	various		take courses
quizzes	buy	formal		complete requirements
certificates	relax	informal		social lives
a system		individual		financial aid
scholarships		relaxed		take an exit exam
grants		available		business clothes
loans		audio		academic lectures
methods		video		learning resource
styles				centers
titles				a course plan
instructors				educational software
facilities				programs
services				the World Wide Web
resources				the Internet
materials				swimming pools
points				tennis courts
scores				snack bars
assignments				distance learning
equipment				

Read

2   **Recognizing Topic Sentences.**   The word *topic* means "the subject of speech or writing." A paragraph usually tells about one topic. Sometimes the title of a paragraph tells the topic. And sometimes one sentence is the "topic sentence." In a general way, the topic sentence tells the point or main idea of the topic. The topic sentence is often the first sentence of a paragraph, but not always. The other sentences usually give examples or facts or reasons for the main idea. They are the single or specific details.

Example:

Kinds of University Classes in the United States

<u>There are several different kinds of classes on university campuses in the United States</u>. Professors usually teach large undergraduate classes. They give formal lectures. Students listen and write things down. Then they attend discussion groups with teaching assistants. In graduate seminars, small groups of students discuss information and ideas with their instructor and classmates. Distance-learning and online students do most of their work individually in other places. But they sometimes come to a campus for group meetings.

In this example, the title of the paragraph is the topic. It is "Kinds of University Classes." The first sentence is underlined. It is the topic sentence of the paragraph. It gives the main idea of the topic. The other sentences give details about these kinds of classes. They give examples.

Read the following paragraphs quickly. Then underline the topic sentence in each paragraph. The first paragraph is done as an example. Remember that the topic sentence is not always the first sentence.

College Life Around the World

Similarities in Student Life

[A]   At colleges and universities around the world, students from other places live in student housing, apartments, or the private homes of other people. They walk to school or get there by bicycle or by car or with public transportation like the bus or subway. They take courses and attend classes. They study and take quizzes or tests or exams. They complete requirements. After years of study, they get certificates or college degrees. Outside school, they have other interests and family or social lives. <u>In some ways, life on the campuses of institutions of higher learning is the same everywhere in the world</u>.

Systems of Higher Education

[B]   Maybe student life is similar, but the system of higher education differs in countries around the world. For example, in the United States, postsecondary students can live at home and go to community colleges for two years or more. Or they can choose four-year state or private colleges or universities. They can get financial aid, like scholarships, grants, or loans. With undergraduate degrees, they can attend graduate school. The system is different in some countries of Asia or the Middle East, like Iran. There students take an exit exam in their last year of high school. The people with the highest scores attend the best universities in the country. Other students can go to other kinds of colleges or get jobs. There is another system in Germany. In that country, most graduates of academic high schools go to public universities or technical colleges. These school don't charge high tuition or educational fees, and students can stay in school for many years.

Differences in Teaching and Learning Styles

[C]   But not only the system of higher education can vary. Teaching and learning methods and styles differ in various cultures, at different colleges and universities, and in individual courses. For example, the atmosphere in many classrooms is very formal. Students use titles for their instructors, like "Professor

Smith," "Mrs. Jones," and so on. Some teachers wear business clothes and give academic lectures. Other classrooms have an informal atmosphere. Instructors dress casually, and students use their first names. In this relaxed atmosphere, class members work together in groups. They give their opinions and talk about their ideas. Some teachers always follow a course plan or the textbook. They give a lot of assignments. They give points, scores, or grades for homework. In their courses, students take many quizzes, tests, and exams. All over the world, there are teaching and learning differences.

Campus Facilities and Services

[D] And what about the facilities and services available to students at college and university campuses around the world? At many institutions of higher learning, resources for learning and recreation are available to students. At libraries, they can read and study books and other materials. At learning resource centers, they can often work on computers. Maybe they can use educational software programs or the World Wide Web or Internet. Sometimes audio or video equipment is available. And people can buy books, supplies, and other things at campus stores. Also, learners can get advice from counselors and individual help with their courses from tutors. Maybe they can relax and have fun on campus too. Some schools have swimming pools, tennis courts, and other sports facilities. Most have snack bars, cafeterias, or other eating places. And at some schools, not all students go to the campus. They take Internet courses by computer, see and hear lectures on television, or use other kinds of distance learning.

After You Read

3 **Learning to Summarize.** How can you show your understanding of reading material? You can summarize it. A summary is a short statement of the main points and important information (details) of reading material. It has some words from the reading and some not from the reading. A summary of a paragraph has only a few sentences. Here is a possible summary of Paragraph A from the reading "College Life Around the World."

In many ways, college life is the same in different places around the world. Students live in similar kinds of places and get to school in similar ways. They attend classes, study, and get certificates or degrees for their hard work. And they have interests and lives outside school too.

How do you learn to summarize? You think about the meaning of reading material in English. Then you tell the main point and the important details in your own words.

Work in groups of four. Choose a different paragraph (A, B, C, or D) from the reading "College Life Around the World." Read it carefully. Begin with the topic or title. Summarize the main idea and important details from your paragraph. Then tell or read your summary to your group.

Discussing the Reading

4   In small groups, talk about your answers to these questions. Then tell the class the most interesting information.

1. Talk about your student life. Where do you live? How do you get to school? What do you do there? What other interests and family or social life do you have?
2. Talk about the system of higher education in your native country or culture. What kinds of colleges and universities are there? What are the requirements for admission? Do they charge tuition or fees? Is there financial aid?
3. Talk about the teaching styles and methods of your instructors. Are they formal or relaxed? Do they use course plans and textbooks? Do they give assignments, test, and grades? Tell about your learning style.
4. What campus facilities and services does your school have? What learning and recreational resources do you use? Where are they?

Talk It Over

What do you prefer in student life? From each box, choose one or two preferences. Circle those words and phrases. In groups, tell your preferences and the reasons for them. Compare your answers with the choices of your classmates.

1. Housing	2. Transportation	3. Activities
Home life with my family Student housing Apartment life The private homes of other people	Walking Bicycle Car The bus, subway, or other public transportation	Taking courses and attending classes Individual study Student recreation or sports Other interests outside school
4. Kinds of Schools	**5. Charges and Payments**	**6. Teaching and Learning Styles**
High school or secondary school A community or technical college A public or government or state university A private school	High tuition and fees Low education charges Scholarships, loans, and other financial aid Private, individual payment of costs	Formal lectures and atmosphere Informal group work with discussion of ideas and opinions A course plan and textbook Individual assignments, homework, grades, and exams
7. Facilities	**8. Services for Students**	**9. Other Choices and Preferences**
A library with books and other reading material A learning center with audio, visual, and computer equipment Swimming pools, tennis courts, and other sports facilities A snack bar, cafeteria, or other eating place	Academic counseling Tutoring help or study groups Individual help with personal and real-life problems A student store with supplies and other things	A casual, relaxed student life A hard program of study A good family or social life Others _____

PART 3	# Vocabulary and Language Learning Skills

1 **Finding Definitions of Vocabulary Items.**   Most language learners want the definitions of new words and phrases. A definition can be a short or long phrase. A good definition explains a meaning in simple words.

Match the definitions in Column B with the vocabulary items in Column A.

Column A

1. __i__ international students
2. __d__ postsecondary
3. __b__ abroad
4. __a__ certificates and degrees
5. __e__ college tuition
6. __j__ academic lectures
7. __f__ campus facilities
8. __c__ transportation
9. __g__ distance learning
10. __h__ the Internet

Column B

a. papers saying you have completed a course of studies

b. out of your country or in foreign places

c. methods or ways of going from one place to another, like cars, bicycles, and buses

d. after high school

e. charges or fees for instruction

f. the buildings and equipment of a school, college, or university

g. courses given by means of video, video conferencing, or computers to students in various locations

h. a system of instant communication by computer

i. college or university learners from other countries

j. formal talks by professors or instructors on subjects of study

For more vocabulary practice, give the reasons for your answers. Cover the items in Column A and try to remember them from the definitions in Column B. Or cover the definitions and give definitions for the Column A items in your own words. And ask for and give definitions of other vocabulary items in Chapter 1.

2 **Recognizing Words with the Same or Similar Meanings.**   The definition of a vocabulary item is an explanation of its meaning in a phrase. Some words in a definition can have the same meaning as the vocabulary item. Or they can have a similar meaning in some but not all contexts. The word *similar* means "alike but not exactly the same."

In each group of vocabulary items from Chapter 1, find the three words with the same or similar meanings. Cross out the word that doesn't belong.

1. country   nation   ~~software~~   culture

2. students   atmosphere   learners   class members

3. teachers   instructors   professors   undergraduates

4. ~~higher~~   ways   methods   styles

5. individual   casual   informal   relaxed

6. a quiz   a cafeteria   a test   an exam

7. a score   the textbook   points   a grade

8. scholarships   titles   loans   financial aid

9. technical   assignment   homework   requirement

10. exit   differ   vary   be different

For more practice, give the reasons for your answers. Give more words and phrases with the same meanings as other vocabulary items in Chapter 1.

3 **Real-Life Reading: School Materials.**   Learners often find new vocabulary items in real-life reading material. They can find out the definitions of these words and phrases in the context. They can learn other new words and phrases with the same or similar meanings.

On page 14 is list of facilities and services at a community college. There is also a campus map with the names of places on it. Which words do you know? Underline them. Which words are new or difficult for you? Circle them. In groups or in class, ask for their meanings. Work with your classmates and instructor. Think of possible definitions and words or phrases with the same or similar meanings.

For more vocabulary practice, make questions with some of the words and phrases like this:

Where is/are (the) _____ on campus?

Answer the questions with information from the campus map or with real facts about your school.

College Facilities and Services

Admissions and Records
- Add Forms for Classes
- Applications for Admission
- College Registration
- Enrollment in Courses
- Grade Transcripts

Administration, Business Services
- Administrative Offices
- Applications for Public Transportation Passes
- Parking Permits
- Payment of Registration Fees and Tuition

Athletics
- The Gymnasium
- The Locker Rooms
- The Physical Education Offices
- The Swimming Pool
- The Stadium and Track
- The Tennis Courts

Bookstore
- Books, Magazines, and Newspapers
- School Supplies
- School Clothing
- Coffee and Snacks
- Textbooks for Courses
- Used Book Buyback

Community Services
- The Amphitheater
- The Planetarium
- The Art Gallery
- Non-Credit Courses
- The Performing Arts Center
- Sports Events

Counseling
- Academic Counseling
- Career Planning
- Graduation Requirements
- Help with Personal Problems
- Student Educational Plans
- The Transfer Center (to Four-Year Universities)

Library Building
- The Audio and Video Center
- Books
- Magazines and Newspapers
- The Computer Center (Educational Software and the Internet)
- The Learning Resource Center

Police and Campus Operations
- Emergency and Safety Solutions
- The Emergency Health Center
- Lost and Found
- Maintenance
- Payment of Parking Violations
- Shipping and Receiving

Student Services and Activities
- The Associated Students Organization (ASO)
- The Child Care Center
- The Disabled Students Center
- Financial Aid (Scholarships, Grants, Loans)
- Student Clubs and Organizations

Campus Map

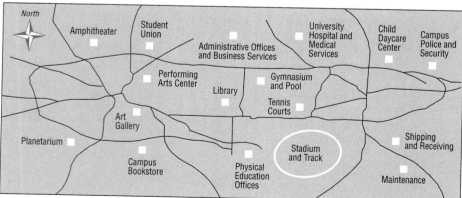

4   More Real-Life Reading.   Here are some kinds of reading material about college life. Check (✔) the kinds available at your school. Bring some examples to class. Write down the important vocabulary items. Give simple definitions of the words and phrases.

_____ a catalog of courses
_____ a course schedule
_____ a handbook of information for students
_____ a campus map
_____ a list of campus facilities and services
_____ information about educational programs
_____ a page from the school Website
_____ a school newspaper
_____ other _____

| PART 4 |

Personal Stories and Humor

1   The following stories in the reading "Experiences and Opinions of College Life" relate various experiences of college life around the world. They also give different opinions or points of view. Follow these steps for the stories.

1. Read them quickly. Summarize the main ideas.
2. Answer your instructor's questions about the stories, or ask and answer questions of your own.
3. Tell your opinions of the ideas in the stories.
4. Tell or write your own story about education or college life.

Experiences and Opinions of College Life

I am a foreign student from Germany. I like the United States very much, and the university campus is beautiful. My favorite places are the swimming pool, the tennis courts, and the other athletic facilities. The student eating places and store are wonderful. My teachers and classmates are nice too. Even so, I don't like the North American system of courses, assignments, test, and grades. In my country, students have more academic freedom and less structure. We don't have to attend lectures, classes, or seminars every day. We don't do homework or have quizzes in every course. The only requirement is a certificate of completion for a certain number of courses. The certificate is proof of attendance. After three to five years of attendance, we take final exams. If we pass these important tests, we get a university degree. We learn the information and skills, so we graduate. In my opinion, that's a better system.

I am a student at an institution of higher learning in China. In colleges in my country, there is a lot of structure and not much academic freedom. Every day the students walk to school or get there by bicycle or public transportation. They listen carefully to formal lectures. Every professor and teaching assistant follows a course plan. After class meetings the students do their assignments and study. They practice their skills in all subjects. They respect the knowledge and opinions of their teachers very much. Why don't students in China want to discuss their private or individual experiences or ideas? Because they can't create new things and think correctly without perfect knowledge and skills. I want to become a high school teacher so I can use the effective teaching and learning methods of my masters with my learners.

I am a foreign student at a small college in the United States. I am doing well in my engineering and technology courses, and I am on my way to a graduate degree in my major subjects. For me, the system of academic freedom in American higher education is wonderful. So are the facilities and services at my school. But I have a big problem. My home country has big financial problems, so now my money doesn't have much value here. I can't pay the full amount of my tuition and fees. I have to live in a small apartment with other students. I can't go out to restaurants or other eating places anymore, and I don't have any money at all for a social life. Why can't I get financial aid from the government? Why can't I get a job off campus? Because I'm not a U.S. citizen, and I'm not a legal immigrant or resident of the United States. I'm an international student. Some of my classmates have to go home after this semester. Can I stay until the end of my graduate program? No one knows.

The Humor of Higher Education

2   Most reading material has a purpose, a point, a message, or a main idea. Humor needs a point too, or it isn't funny! The point of humorous material is the joke. How can you get the joke of a funny story or cartoon? There is probably no topic sentence.

There are probably no clear details that support the main idea. For the point of humor, you need cultural and life experience. You need your own ideas.

Here are cartoon stories about higher education and school life. Discuss your answers to these questions:

1. What is the point or joke of each cartoon? Why do you think so?
2. Does the cartoon remind you of your own school life? Why or why not?
3. Do you think each cartoon is funny? Why or why not?
4. In what other ways is the topic of higher education funny for you? Give your ideas or experiences.

DRABBLE By Kevin Fagan

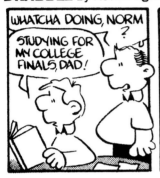   

Video Activities: Exchange Students

Before You Watch.   Discuss these questions in a group.

1. Did you have exchange students in your school?
2. What are the advantages and disadvantages of studying in an overseas high school?
3. How do students celebrate graduation from high school?

Watch.   Write answers to these questions.

1. Where does Eda come from?
2. How old do you think she is?
3. Where does she live?
4. What event is Eda going to?
5. At the end of their year in the U.S., how do the visiting students feel about going back to their home countries?

Watch Again.   Read the following statements. Are the statements true or false? Write T for true, F for false.

1. _____ Brian thinks Turkish people are very different from American people.

2. _____ Eda is not homesick because she talks to her parents frequently.

3. _____ About 12 foreign students are studying in San Diego.

4. _____ The students are going to return to their countries in five months.

5. _____ The students are planning to meet again in the future.

After You Watch.   Phrasal verbs consist of two words together, a verb and a preposition. The underlined phrasal verbs on the left are from the video segment. Use the context to match them with their definitions on the right.

1. _____ Eda is <u>getting ready for</u> her prom.

2. _____ Eda wants her mother to <u>put the video camera away</u>.

3. _____ Eda doesn't want to <u>go back</u> to Turkey.

4. _____ Brian will <u>take care of</u> Eda at the prom.

5. _____ After they return, the students will need to <u>adjust to</u> life in their own countries.

a. become comfortable with something

b. return something to its original place.

c. preparing

d. return

e. protect, be responsible for (someone)

Chapter 2

Experiencing Nature

IN THIS CHAPTER

You will read about the effects of weather on people. You will also learn about possible global changes in climate. And you will look at various people's experiences with nature and their views and opinions of it.

| PART 1 | # The Powerful Influence of Weather |

تؤثرى

Before You Read

1 Discuss the pictures in small groups.

   1. Describe the people. What are they wearing or carrying? How are they feeling? How do you know?
   2. Describe the kinds of weather. Which kind do you like best? Why?

2 Think about the answers to these questions. The reading "The Powerful Influence of Weather" answers them.

منظمى الجويات البيولوجية

   1. What are biometeorologists?
   2. What are the possible health effects of some kinds of wind?
   3. How might other weather conditions influence human health?
   4. What is an example of a winter mood disorder in northern areas of the world?

3 **Vocabulary Preview.** Discuss these vocabulary items in small groups. You can learn them now or come back to them later.

Nouns	Verbs	Adjectives	Phrases
an influence	affect	powerful	in response to
an effect	influence	physical	atmospheric conditions
personalities	become	warm/warmer	according to
scientists	increase	dry/drier	temperature changes
researchers		southern	blood pressure
conditions		northern	forces of nature
mountains		sudden	
headaches		forceful	
increase		depressing	
colds		nervous	
diseases		humid	
a disorder		clear	
		usual	
		even	
		moody	

Read

4 Read the following material quickly. Then read the explanations and do the exercises after the reading.

The Powerful Influence of Weather

[A] Weather has a powerful effect on the physical world. It also affects people's personalities. How do we know about the effects of weather on people? We know from *biometeorologists*. These scientists are weather researchers. They study human health and emotions in response to atmospheric conditions. The word *atmosphere* means "the air around the earth." "Atmospheric conditions at a time or place" is a definition of the word *weather*. Some examples of these conditions are sun, wind, rain, snow, humidity (the amount of moisture in the air), and air pressure (the force of air). The weather conditions of the atmosphere greatly influence people's health, thinking, and feelings.

[B]   All over the world winds come down from high mountain areas. The winds fall faster and faster, and the air becomes warmer and drier. What do scientists say about the health effects of this kind of weather? According to biometeorologists in Russia, powerful winds from the mountains increase the number of strokes (blood vessel attacks in the brain). Also, sometimes strong southern winds blow north over Italy. During these times, researchers say, Italians have more heart attacks (sudden stopping of the heart). People everywhere have bad headaches during times of forceful winds. And Japanese weather scientists say there is an increase in the number of asthma attacks. (Asthma is a lung disorder. It causes breathing problems.)

[C]   Do other kinds of weather influence physical health? Sudden temperature changes in winter are often associated with colds or flu. (*Influenza* is a viral disease.) However, colds and flu probably increase because people are in close contact indoors in cold weather. Colds and flu may even lead to pneumonia (another lung disease). Other illnesses also increase during long periods (times) of cold weather. In most places, diseases of the blood and heart attacks are more common in winter. But in some very hot and humid (wet) regions, there are more heart attacks in summer. Many people have high blood pressure (a health condition). In three out of four people, blood pressure falls (goes down) in warm weather. But *some* people have lower blood pressure in the cool or cold times of the year.

[D]   These forces of nature greatly affect people's moods (emotional conditions and feelings) too. For many people, winter in the northern regions is very depressing. They eat and sleep a lot, but they usually feel tired. They are nervous and can't work well. They are irritable (not very nice to other people). Biometeorologists even have a name for this condition. The name is Seasonal Affective Disorder (SAD). Scientists think the cause of this mood disorder is the long periods of darkness. Even during the day, it is often cloudy or gray. What can people with SAD do about their moods? Naturally, they need more light! On bright days they feel better. But people don't work very well on sunny, hot, and humid days. The best weather for good work and thinking is cool and clear.

[E]   Are the people around you becoming sick more often? Are they getting more colds or the flu or even pneumonia? Are they having more health problems like headaches or asthma attacks or heart disease? Or are *you* becoming moody? Are you getting more tired or depressed (low in mood) or sad? Remember—according to biometeorologists and other weather scientists—the cause may be the atmosphere!

After You Read

5 **Recognizing Paragraph Topics.**   In most reading material with structure, the information in each paragraph is about a different topic or subject. Most often, the topic is a word or a short or long phrase. It is not a full sentence. What is the topic of each paragraph from the reading selection "The Powerful Influence of Weather"? Write the paragraph letter on each line.

1. __B__   the effects of strong winds from mountain regions on health

2. __D__   some human emotional responses to atmospheric conditions

3. __C__   some other kinds of weather with an influence on physical health

4. __E__   the conclusion of the reading selection

5. __A__   some definitions of important words on the topic of weather

6 **Understanding the Main Idea.**   Usually, the information in each paragraph of a reading answers a different question. A one- or two-sentence answer to the question can be a statement of the point of the paragraph.

Here are some possible main-idea statements about the topics of the paragraphs in the reading "The Powerful Influence of Weather." The sentences are in the same order as Paragraphs A–E. Write T (true) or F (false) on each line.

1. __F__ Biometeorologists are "researchers into human responses to academic lectures." A definition of weather is "places on the earth like mountains, countries, and communities.

2. __T__ During times of fast, strong winds from high mountain areas, there are more health problems like strokes, heart attacks, headaches, and asthma.

3. __T__ Sudden winter temperature changes, long cold periods, or heat and humidity can bring illnesses and health problems like colds, flu, or pneumonia.

4. __F__ The atmosphere and weather don't affect people's moods. People in the northern regions eat and sleep a lot, work badly, are tired, and feel depressed all the time.

5. __F__ According to scientists, the cause of health problems and sad moods may be higher education around the world!

Change each false statement in Exercise 6 Understanding the Main Idea to a true statement of the point of the paragraph. Then ask a different question for each of the five answers. (You can add the words What is . . .? or What are . . .?) The question and the answer go together. Example:

> *Question:* What are some definitions of important words on the topic of weather?
>
> *Answer:* *Biometeorologists* are "researchers of human responses to weather." A definition of *weather* is "atmosphere conditions like sun, wind, and temperature."

7 **Finding Definitions and Words with Similar Meanings.** You can often find the meanings of new vocabulary items from the context (the other words in the sentence or paragraph). There may be a definition (a statement or explanation of meaning) in the context. Definitions can come after the words *be* or *mean* or in parentheses.

Example: We know from biometeorologists. These scientists are weather researchers.

Or there might be other words with the same or similar meanings. In Paragraph B, the phrases *powerful winds, strong southern winds,* and *forceful winds* occur. The three phrases have similar meanings.

In the reading selection "The Powerful Influence of Weather," there are some definitions of new vocabulary in the context, sometimes in parentheses. There are also words with the same or similar meanings. Finish these sentences. (The letters refer to the paragraphs of the reading.)

1. These weather researchers study health and emotions in response to atmospheric conditions. They are (A) __biometeorologists__ .

2. This word means "the air around the earth." It is the (A) _atmosphere_ .

3. Some examples of kinds of atmospheric conditions are sun, wind, (A) ____rain____ , ___humidity___ , and ____snow____ .

4. Another word for "atmospheric conditions at a time or place" is (A) ____word weather____ .

5. A word for "blood vessel attacks in the brain" is (B) ___strokes___ .

6. A heart attack is a (B) __sudden stopping in the heart__ .

7. A short word for "influenza, a virus illness" is (C) ___flu___ .

8. Pneumonia and asthma are disorders or diseases of the (B, C) ___lung___   ___and feeling___ .

9. The meaning of the word *moods* is (D) _emotional condition_ .

10. The name SAD means (D) "___Seasonal affective Disorder___."
    This condition is a _____ .

For more practice, find definitions of more vocabulary items and more words with similar meanings. Look for these vocabulary items and others: *air pressure, emotions, irritable.*

8 **Recognizing the Main Idea.**   Usually, the material in each paragraph of a reading selection tells more than the main idea. It also gives details of the "message." These details can be examples of the main idea.

Here are some statements of the main ideas of the first four paragraphs of the reading selection in Part 1. Which details are examples of the truth of the statements? Cross out the unrelated sentence as in the first item.

1. There are some important words related to the topic of the powerful influence of weather.
    a. A definition of *biometeorologists* is "researchers with interest in human responses to the weather."
    b. *Atmospheric conditions* is another phrase for weather.
    c. The meaning of the word *mountains* is "very high areas on the earth or globe."
    d. ~~Sun, wind, temperature, air pressure, and the amount of moisture in the atmosphere are some *kinds of weather* with effects on human health and emotions.~~

2. Some kinds of winds might cause illness or health problems.
    a. These winds from mountain regions blow faster and faster. They warm and dry the air.
    b. Researchers say there are more strokes and heart attacks during windy weather of this kind.
    c. Bad headaches and asthma attacks are some possible examples of the effects of the winds.
    d. There are biometeorologists in many countries, like Russia and Italy and Japan.

3. Many other kinds of weather can influence human physical health.
   a. Some people are always sad or depressed or moody. Weather isn't important to them.
   b. Sudden winter temperature changes might bring colds, flu, or pneumonia.
   c. During long cold periods, people have more blood diseases and heart attacks.
   d. Air temperature affects people's blood pressure in different ways.

4. The weather and atmosphere have powerful effects on people's emotions.
   a. In northern areas of the earth, the long periods of darkness influence many people's moods.
   b. People with SAD may feel hungry, tired, nervous, and depressed.
   c. Bright, sunny days and high humidity can also affect human emotions.
   d. Cloudy, gray days often mean rain or snow. There may be sun on those days.

For more practice, turn back to Exercise 2 on page 20 and answer the questions.

Discussing the Reading

9 In small groups, talk about your answers to the following questions. Then tell the class the most interesting information and ideas.

1. Do some kinds of weather (wind, sun, temperature, humidity, rain, snow, air pressure, and other conditions) affect your health, feelings, or mood? In what ways?
2. In your opinion, does the weather greatly influence human health or emotions? Why or why not?

PART 2 # Global Climate Changes

Before You Read

1 **Vocabulary Preview.** Here are some vocabulary items from the next reading, "Global Climate Changes." You can learn them now or come back to them later.

Nouns	Verbs	Adjectives	Adverbs	Phrases
the globe	stay	average	probably	in contrast to
a desert	change	typical	generally	from day to day
gases	believe	tropical	usually	from season to season
blizzards		extreme	greatly	from one to another
		worse		more and more
		major		at least
		common		
		natural		

Read

2 A reading selection of several paragraphs is probably about one general subject. The title of a reading often gives its subject. Each paragraph of the reading is usually about a more specific (narrower) topic within the general (wide) subject. For example, here are four paragraph titles that go with the reading selection "Global Climate Changes."

> General Changes in the Nature of Weather
> The Powerful Effect of People on Nature
> Climate in Regions of the Globe
> Global Warming and the "El Niño" Effect

Notice that the titles are phrases, not full sentences. The important words begin with capital letters. Quickly read each paragraph of the reading. Then choose the best title from the list and write it on the line below the paragraph. Also, underline the topic sentence in each paragraph. Remember—a topic sentence tells the general subject of the paragraph. It is a short statement of the main idea.

Global Climate Changes

The word *weather* means "the atmospheric conditions at a specific place and time." The weather can vary from day to day. In contrast to weather, *climate* is "the general or average atmospheric conditions of a region." <u>In different areas of the globe, the climate generally stays the same from year to year.</u> For example, the climate in the desert is usually very dry. It may be cold in winter and hot in summer, but there is very little rain or humidity. In contrast, in tropical rain forests there is very high humidity. In most other areas of the world, the weather is cool or cold and wet or dry in the winter season. It is warm or hot and dry or humid in the summer months.

Climate in Regions of the Globe

According to some meteorologists (weather researchers), the earth's climate is changing slowly. In most places on the planet, the weather varies from season to season or even from day to day. In contrast, the typical climate is similar every year. Even so, there may be global climate changes from one long time period to another. What are these changes? Some scientists believe the weather is becoming more extreme. There are longer periods of very cold and very hot temperatures. There are more and more powerful hurricanes and tornados (storms with strong fast winds) and blizzards (heavy snowstorms). Floods (large amounts of water on dry land) and long droughts (times without enough rain) are causing greater and greater physical damage to the human communities on earth. These extreme forces of nature will get even worse in the future, say some people. And every change in climate in one part of the globe will bring more extreme changes in other areas.

General changes in the Nature of weather

Global warming and El Niño are having major effects on the earth's atmosphere, the weather, and the changing world climate. At least that's the opinion of many researchers and scientists. What is global warming? It is a slow increase in the average yearly temperature of the planet. The cause is an increase of gases in the atmosphere. What is El Niño? The Spanish phrase means "The Little Boy" or "The Christ Child." It names a weather condition most common in the month of December. This "seasonal weather disorder" is a change in the atmosphere of the tropical areas of the Pacific Ocean. It increases the mount of rain in the Americas and can bring strong winds and hurricanes. In contrast, El Niño may cause drought in the southern and western Pacific (Asia). Blizzards, snow, and long periods of low temperatures may follow in the northern regions of the globe.

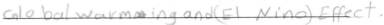
Global warming and (El Nino) Effect.

Not all meteorologists believe there is much natural global warming. According to these scientists, the El Niño effect is not getting stronger. So why is the temperature of the earth going up? Why are tropical storms like hurricanes causing more and greater flood and wind damage? Probably, human beings are the main cause of the extreme effects of weather and climate changes. Cars and factories are putting more and more gases like carbon dioxide (CO_2) into the earth's atmosphere. Coal and oil add carbon dioxide to the air too. Trees and plants take in carbon dioxide, but humans are cutting down the rain forests and putting up buildings where green plants grow. The world has a lot of people now, and it will have a lot more people in the future.

The powerfull Effect of people on Nature.

After You Read

3 **Summarizing Paragraphs.** A summary is a short statement of the most important information in a reading. How can you learn to summarize better? In your own words, begin with the most general point about the topic. Then give the important details or examples of that point. Here is a summary of the first paragraph of "Global Climate Changes."

> All over the world, the typical climate is generally similar every year. It is dry in desert areas and wet in tropical regions. In most places, it is colder in winter and warm or hot in summer.

Work in groups of four. Choose a different paragraph from the reading and read it carefully. Begin with the title or topic. Identify the main idea and the important details. Then tell or read your summary to your group.

Discussing the Reading

4 In small groups, talk about your answers to these questions. Then tell the class the most interesting information.

1. Describe the typical climate in your area of the world. Does the weather change in the various seasons? If so, how?
2. Do you think the earth's climate is changing? If so, how and why is it changing? If not, why not?
3. What are your opinions on the future of the atmosphere and nature?

Talk It Over

People have many different beliefs about nature and the weather. Some ideas come from scientific facts. Others come from people's experiences or culture. In your opinion, which of these statements are true? Explain them to the group, and give the reasons for your opinions.

- In nature, there is no good or bad. There is no right or wrong. There is only the power of cause and effect.
- Why does it rain? It's useless to ask. It just does.
- Meteorologists and other researchers can study the weather, but they can't know or tell about future weather.
- A lot of people complain about the weather. Do they have the power to change it? Of course not.
- Nature doesn't listen to criticism or complaints. Do human beings have to listen to them? No, they can be like nature.
- If you ask for rain, don't be surprised if you get thunder and lightning.
- Why do people get depressed about the rain? Without rain, there would be no rainbows.
- Two people can never see exactly the same rainbow. But they can take a picture of it.
- Do you want sunshine today? Carry a big umbrella and wear a heavy raincoat. Then it won't rain.
- Is your arthritis pain increasing? This means wet weather is coming.

PART 3

Vocabulary and Language Learning Skills

1   **Recognizing Words with the Same or Similar Meanings.**   Students of all subjects want to learn information and get ideas from reading material. For this reason, they read for meaning. Many language learners want to learn the meanings of new words and phrases in the context of reading material. But they don't always need the exact meanings of those vocabulary items. Usually, knowledge of a few words with the same or similar meanings are enough.

In each group of vocabulary items from Chapters 1 and 2, circle the three words with the same or similar meanings. Cross out the word that doesn't belong. The first item is done as an example.

1. region   area   ~~real life~~   place
2. the world   countries and cultures   the globe   the planet Earth
3. ~~condition~~   affect   influence   have an effect on
4. ~~global~~   powerful   physically strong   forceful

5. human emotions   feelings   moods   ~~physical health~~
6. fall   go down   get lower   ~~increase~~
7. diseases   sicknesses   health disorders and problems   ~~science~~
8. sad   ~~common~~   depressed   low in mood
9. season   time of year   ~~air pressure~~   three-month period
10. ~~human beings~~   meteorologists   weather researchers   scientists

For more practice, give the reasons for your answers. Find more words and phrases with the same meanings as other vocabulary items in Chapter 2.

2   **Recognizing Word Meanings.**   A definition of the word *example* is "a typical member of a group or class." Sometimes, examples can explain a word or phrase. For example, sun, rain, and wind are examples of kinds of weather.

Match the examples in Column B with the vocabulary items in Column A. Write the letters of the meanings on the lines in Column A like the example.

Column A

1. __d__ atmospheric conditions
2. __f__ kinds of extreme weather
3. __i__ air temperatures
4. __b__ earth's natural materials and gases
5. __g__ countries of the world
6. __c__ the largest areas of the globe
7. __j__ diseases or health disorders
8. __e__ how people feel (adjectives)
9. __h__ seasons of the year
10. __a__ natural areas or regions of the earth

Column B

a. the ocean, seas, islands, deserts, forests
b. coal, oil, carbon dioxide, air, water
c. Asia, Europe, Africa, the Americas
d. sun, rain, snow, wind, humidity
e. happy, tired, sad, depressed, nervous, irritable
f. blizzards, tornados, hurricanes, floods, droughts
g. Japan, China, Russia, Italy, Germany, the United States
h. winter, spring, summer, fall
i. hot, warm, cool, cold
j. stroke, asthma, influenza, pneumonia, headaches, high blood pressure, arthritis

For more practice, give more examples for the items in Column A of Exercise 2. Can you explain other vocabulary in Chapter 2 with individual examples?

3   **Real-Life Reading: Nature Map.**   Language learners often find new vocabulary items in real-life reading material. You can find definitions of these words and phrases in the context. You can also use words and phrases with the same or similar meanings. And you can use examples to help you understand the meaning of new words or phrases.

Here are some lists of vocabulary items on the subject of global nature and weather. Which words do you know? Underline them. Which words are new or difficult for you? Circle them. In groups or in class, ask for their meanings. Think of possible definitions and words or phrases with the same or similar meanings.

Places on the Earth
the Equator
the Poles (North and South)
the Tropic of Cancer
the continents
peninsulas
islands

Kinds of Weather (Nouns)
sun
rain
showers
snow
frost
ice
an air mass (a front, a high, a low)
fog
smog
clouds

Bodies of Water
the oceans
seas
lakes
gulfs
bays
rivers
swampland

Weather Events
hurricanes
tornados
cyclones
winds
blizzards
snowstorms

Natural Regions and Areas
deserts
jungles
forests
mountains
hills
flatlands
plains

Climate and Temperature Words (Adjectives)
tropical
polar (arctic)
temperate
cold
cool
warm
hot
humid
dry
sunny
overcast
severe
mild

Find examples of some of the words in the lists on the map. Write the words in the right places on the map.

For more vocabulary practice, name the biggest oceans, seas, lakes, continents, countries, cities, mountain regions, rain forests, deserts, and rivers on the globe. Write their names on the map too.

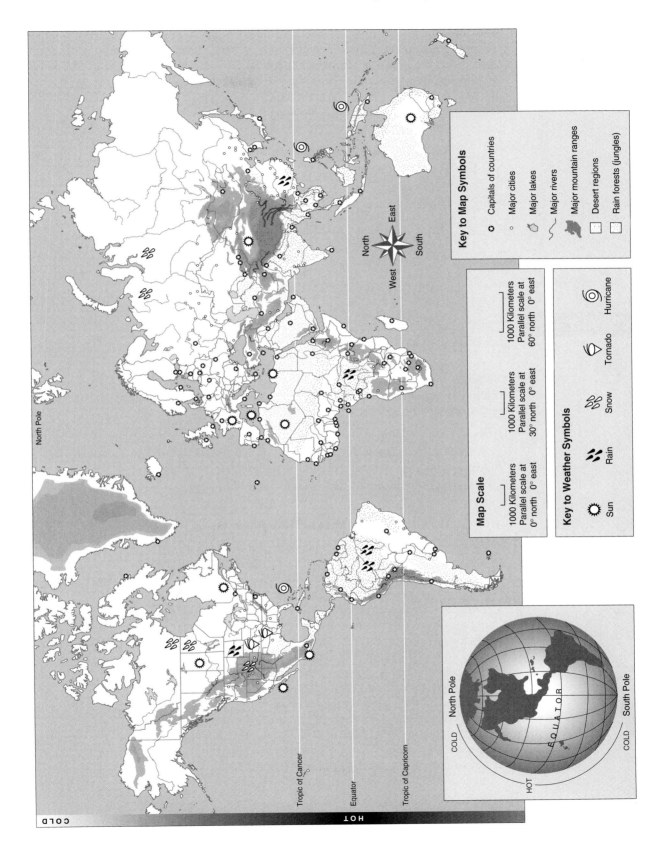

4 **More Real-Life Reading.**   Here are some kinds of reading material about weather and nature. Check (✔) the kinds available to you. Bring some examples to class. Write down the important vocabulary items. Give simple definitions of the words and phrases. Talk about the main idea of each piece.

- ■ _____ political maps with the names of continents, countries, cities, and so on

- ■ _____ physical maps with mountain regions, rivers, and so on

- ■ _____ weather maps and other special maps

- ■ _____ nature postcards

- ■ _____ travel brochures about nature

- ■ _____ other _____

PART 4   # Personal Stories and Humor

---

1 The following stories give various people's experiences of nature. They give different opinions or points of view of the weather, climate, and other natural forces. Follow these steps for the stories.

1. Read them quickly. Summarize the main ideas.
2. Answer your instructor's questions about the stories, or ask and answer questions of your own. Give your opinion of the ideas in the stories.
3. Tell or write your own story about weather and other forces of nature.

Three Views of Nature

I live in a small apartment on the beach on a beautiful tropical island in the Pacific Ocean. I love my relaxed life in this perfect place! The sky and the water are always bright blue and clear, and most days are sunny and warm. With the cool sea air, the nights are nice and comfortable. For me, nature is completely right and good. Of course, we experience one or two forceful tropical storms every year, and occasionally there is a powerful hurricane. Sometimes floods cause major damage to the communities on the island. The people fix or rebuild their homes, but then they get irritated or even angry at the forces of nature. Why, I wonder? Nature is never bad or wrong. With extreme weather, nature creates perfect balance in the world. Only human beings are out of balance with nature.

It's hot and humid in my city in the summer, and there are too many moody, nervous people. The weather has a strong influence on my feelings, and I often feel depressed or irritable during the summer. But this summer will be wonderful! My friends and I are experiencing nature in all its best forms. We're going to the mountains, the ocean beaches, and the high desert. During the day we'll enjoy the warm sunshine and the perfect temperatures. At night we'll take in the cool open air under the clear sky. We can move from place to place according to the weather reports, so we won't experience any rainstorms or strong winds or other kinds of extreme conditions. (We can find out the weather from the satellite pictures on the Internet on our computer.) And what

fun it will be! We'll park our mobile home in the places with the most beautiful views. We can walk and swim and play and ride our bicycles in the beauty of nature. We can take the best rocks and plants and other natural things home with us. Nature is great. And what is its purpose? Nature is for human beings!

Do we enjoy nature outside in the hot, humid summer and the cold, windy winter? No way! We live in Japan, and we prefer our nature indoors. Even at the hottest times, our little house is nice and cool, and our three air conditioners help. During long, cold periods, this same equipment warms our home. But even better are the electric carpets. They warm our feet, and our heads stay cool and comfortable. In wonderful, natural comfort, we can read and study and work on our computers. Our audio and video equipment brings us the best sounds and great views of nature (the ocean and the forest and the desert and more). Of course we love our *kotatsu* (low table with a cover and an electric heater). On cold nights, we all sit around the kotatsu and enjoy time together. We enjoy the "nature" of the people in our family. For us, this is the best kind of nature!

The Humor of Nature

2   Sometimes humor differs in various cultures around the world. How can you get the point of a funny story or cartoon? Often you need knowledge of that specific country or culture. In contrast, some humor is the same or similar all over the globe. With general experience and your own ideas, you can understand the point.

Here are three cartoon stories about nature and the weather. Discuss your answers to these questions:

1. What is the point or joke of each cartoon? Why do you think so?
2. Does the cartoon remind you of your own experiences with nature? Why or why not?
3. Do you think each cartoon is funny? Why or why not?
4. In what other ways is the topic of nature or weather funny for you? Tell your ideas or experiences.

Video Activities: Winter Storm

Before You Watch.

1. The following places are mentioned in the video. Find them on a map of the United States before you watch: Washington, D.C.; New York; Ohio; New England; North Carolina.

2. Work in a group. Make a list of words to describe winter weather in a cold climate.

   Examples: snow   icy   freezing

Watch.

1. This video mainly shows a storm in the _____ part of the U.S.

   a. southern   b. western   c. northern   d. eastern

2. Which of the following words describe the weather conditions you saw in the video?

   snow   rain   wind
   fair   icy   warm
   storm   freezing   humid

Watch Again.   Match the places on the left with the weather conditions on the right.

Place

1. _____ Washington, D.C.

2. _____ New York City

3. _____ New England

4. _____ North Carolina

5. _____ Long Island

Weather Conditions

a. 12 inches of snow are expected

b. drivers of salt trucks and snow plows didn't go to work

c. 5 inches of snow are expected

d. 6 inches of snow fell

e. schools, businesses, and government offices closed

f. slush

After You Watch.   Read about the weather in cities throughout the world in an English language newspaper, magazine, or on the Internet. Then describe the weather in one region or one city of the world to your classmates.

Chapter 3

Living to Eat or
Eating to Live?

IN THIS CHAPTER

You will read about the growth of fast food around the world and various opinions of its nutritional value. You will also read about changes in the diets of various countries and their consequences. Four interesting paragraphs about food end the chapter.

| PART 1 | # The Changing Global Diet |

Before You Read

1 Discuss the pictures in small groups.

1. Where are the people in each scene and what are they doing?
2. How are the foods in each picture similar? How are they different?

2 Think about the answers to these questions. The reading "The Changing Global Diet" answers them.

1. What might the word *diet* mean?
2. How is "fast foods" becoming the same around the globe?
3. Why might people like or dislike quick and convenient eating places?
4. How are fast foods and convenience foods becoming more nutritious?
5. How are global eating customs and food choices changing?

3 Vocabulary Preview. Here are some vocabulary items from the first reading. You can learn them now or come back to them later.

Nouns	Verbs	Adjectives	Adverbs	Phrases
choices	include	basic	typically	lose weight
habits	grow	certain	quickly	go on a diet
nourishment	prepare	expensive	generally	food stands
nutrition	serve	universal	widely	fast-food chains
menus	contain	famous	perfectly	have the same look
style	snack	convenient		home-cooked meals
taste	produce	cheap/cheaper		convenience foods
customers		familiar		salad bars
value		nutritional		junk food
vitamins		fresh		nutrition bars
minerals		canned		for instance
dairy		frozen		
elements		packaged		
ingredients		healthful		
markets		nourishing		

Read

4 Read the following material quickly. Then read the explanation and do the exercises after the reading.

The Changing Global Diet

[A] Most words in the English language have more than one simple, or basic, meaning. One example is the word *diet*. The most general definition of the noun is "a person's or a group's usual food choices and habits." In a more specific definition, *diet* means "an eating plan with only certain kinds or amounts of food." For instance, a diet is often a plan to lose weight. And as a verb, *diet* means "go on a diet."

[B] All over the world, the global diet includes *fast food*—prepared items from inexpensive restaurants, snack bars, or food stands. Some examples of typically American fast food are *hamburgers, hot dogs, sandwiches, fried chicken,* and so on. Some types of international fast foods might be German *sausage* and *schnitzel,* Italian *pizza* and *pasta,* Mexican *tacos* and *burritos,* Middle Eastern *shish kebob* and *falafel*, Japanese *sushi* and *tempura*, Chinese *eggrolls* and *noodles*, and the like. The variety of fast foods available on the planet is growing. Even so, this kind of style of nourishment is becoming *universal*, or worldwide. Fast-food places usually prepare and serve the items quickly. Many are part of *fast-food chains* (eating places with the same name and company owner). For instance, the biggest and most famous American fast-food chain serves hamburgers in every continent on the planet except Antarctica. In over 120 different countries, its 25,000 eating places have the same look. They have a similar atmosphere. The menu items may not be exactly alike from one culture to another, but the style and taste of the foods don't differ much.

[C]   For several reasons, many people choose fast food. First, it is quick and convenient. Second, it is cheaper than special home-cooked meals or formal restaurant dinners. And third, it is identical in every eating place with the same company name. The atmosphere and style of most fast-food places is casual, comfortable, and familiar. So why do other eaters dislike or stay away from this fast, easy kind of nourishment? The main reason is its low nutritional value. Fast food doesn't contain large amounts of *fiber, vitamins, minerals,* and the like—elements necessary for good nutrition and health. In contrast, most types of fast food have a lot of fat, cholesterol, sugar, or salt in them. Possibly, these substances can cause or increase health disorders, like heart disease, strokes, and some kinds of cancer.

[D]   Some people believe food should be perfectly fresh and "natural." According to natural food eaters, fast food is not good for human beings. They don't believe *convenience foods*—canned, frozen, or packaged in other ways—are very nutritious either. On the other hand, these quick and easy kinds of worldwide nourishment are generally getting better and more healthful. For instance, many fast-food restaurants now have salad bars and put vegetable items on their menus. In some places, customers can get fish or *vegieburgers* instead of hamburgers, and grilled chicken instead of fried. Also, some newer kinds of packaged and prepared foods contain less fat, cholesterol, sugar, or salt than before. Of course, people everywhere like to snack on *junk food* (*candy, cookies, potato chips, ice cream,* and other things without much nutritional value). For health and sales reasons, some snack food companies are producing packaged items with less fat, sugar, or salt. And *nutrition bars*—snacks with a lot of *protein, vitamins,* and other nourishing food elements—are becoming more widely available.

[E]   Of course, human beings around the world don't always eat in fast-food places. They don't buy only canned, frozen, or packaged convenience items from stores or machines. A few families are producing food on their own, but most people buy it from markets in their communities. Some choose only *natural food,* items without chemical substances. Many families prepare good meals at home. Other people are restaurant customers. Universally, more meals include the basic necessary food elements—*protein, carbohydrates,* and *fats.* A greater number of dishes contains the necessary vitamins and minerals. Almost everywhere, some kind of meat, fish, dairy product, or another protein food is part of a good breakfast, lunch, or dinner. There are also grains, breads, vegetables, fruit, and the like. The variety of food choices is large now and is probably going to increase. The number of food preparation methods is growing too. Cooking customs, eating habits, and food preferences all over the world are becoming more healthful. In these and other ways, the global diet is changing.

After You Read

5 **Recognizing Paragraph Topics.** A well-structured paragraph has a clear topic. Within the subject of the reading, it is about a different topic from all the other paragraphs. The material in each paragraph answers a question about that topic.

What is the topic of each paragraph from the reading "The Changing Global Diet"? Write the paragraph letter on each line.

1. _____ ways the global diet is changing

2. _____ why people choose or stay away from fast food

3. _____ how convenience foods are becoming more nutritious

4. _____ how fast food is the same around the globe

5. _____ some definitions of the word *diet*

For each of the five topics, make a different question about the material in the reading. Remember—for questions, you'll have to change the word order or add words to the topic phrases. Examples:

1. In what ways is the global diet changing?
2. Why do people choose or stay away from fast food?

6 **Understanding the Main Idea.** Usually, a main-idea statement is a good answer to a question about the topic of each paragraph of reading material. This one- or two-sentence answer also tells the point or message of the paragraph.

In order A–E, here are some possible main-idea statements about the topics of the paragraphs in the reading "The Changing Global Diet." Write T (true) or F (false) on each line. Change the false sentences to true statements of the main idea. Then use them as answers to the five questions in Exercise 2.

1. _____ The word *diet* has two basic definitions—"usual food choices" and "an eating plan."

2. _____ Fast food has very little variety around the world. It is always hamburgers, hot dogs, and fried chicken. But the style of the nourishment and the atmosphere of the eating places varies a lot in different countries.

3. _____ Some eaters enjoy the convenience, price, and familiar comfort of fast food. Other people dislike its low nutritional value.

4. _____ Fast foods and convenience foods are getting less and less healthful. The restaurant items are always fried, and there are no vegetables. The packaged items are going to contain more fat, sugar, salt, and so on.

5. _____ The global diet is changing mostly in bad ways. Few people buy fresh, natural foods at markets. No families cook at home. Not many meals contain the necessary food elements. And there is a smaller variety of food choices and preparation methods.

7   Getting Meaning by Using Punctuation Clues.   Often, the context of reading material contains clues to the meanings of vocabulary items. New or unusual words or phrases may be in italics. Short definitions, similar words, explanations of the items, or examples of their meanings might come between certain kinds of punctuation marks, like quotation marks (" ") or parentheses ( ). They can also appear after a comma (,) or a dash (—).

In the reading selection "The Changing Global Diet," some of the new or less common vocabulary items are in italics. Short explanations of their meanings may appear between or after various kinds of punctuation marks. For each of these definitions, find the words and phrases. (The letters in parentheses are the letters of the paragraphs.) Write them on the lines, as in the example.

1.   a person's or group's usual food choices or habits: (A) _____ *diet* _____

2.   an eating plan with only certain kinds or amounts of food: (A) __ *diet* __

3.   prepared items from inexpensive restaurants, snack bars, or food stands: (B) __ *fast food* __

4.   another word for worldwide: (B) __ ~~global~~ *global* __

5.   eating places with the same name and company owner: (B) __ *fast-food chain* __

6.   elements necessary for good nutrition and health: (C) _____

7.   prepared canned, frozen, or packaged items: (D) _____

8.   candy, cookies, potato chips, ice cream, and other things without much nutritional value: (D) _____

9.   snacks with a lot of protein, vitamins, and other nourishing food elements: (D) _____

10.   food items without chemical substances: (E) _____

For more practice, find other vocabulary items in italics, such as *hamburgers, hot dogs, sandwiches, fried chicken, sausage, schnitzel, pizza, pasta, tacos, burritos, shish kebob, falafel, sushi, tempura, eggrolls, vegieburgers, candy, cookies, potato chips, ice cream, protein, carbohydrates, fats, fiber, vitamins, minerals,* and the like. For each item and others, you can explain the meaning in a sentence like this.

Hamburgers are a kind of typical American fast food.
Sausage is a type of German fast food.
Protein is an example of a necessary food element.

(A/An) _____ is/are   a kind   of _____ .
                                  a type
                                  an example

8   **Recognizing Supporting Details.**   Usually, each paragraph of a reading includes not only a main idea but also details about it. These details support the main idea of the paragraph with specific facts, examples, reasons, or the like. The supporting details are answers to a question about the main idea. A paragraph may also contain other information or ideas, but these are not part of the main idea.

Here are five different questions about the information in the reading "The Changing Global Diet." Which details answer each question? Cross out the unrelated sentence.

1. What are some examples of possible meanings of the word *diet?*
    a. ideas or information to think about
    b. a person's or a group's usual food choices or habits
    c. an eating plan with only certain kinds or amounts of food
    d. a way to lose weight

2. For what reasons is fast food becoming the same or similar in various cultures around the globe?
    a. It includes typically American kinds of food like hamburgers, hot dogs, and fried chicken.
    b. Quick and convenient items from Germany, Italy, Mexico, China, and other countries are available too.
    c. Formal restaurant meals can be expensive or cheap, fast or slow, nutritious or low in fiber.
    d. The eating places have a similar look and atmosphere, and they may be part of a chain.

3. Some people like to eat fast food, but others don't. What are the reasons for their preferences?
    a. Fast food is usually quick, convenient, and inexpensive.
    b. Fast-food restaurants, snack bars, and other eating places are informal, comfortable, and familiar.
    c. Fast food may not contain the necessary elements or substances for good nutrition and health.
    d. People can't get vegetables and fruit or other kinds of nourishment from stores or machines.

4. In what ways are fast foods and convenience foods becoming better and more healthful?
    a. Some people buy and eat only natural foods without chemicals of any kind.
    b. Many fast-food eating places have salad bars and include vegetables on their menus.
    c. Instead of hamburgers high in fat and cholesterol, customers can get fish or vegieburgers or grilled chicken.
    d. Some newer kinds of packaged foods contain less fat, sugar, or salt than before.

5. The global diet is changing in some good ways. What are some examples of these changes for the better?

   a. A few families are producing their own food, and many more are buying natural or nutritious food from markets.

   b. Health disorders like heart disease, strokes, and cancer are no longer related to food and eating.

   c. Many people are preparing, cooking, and eating healthful meals in their own homes.

   d. The available variety of healthful nourishment choices—protein foods, grains, vegetables, and fruits—is large and growing.

For more practice, turn back to the Before You Read section on page 38 and answer the questions.

Discussing the Reading

9 In small groups, talk about your answers to the following questions. Then tell the class the most interesting information and ideas.

1. What are your opinions of fast food and fast-food eating places? Give reasons for your answer.
2. What kinds of food do you usually buy from machines, stores, or markets? How do you prepare or cook it? When and where do you eat it? Give examples of your food customs and habits.
3. In general, do you think the global diet is changing? In the same ways or in different ways? In good or bad ways? What are the reasons for your opinions?

PART 2   # Facts About Food

Before You Read

1 **Vocabulary Preview.**   Here are some vocabulary items from "Facts About Food," the next reading selection. You can learn them now or come back to them later.

Nouns		Verbs	Adjectives	Adverb	Phrases
specialists	legs	allow	opposite	financially	brain power
nutritionists	ants	last	high-protein		the B-vitamins
nutrients	caterpillars	damage	high-fiber		whole grains
ingredients	worms	support	dried		tomato sauce
broccoli	bugs		industrialized		hot-pepper sauce
decrease	insects		related		island country
memory	desserts				
ability	cheese				
caffeine	diabetes				

Read

2 **Choosing Paragraph Titles.**   Often, the title of reading material tells its topic. Even so, a title should look or sound interesting. For this reason, readers might not know the meaning of a short title phrase—the subject of the reading—at first. On the left are four examples of interesting titles on the subject of food and eating. On the right are less interesting but clearer topic phrases. Match them with lines, as in the example.

Food for Thought   The Effects of the Changing
                                  Global Diet in Different Cultures

The Fat of the Land   Cooking and Eating Insect Foods
                                  for Good Nutrition

Food Fights   Opposite or Contrasting Views on
                                  the Best Eating Habits

Getting the Bugs Out   Brain Foods and Other Nutrients
                                  for the Mind and Memory

3   Here are four paragraphs with the general title of "Facts About Food." Quickly read the information and ideas. On the line over each reading, you can write a possible title from the columns in Exercise 2. Can you find a topic sentence—a wider statement of the point instead of a specific fact, reason, example, or other detail—in each paragraph? Underline your choice of a topic sentence.

Facts About Food

Food Fights
_____

Everywhere on earth there are "food specialists" with different or opposite views on the best kinds of nutrition for various purposes. A lot of people believe the most healthful diets are high in fiber, vitamins, and minerals but low in fat, cholesterol, sugar, and salt. Some nutritionists say the perfect eating plan contains mostly carbohydrates without much protein. In contrast, other scientists say people need high-protein meals with meat, chicken, fish, or milk products and only small amounts of grains, potatoes, breads, rice, and noodles. One famous diet plan allows only certain foods at certain times—protein with protein, carbohydrates with carbohydrates, fruits alone, and so on. Some eaters stay away from all meat and maybe even fish and milk products. They get their protein from plants, mostly beans. Others want only high-fiber food. These people may not eat white bread or white rice or even cooked vegetables. So what is the best way to eat and be healthy? The discussion of this topic will go on far into the future.

The necessary substances and elements for human life and health are water, protein, carbohydrates, fats, vitamins, and minerals. Most kinds of food contain some or all of these nutrients, but they are not all the same in their effects on people. Various ingredients and dishes affect the mind in different ways, and some kinds of nourishment have better effects on the brain than others. For instance, can broccoli increase brain power? Maybe so. Low levels of some of the B-vitamins can cause a decrease in memory and thinking ability, nutritionists say, but dark green vegetables contain a lot of these nutrients. Another example of a "memory helper" is lecithin—a substance from soybeans, also found in high-fiber foods like nuts and whole grains. High-protein foods influence the mind in more helpful ways than dishes high in sugar and carbohydrates. And the caffeine in coffee or tea may help thinking. Of course, its effects don't last long.

In many places outside big cities, food with more than four legs is part of good, nutritious home cooking. Fried or grilled ants are a tasty but expensive snack in Columbia, South America. In various parts of Mexico, over 300 types of insects serve as food. In southern Africa, many people like to eat at least one kind of caterpillar or worm. They enjoy it fried, dried, or cooked in tomato sauce. In Thailand, cooks create a spicy hot-pepper sauce with water bugs. In Vietnam, grasshoppers filled with peanuts are a special dish. And in some regions of China, bugs are not only a part of meals but an important ingredient in medicine too. Most kinds of insects have high nutritional value. They contain a lot of protein, vitamins, and minerals. Many people like their taste. They are everywhere on the planet. They add to the variety of people's diets. For several reasons, insects are an important kind of food in the global diet, and they will become a more common ingredient in the future.

The growing similarities in diet and eating habits around the world are influencing people of various cultures in different ways. For example, Western foods are damaging health in the industrialized island country of Japan. Instead of small meals of seafood, rice, and vegetables, the typical Japanese diet now includes large amounts of meat, dairy products (like whole-milk ice cream), and desserts like tiramisu, a rich Italian dessert full of chocolate, cheese, and sugar. According to Japanese health researchers, such changes in eating habits are related to a great increase in health problems such as heart disease, strokes, cancer, and diabetes. On the other hand, the changing global diet is having the opposite effect on the people in the Czech Republic. The government of this European nation no longer supports meat and dairy products financially, so the cost of these foods is going up. In contrast, fresh fruits and vegetables are becoming more widely available from private markets and stands. Cooks are even serving salads to schoolchildren, and families are eating more nutritious home-cooked meals. For these reasons, fewer Czech men are having heart attacks, the women are losing a lot of weight, and most people are living healthier lives.

After You Read

4   **Learning to Summarize.**   What is another way to learn to summarize better? You can ask a paragraph question and begin your summary with a one-sentence general answer to the question. Which information and ideas (facts, examples, and reasons) from the reading support your first statement? Add those in a clear order to your summary. Here is a possible summary of the first paragraph of the selection "Facts About Food."

What do food specialists around the world believe about nutrition? They may agree on the basics, but they can have very different opinions about the best kinds and amounts of foods for human health. Some people say to eat mostly carbohydrates; others believe in high-protein eating plans; and still others think fiber is the most important element.

Work in groups of four. Choose a different paragraph from the reading selection "Facts About Food." Read it carefully. Begin with the topic or title. Summarize the main idea and important details. Then tell or read your summary to your group.

Discussing the Reading

5   In small groups, talk about your answers to these questions. Then tell the class the most interesting information.

1.   What are your ideas about good food and nutrition? Is there a "perfect" diet for health and long life? Why do you think this way?

2.   In your opinion, do certain foods increase or decrease brain power (memory and thinking ability)? If so, which ones? Give examples of your experiences with food.

3.   In big cities and industrialized areas of the world, people don't generally cook or choose insect dishes. What are your feelings about unusual foods of this kind? Give reasons for your answer.

4.   How are changes in diet and eating habits affecting people in your country or culture? Why do you think so?

Talk It Over

Food and eating are common topics of discussion everywhere. People are always talking about tasty and unusual dishes, good (and bad) restaurants, new diet plans, and their ideas about health and nutrition. But not all talkers have the same information or know the same facts. From your knowledge and experience, which of these statements are true facts? Which are unproven opinions? (Write F for fact or O for opinion on each line.) Then explain your reasons to the group.

1.   _____ Fresh, uncooked natural foods are always best for the health. Cooking takes away vitamins and other nutrients.

2.   _____ Hot, spicy foods damage the stomach. Chili peppers or similar ingredients don't belong in family dishes.

3. _____ Nuts are bad for people. They contain fat, so they raise cholesterol levels.

4. _____ Many kinds of foods are related. For instance, prunes are dried plums, and raisins are dried grapes. Tofu looks like cheese, but it really comes from soybeans.

5. _____ More coffee comes from Brazil than from any other place, and most the world's tea comes from India.

6. _____ For various reasons (color, taste, safety, etc.), companies add natural substances from seaweed, insects, trees, flowers, and so on to packaged foods.

7. _____ With added vitamins, minerals, and nutrients, snack foods like candy, cookies, chips, and soft drinks can and will become the new "health foods."

8. _____ Even a simple, basic food like rice has many varieties—such as white, brown, black, basmati, long-grain, short-grain, and so on. There are various ways to cook and include rice in menus and meals.

9. _____ Japanese men smoke twice as much as Western men. Even so, they have a lot less lung cancer. The reason is green tea. It protects them.

10. _____ For good health and long life, there are a number of "perfect" foods. Some examples are vegetables like broccoli and cabbage, red grapes, citrus fruits, onions, garlic, and soybeans.

Are your beliefs about food and eating mostly scientific facts, or are they personal opinions? Give some more information like Nos. 1–10. Who agrees with your statements? Who disagrees, and why?

PART 3 # Vocabulary and Language Learning Skills

1 **Recognizing Meaning Categories.** Most language learners want to learn a lot of vocabulary as quickly as possible. How can they do this? One way is to learn several words with the same or similar meanings at the same time. Another possibility is to learn words in meaning categories. A category is a class or group of items in a system of classification. It is a kind or type of thing, person, idea, and so on. For instance, the items meat, dairy products, vegetables, and fruit are members of the category "kinds of food." Protein, carbohydrates, fats, vitamins, and minerals belong to the category "necessary nutrients in food."

Here are a large number of vocabulary items from Chapters 1 to 3. They all belong to various categories. Possible names for these categories appear in the boxes. Work in small groups. Write the words on the lines in the correct boxes. Cross out the words on the list.

college students   sushi and tempura   teachers   scientists
beef and pork   a classroom   heart disease   flu or pneumonia
citizens   swimming pools   headaches   developing nations
school   graduates   high blood pressure   tennis courts
a college campus   mood disorders   grains and breads   snack bars
chicken and duck   classmates   dairy products   sadness or depression
hamburgers   candy and cookies   professors   continents
teaching assistants   salads   asthma   researchers
meteorologists   vegetables   language learners   emotions
restaurants   immigrants   a university   doctors
sickness or illness   foreigners   European countries   ice cream
academic freedom   the whole world   mountain areas   hunger
desert regions   food markets   a tropical island   specialists
sandwiches   fruit   potato chips   shellfish
anger   perfect health   diabetes   rice and pasta

Meaning Categories			
People	**Places**	**Possible Foods**	**Human Conditions**
college students	school	beef and pork	sickness or illness
_____	_____	_____	_____
_____	_____	_____	_____
_____	_____	_____	_____
_____	_____	_____	_____
_____	_____	_____	_____
_____	_____	_____	_____
_____	_____	_____	_____
_____	_____	_____	_____
_____	_____	_____	_____
_____	_____	_____	_____
_____	_____	_____	_____
_____	_____	_____	_____
_____	_____	_____	_____
_____	_____	_____	_____

2   The categories in the chart in Exercise 1 are general (wide) classifications. In the left column here in Exercise 2 are some vocabulary items for more specific (narrower) categories. These are in a list on the right after the letters a–j. For each group of words or phrases, write the matching letter on the line.

Vocabulary Items

1. _____ summer, fall (autumn), winter, spring

2. _____ breakfast, lunch, dinner, supper, snacks, and the like

3. _____ broccoli, cabbage, beans, potatoes, onions, green peppers, etc.

4. _____ business, engineering, technology, computer science, etc.

5. _____ Canada, Brazil, Great Britain, Germany, Russia, Korea, etc.

6. _____ sun, rain, snow, ice, wind, humidity, drought, fog, clouds, etc.

7. _____ restaurants, fast-food chains, snack bars, food stands, markets, etc.

8. _____ protein, carbohydrates, fats, cholesterol, vitamins, minerals, etc.

9. _____ North America, South America, Europe, Asia, Africa, a few others

10. _____ water, coffee, tea, wine, beer, juice, soft drinks, and other beverages

Meaning Categories

a. continents

b. countries

c. subjects of college study

d. seasons of the year

e. weather conditions

f. eating places and food stores

g. kinds of meals

h. vegetables

i. beverages

j. nutrients and food elements

For more practice, say or write more items for the categories. Phrases such as *and the like, and so on, and others,* and *etc.* mean there are other members of that group of items. Another practice activity is to list typical vocabulary items (examples of members of a class or group) for others. Your classmates can try to name the category.

3   **Real-Life Reading: Menus and Food Labels.**   In many kinds of real-life reading material, you will find vocabulary items that can be grouped under categories. For instance, the listings on a menu are names of dishes and other food items. The words on a food label are ingredients or nutrients.

A menu and a label from a food container are shown on page 51. Which words and phrases do you know? Underline them. Which words are new or difficult for you? Circle them. In groups or in class, ask for their meanings. Work with your classmates and instructor. Figure out the general or specific categories of the items. Try to explain their meanings in your own words. Remember—the exact meaning may not be important. Often, the general sense is enough.

For more practice, make questions with some of the words and phrases like this. Answer the questions with information from this menu or label or from others.

What kind of food is the _____?

How much/many is/are _____ on the menu?

According to the label, how many/much _____ is/are in this container?

MENU

Steve's
C   A   F   E

BURGERS

The American Tradition . . . . . . $ 3.50
Plain burger, nothing but a pickle

Cheese Burger 3.95
You pick the cheese— and still get the pickle

Vegie Burger 3.75
With fresh lettuce and tomato

HOT DOGS

Traditional Dog . . . . $ 2.50
Plain hot dog, nothing but a pickle

Turkey Hot Dog 2.75
Smothered in cheese sauce

Tofu Hot Dog 2.95
Cheese, and onions, of course

SOUPS

Soup of the Day . . . . $ 1.25

Cheese Soup 1.50

Homemade Chili 1.75

SALADS

An American Chef . . . .$ 5.50
Garden greens with turkey, beef, cheese

Golden Gate 5.75
Fresh pineapple stuffed with almond chicken salad

Tutti-Fruiti 5.75
Fresh fruits served with cottage cheese

SANDWICHES

Baked Tuna Melt . . . . $ 4.50
Tuna Salad with Swiss cheese on rye

Chicken Heaven 4.95
Bar-BQ chicken on a multi-grain bun

South Philly Steak 5.75
Ribeye steak, onions, cheese, marinara sauce

HOUSE SPECIALTIES

All entrees served with your choice of coleslaw, cottage cheese, tossed salad, choice of potato, roll and butter

Walley's Pike . . . . $ 8.95
Broiled or pan-fried walleye pike

Ribeye Steak 10.75
Grilled to order

Fantail Shrimp .
Broiled with butter an

Ask About Our Delicious Desserts!

HOMOGENIZED HALF AND HALF

INGREDIENTS: MILK & CREAM

NUTRITION INFORMATION PER SERVING

Serving Size . . . . ONE HALF CUP (4 fl. oz.)
Servings per Container 4
Calories 160   Carbohydrate . . 5 grams
Protein . . . . 4 grams   Fat . . . . 14 grams

PERCENTAGE OF U.S. RECOMMENDED DAILY ALLOWANCES (U.S. RDA)

Protein 10	Vitamin D 4
Vitamin A 8	Vitamin B$_6$ 2
Vitamin C 2	Vitamin B$_{12}$ 6
Thiamine 2	Phosphorus 10
Riboflavin 12	Magnesium 4
Niacin . . . . *	Zinc 2
Calcium 15	Pantothenic
Iron . . . . *	Acid 2

*Contains less than 2% of the U.S. RDA of these nutrients

4 **More Real-Life Reading.** Here are some kinds of reading material about food and nutrition. Check (✔) the kinds available to you. Bring some examples to class. Write down the important vocabulary items. Give simple definitions of the words and phrases. Talk about the point of each piece of material.

■ _____ menus from restaurants

■ _____ food lists from fast-food places

■ _____ labels on packaged convenience foods

■ _____ newspapers food advertisements

■ _____ recipes

■ _____ diet plans

■ _____ other _____

| PART 4 | # Personal Stories and Humor |

1 The following stories give different thoughts, ideas, and opinions of food and nutrition. Follow these steps for the stories.

1. Read them quickly. Summarize the main ideas.
2. Answer your instructor's questions about the stories, or ask and answer questions of your own.
3. Give your opinions of the ideas in the stories.
4. Tell or write your own story about food, nutrition, and eating.

Food Groups

Usually, the phrase *food group* means "a category of foods according to their nutrients." For instance, meat, fish, eggs, and beans belong to one food group, and vegetables are part of another. But I belong to a different kind of food group. It's an organization called Slow Food. Its members live in Italy, France, Hungary, Spain, Argentina, Brazil, the United States, Japan, and other countries. What are our purposes? First, we need to protect the human  rights to the enjoyment of food! People want to buy and cook perfect fresh and natural ingredients in season. They like to experience relaxed meals with family and friends. Second, we have to save people from the unhealthful conditions and requirements of today's fast lifestyle. A fast life with only quick and convenient food makes people nervous, irritable, moody, depressed, or sick. A third reason for our group is the education of children in cooking and eating. Slow food preparation and long, happy dinners are important parts of a happy, nourishing family life. And a fourth purpose is to keep and increase the great variety of ingredients and food preparation methods worldwide. Food and eating customs and habits belong to individual cultures. They should not become identical all over the planet.

We live in a big city in the United States, but our community and its food culture are completely Asian. There are hundreds of Chinese, Vietnamese, Korean, Japanese, and Thai restaurants, snack bars, fast-food stands, markets, bakeries, convenience stores, and other kinds of eating and food-shopping places in our neighborhood. People come from far away to taste and experience the great variety of Asian-style dishes. There are so many good things to eat! We choose from tasty and healthful seafood, beef, pork,

chicken, and duck main dishes, spicy soups, various types of rice and noodle meals, snacks and desserts—and even unusual treats like peanut-filled grasshoppers in a hot-pepper water-bug sauce. We eat out often and enjoy many of these wonderful foods at home too. But where do we go for a really great meal on special family occasions? We visit the nearest "Hometown Buffet," a big family restaurant in a worldwide chain. There we fill up on hamburgers, fried chicken, mashed potatoes, pizza, pasta, sausage, tacos, and so on. These are the real and true international foods!

I love American fast food, especially cheeseburgers. A big salad with lots of ham and cheese is my idea of a perfectly enjoyable meal. In my opinion, the tastiest Chinese dishes contain lobster, shrimp, or pork. And after a great steak dinner, the best dessert is ice cream with chocolate sauce. Even so, I stay away from some of these foods, and I don't eat the others at the same meal. I keep kosher. I follow the laws of Jewish food preparation and eating. These laws

don't allow pork or bacon or other meat from pigs. They don't permit dishes with shellfish or snake or insect ingredients. And I can't have chicken at dairy meals or add milk or cheese to my enjoyment of meat. Don't get me wrong. For me, kosher food isn't health food. It isn't the "cleanest" food in the world. It's not the least expensive, and it doesn't always taste so good either. So why do I choose to keep these difficult requirements? They are an expression of my values and beliefs. Through them, I can prove my respect for life. The laws give me fewer choices, so I have less freedom in my tastes and preferences. For me, this structure is a good thing. It is right and correct. It makes me a better person.

The Humor of Food

2 In cartoon strips like those at the end of Chapters 1 and 2, readers get the joke from the order of the pictures and the words of the people in them. But some kinds of humor appear in one-picture cartoons. There may or may not be words in or under the pictures. Readers have to understand the humorous point with less information. On the other hand, food and eating are universal topics, so humor on these subjects is easy to understand.

Here are three cartoon stories about food topics. Discuss your answers to these questions.

1. What is the point or joke of each cartoon picture? Why do you think so?
2. Does the cartoon remind you of your own experiences with food and eating? Why or why not?
3. Do you think each cartoon is funny? Why or why not?
4. In what other ways is the topic of food or eating funny for you? Give your ideas or experiences.

REAL LIFE ADVENTURES By Wise and Aldrich

© 1991 GarLanCo/Distributed by Universal Press Syndicate.

One smack too many

The Futile Gourmet.

BENT OFFERINGS By Don Addis

TV DINNER. SOMEBODY LIVES BY HIMSELF, I SEE.
DEODORANT. SOMEBODY'S GOT A DATE TONIGHT.
CIGARETTES. CAN'T QUIT, EH? BRAN MUFFINS.
SOMEBODY'S ON A DIET. AFTER SHAVE. AREN'T
WE THE LADY KILLER! SPAGHETTI SAUCE...

Video Activities: Treat Yourself Well Campaign

Before You Watch.   Discuss these questions in a group.

1.   What is the difference between "healthy" and "unhealthy" food?
2.   Do you think low-fat or nonfat food can be delicious?
3.   Do you like American fast food?

Watch.   Write answers to these questions.

1.   What kind of food do the Wood brothers like to eat?
2.   Describe some of the dishes that the tasters are eating.

Watch Again.   Complete the following statements.

1.   The Wood brothers don't eat light dishes because

   a. they're more expensive than fast food

   b. they don't taste as good as "fat" food

   c. they don't care if they get fat

2.   "Healthy" food contains

   a. butter

   b. cream

   c. vegetables

   d. lots of salt

3.   The pizza does <u>not</u> contain

   a. nonfat cheese

   b. vegetables

   c. nonfat dressing

   d. low-fat sausage

After You Watch.   Bring a menu to class from a restaurant you like. Work in small groups. Your teacher will divide the menus among the groups, and you should read them together. Decide which restaurant has the healthiest food. Tell the class about it. When all the groups have told about their restaurants, the class should vote for the "best" restaurant. Maybe you can go there together for lunch or dinner!

Chapter 4

In the Community

IN THIS CHAPTER

In what ways do people in various places give directions? The first reading "How Can I Get to the Post Office?" will tell you. Next, you will find out about differences in local laws in communities around the world. Finally, you will read different opinions about cities.

| **PART 1** | # How Can I Get to the Post Office? |

Before You Read

1 Discuss the picture in small groups.

1. Who are the two young travelers? What are they doing? What is their problem?
2. What are the other people in the picture doing?
3. Does this situation ever happen to you? Do you use a map or ask for directions—or both? Do people sometimes ask you for directions? What do you answer?

2 Think about the answers to these questions. The reading selection "How Can I Get to the Post Office?" answers them.

1. How do people in different places give directions?
2. Sometimes you might ask, "How can I get to the post office?" What if a person doesn't know the answer? What might he or she do?
3. How can body language help you in getting around the community?

3 **Vocabulary Preview.**   Here some vocabulary items from "How Can I Get to the Post Office?" You can learn them now or come back to them later.

Nouns	Verbs	Adjectives	Adverbs	Phrases
advantages	find out	confused	straight	ask for directions
tourists	measure	flat	seldom	the American Midwest
travelers	motion	impolite	rarely	a sense of direction
the countryside	gesture			get lost
the flatlands	lead			have a good time
gestures	guess			body language
motions				facial expressions
movements				

Read

4 Read the following material quickly. Then read the explanations and do the exercises after the reading.

How Can I Get to the Post Office?

[A] I have a special rule for travel: Never carry a map. I prefer to ask for directions. Sometimes I get lost, but I usually have a good time. And there are some other advantages: I can practice a new language, meet new people, learn new customs, and the like. I can find out about different "styles" of directions every time I ask, "How can I get to the post office?" Here are some illustrations of those differences.

[B]   Tourists are often confused in Japan. That's because most streets there don't have names; outside big cities, people most often use landmarks in their directions. For example, the Japanese might tell travelers something like this: "Go straight down to the corner. Turn left at the big hotel with the sushi bar and go past the fruit market. The post office is across from the bus stop—next to the fast-food fried chicken place."

[C]   In the United States, people might give directions in different ways according to their region or community. As an example, in the countryside of the American Midwest, there are not usually many landmarks. There are no mountains, so the land is very flat; in many places there are no towns or buildings for miles. Instead of landmarks, residents of the flatlands will tell you directions and distances. In the states of Kansas or Iowa, for instance, people will say, "Go straight north for two miles. Turn right, and then go another mile in a northeast direction."

[D]   On the other hand, people in Los Angeles, California, have no idea of directions or distance on the map. Residents of this Pacific coast area are almost always in their cars, so they measure distance in time. "How far away is the post office?" you ask. "Oh," they might answer, "I guess it's about five minutes from here." You say, "Yes, but how many miles away is it—or how many kilometers or blocks?" They rarely know—or can seldom say.

[E]   Sometimes, people in the European country of Greece do not even try to give directions; that's because tourists seldom understand the Greek language. Instead, a Greek may motion or gesture or say, "Follow me." Then that person will lead you through the streets of a city to the post office.

[F]   What if a person doesn't know the answer to your question about the location of a place? A New Yorker might say, "Sorry, I have no idea" and walk away quickly. But in Yucatan, Mexico, not many residents answer, "I don't know." People in Yucatan may believe that a quick "I don't know" is impolite; they might stay and talk to you—and usually they'll try to give an answer, sometimes a wrong one. A tourist without a good sense of direction can get very, very lost in this southern region!

[G]   One thing will help you everywhere—in Japan, the United States, Greece, Mexico, or any other place. You might not understand a person's words, but you can probably understand the body language—the facial expressions, gestures, motions, movements, and so on. He or she will usually turn and then point. Go in that direction and you'll find the post office—maybe!

After You Read

5   **Recognizing Paragraph and Whole Reading Topics.**   Reading material with simple, basic structure might begin with an introductory paragraph and end with a short conclusion. The several paragraphs between the first and the last might give the same *kind* of information—for instance, illustrations of the main point of the whole reading. (An illustration serves as an example or proof of an idea or statement.) Each of the paragraphs will give *different* illustrations of the message.

Of course, the subject of a *whole* reading should be more general than the specific topics of the individual paragraphs. It should be clearly related to the narrower topics.

In the reading "How Can I Get to the Post Office?" there is a capital letter next to each of the seven paragraphs. Write the specific topic of each paragraph next to its letter. A and B are done as examples.

A.   _The Introduction to the Reading_

B.   _Directions in Japan_

C.   _____

D.   _____

E.   _____

F.   _____

G.   _____

Which phrase best tells the subject of the whole reading "How Can I Get to the Post Office?" Circle its letter. Give the reasons for your answer.

a.   the importance of body language for tourists and travelers

b.   how people give street directions in various places in the world

c.   different kinds of maps for travel and weather

6 **Understanding the Main Idea.**   How can readers get and tell the point of reading material in a simple way? One basic method is to ask one question about the information in each paragraph—and then a general question about the point of the whole reading. A one- or two-sentence answer to each question gives the main idea.

For each of the paragraph topics from the reading "How Can I Get to the Post Office?," complete a different question about the information. (Write the necessary words on the lines.) Also, finish the question about the main idea of the whole reading. Two items are done as examples.

A. _____What is the point of_____ the introduction to the reading material?

B. _____How do people often give_____ directions in Japan?

C. _____ directions in the region of the American Midwest?

D. _____ directions in the city of Los Angeles, California?

E. _____ directions in European country of Greece?

F. _____ directions in some areas of Mexico like Yucatan?

G. _____ the conclusion to the reading material?

In what ways _____ directions in various cultures around the world?

7 In order, here are some false sentences about the information in paragraphs A–G of the reading. The possible statement of the point of the *whole* reading is not right, either. Change the eight wrong sentences to true statements of the point. Then use them as correct answers to the eight questions in Exercise 6.

1. If you don't carry a map on your travels, you won't have to ask for directions.
2. In Japan, people most often use street names in their directions.
3. In the mountainous land of the American Midwest, people will tell you directions with landmarks.
4. In Los Angeles, California, the most common way to give directions is in kilometers.
5. Even if visitors to Greece don't understand the language, the people will usually give directions with a lot of words in long sentences.
6. In some parts of Mexico, people may be impolite, so they always say "I don't know" in answer to questions about directions.
7. All over the world, words in sentences are easier to understand than body language.

In various cultures around the world, people give directions to travelers and tourists in exactly the same way.

8 **Finding Illustrations of Word Meanings.**   Sometimes illustrations of the meaning of vocabulary items are in another sentence or sentence part. The words *for example, for instance, as an illustration, like,* and *such as* can be clues to meaning through illustrations.

Example: People in Los Angeles talk about <u>distance in time</u>. They'll say such things as "It's about five minutes from here." (An illustration of distance in time is the phrase "about five minutes from here.")

On the lines, write illustrations of the words from the reading material. (The letters in parentheses are the letters of the paragraphs.) Some items are partly done as examples.

1. landmarks: (B) ___the corner___ , ___the big hotel with the sushi bar___ ,

   _____ , _____ ,

   _____ , and so on.

2. directions: (C) ___straight north___ , _____ ,

   _____ , _____ ,

   _____ , and so on.

3. distances: (C) _____ , _____ ,

   _____ , _____ , and the like.

4. body language: (G) _____ ,

   _____ , _____ , and so on.

For more practice, find other illustrations of vocabulary items, such as names of countries, names of nationalities, names of American states, names of regions, kinds of places, phrases in street directions, and the like.

9   **Recognizing the Relationship of Detail to the Point.**   Punctuation marks might show the relationship between the point of reading material and some of the supporting detail. For instance, a colon (:) can introduce a list of things—usually illustrations or examples of an idea. Commas (,) can separate the different items of the list or series.

Example: In Japan, people typically use *landmarks* in their directions: they talk about hotels, markets, bus stops, and so on. (What are some examples of landmarks for directions? *Hotels, markets,* and *bus stops.*)

A semicolon (;) can separate two closely related sentence parts. The second sentence part can explain or add useful information to the point of the first.

Example: In the American Midwest, there are no mountains and few hills; the land is very flat. (The word *flat* can mean "without mountains or hills.")

Quotation marks separate direct quotes (people's exact words) from the rest of the sentence.

Example: A Greek will say, "Follow me." (What does a Greek often say instead of giving directions? "Follow me.")

Here are some questions about the supporting details of the reading "How Can I Get to the Post Office?" Look at the punctuation and related sentence parts. Then find the answers to these questions in the material. With words from the paragraphs and your own words, write the answers on the lines.

1. The writer of the reading material has a special rule for travel. What is it?

   _____

2. What are some advantages of travel without maps?

   _____

   _____

3. Why are foreign tourists often confused in Japan?

   _____

   _____

4. What are some illustrations of Japanese directions?

   _____

   _____

5. What directions might residents of the American Midwest give people? (Tell some examples.)

   _____

   _____

6. Why don't people in Los Angeles give directions in miles, kilometers, or blocks?

   _____

7. Why do Greeks seldom give foreigners directions in words and sentences?

   _____

   _____

8. If a resident of New York City doesn't know the location of a place, how might he or she answer a question about directions?

   _____

   _____

9. Why won't a polite resident of Yucatan answer a lost tourist, "I don't know"?

   _____

   _____

10. How does a person give directions with body language?

    _____

For more practice, turn back to the Before You Read section on page 58 and answer the questions in your own words.

Discussing the Reading

10 In small groups, talk about your answers to the following questions. Then tell the class the most interesting information and ideas.

1. Do you ever get lost—in our own town, city, region, or in new places? If so, do you ask for directions? Why or why not? If so, in what way?
2. How do most people give directions in your city or in the countryside? Do you give directions the same way? Why or why not?
3. In your opinion, why do people in different places give directions in different ways?
4. Do you have a good sense of direction? Can you find new places quickly and easily? Explain your answer with examples.

PART 2   # The Laws of Communities

Before You Read

1   **Vocabulary Preview.** Here are some vocabulary items from "The Laws of Communities," the next reading selection. You can learn them now or come back to them later.

Nouns		Verbs	Adjectives	Phrases
murder	activity	smoke	local	make sense
robbery	traffic	drive	legal	fifteen-year-olds
violence	teenagers	park	illegal	driving permits
safety	regulations	hit	serious	make a right turn
order	container	punish	licensed	a full stop
relationships	workplaces		religious	a traffic light
alcohol	airports		strange	against the law
shopping	airlines		married	helmet laws
offenses	flights			get a ticket
action	wives			in effect
				hold hands
				train stations
				go camping

Read

2   **Skimming for Topics and Main Ideas.** Every reading—and every part of a reading—should have a clear topic or subject. The *title* of a piece of writing may tell or suggest its topic. On the other hand, without a title, readers need to figure out the topic on their own. Similarly, not every piece of information contains a clear topic sentence, so readers may have to get the main idea or point or message of the material without it. One way to figure out topics and main ideas is to *skim. Skimming* is fast reading for a purpose. A common reason to skim is to find out the topic or to get the main idea of some reading material.

Following are four paragraphs with the general title of "The Laws of Communities." Quickly skim the information. Before each of these topic phrases, write the paragraph letter A, B, C, or D.

_____ Strange or Unusual Laws About People's Relationships

_____ Traffic Laws for Drivers, Riders, and Walkers

_____ Drinking and Smoking Laws and Customs Around the World

_____ The Laws of Communities in Many Areas of Life

Now read each paragraph quickly a second time. Following the material are three possible main-idea statements. In your opinion, which sentence or sentences best express the point of each paragraph? Circle the number 1, 2, or 3. Then tell the reasons for your choices.

The Laws of Communities

[A]   Laws are rules for people in communities. For instance, in every country and culture of the world, there are laws against serious offenses: murder, robbery, violence against people, and the like. These laws make sense. They are necessary for safety and health, for community order, and for good human relationships in communities; they are probably similar all over the world. On the other hand, many laws and rules differ from country to country, from area to area, or even from one community to another. Some common illustrations of this variety are laws about driving, drinking alcohol, eating, smoking, shopping, money, people's rights, and many others. For example, a legal action in Lima, Peru, may be against the law in Seoul, Korea—and an illegal activity in an Asian community may be perfectly legal in a European city. On the other hand, laws may be the same in various countries but vary in different cities or states of the same nation.

1. Laws should always make sense; if they don't, people won't follow them. They will drink alcohol, eat too much, and smoke.
2. Laws in Lima, Peru, keep community order better than the laws in Seoul, Korea, and other communities or countries of Asia.
3. Laws against the most serious crimes may be similar everywhere, but the rules of most areas of life differ from one place to another.

[B]   Traffic laws—rules about driving and parking cars, riding bicycles, walking, and so on—vary in communities around the world. Here are some examples from the United States. In some rural (country) communities, teenagers with driving permits can drive alone after the age of fourteen; in most towns fifteen-year-olds can drive only with a licensed diver in the car; in still other places, the lowest legal driving age is sixteen or eighteen. In some states, drivers can make a right turn after a full stop at a red traffic light, but in other states drivers may turn only at a green light. In many places, but not everywhere, it is against the law to drive or ride without a seat belt. As another example, some communities have helmet laws: motorcycle riders and bicycle riders under a certain age have to wear these hard hats for safety. There are even laws for walkers: in many U.S. cities you can get a ticket for jaywalking (crossing the street in the middle instead of at the corner). Of course, other countries may have similar traffic laws. For instance, jaywalking is against the law in Russian cities too. What happens if a car hits a jaywalker? The walker has to pay a fine, but not the driver!

1.   Traffic laws are for drivers, riders, and even walkers; these laws may be the same or very different in various communities around the world.

2.   Laws about the lowest legal driving age are higher in rural areas than in towns and big cities, but they make good sense everywhere.

3.   Laws about car seat belts, motorcycle or bicycle helmets, and jaywalking are for safety purposes, but laws about right turns are not.

[C]   What about regulations and customs in other areas of people's lives? Some communities have a lot of rules about legal and illegal individual activities— even drinking and smoking. For instance, in most places in the United States, no one under twenty-one can buy or drink alcohol legally—even beer or wine. In some communities, it's illegal to drink a can of beer on a public street; it's also against the law to have an open alcohol container in a car. Similarly, smoking is no longer legal in public places—such as workplaces, restaurants, airports, and on airline flights within the United States. In Japan and other places, there is a legal age for smoking; in some Moslem countries, all smoking is against religious law. On the other hand, many people around the world drink and smoke—including more and more teenagers and young people. Customs and habits do not always go along with health or safety regulations or laws.

1.   People should not drink, smoke, or eat too much. These are not good health habits, but they are never against the law.

2.   Around the world, there are many laws about individual activities like drinking and smoking; many people still do these things— sometimes legally but not always.

3.   Workplaces, airports, airplanes, and restaurants are public places; for this reason, people over the legal age can drink beer and wine and smoke cigarettes there.

[D]   In the beginning, most local laws have a clear purpose or reason; even so, after many years, these same regulations can seem very strange or unusual. Here are some examples of old rules about personal relationships. In the back country of New Zealand, a man with many sisters can have the same number of wives. How is this custom legal? The man can give one sister to each of his wives' families! In some Indian communities, it is illegal for a young man and woman—married or not, to hold hands in a bus or train station; if they do, they have to pay an expensive fine. The law in some Chinese towns doesn't allow a man to give a woman a chicken leg during a meal; he can give her other chicken parts, but not a leg. And in Worland, Wyoming (a state in the United States), no married man may go camping alone or with his friends; he has to take along his wife! These old laws are probably still in effect, but not many people follow them.

1. After a long time, old local laws about relationships can seem very strange; they may not make sense in today's world.
2. All over the world, regulations for married men and women are different from rules for unmarried people—especially in bus or train stations.
3. Old local marriage and relationship rules are all the same: people follow them everywhere because they make good sense.

After You Read

3   **Learning to Summarize.**   In Chapter 3, you learned how to summarize by asking a question about a paragraph. Another way is to paraphrase the main idea and the important supporting details. A *paraphrase* is a restatement in other words. First, be sure you understand the correct *meaning* of each important idea or piece of information in the material. Then use words and phrases with similar meanings to express the same ideas. Here are phrases from the first paragraph of the reading "The Laws of Communities," with possible ways to paraphrase them.

local law: legal rules of a community, rural or town or city regulations
serious offenses: major illegal actions, very bad activities against the law
make sense: have a real purpose, are necessary for good reasons
are different: differ, vary, appear in various forms

And here is a possible short, paraphrased summary of Paragraph A.

In most communities in the world, the most serious offenses are illegal, so the necessary laws against these terrible acts are similar for good reasons. In contrast, the local rules about activities in everyday life in rural areas, towns, and cities may vary from place to place.

Work in groups of four. Choose a different paragraph from the reading selection "The Laws of Communities." Read it carefully. Begin with the topic or title. Summarize the main idea and important details. Then tell or read your summary to your group.

Discussing the Reading

4   In small groups, talk about your answers to these questions. Then tell the class the most interesting information.

1. Which community's or country's laws and rules do you know the best? Why are you familiar with these regulations?
2. Compare some traffic regulations in two or more communities or cities. Tell about driving, bicycling, parking, walking, and so on. Why do you think different places have different traffic rules and customs?
3. What laws about smoking and drinking alcohol do you know about? Do most people follow these rules? Give examples for your answer.
4. What are some of the laws about relationships in your community? What is their purpose? Are they good laws to follow? Give examples and reasons for your answers.

Talk It Over

All over the world, people like some laws and dislike others. Some rules seem reasonable in certain communities but don't have a real purpose in other places. Also, some regulations are very old, so they don't make sense in today's world. The following local laws may seem strange or unusual. From your knowledge and experience, which laws make sense? Which laws seems senseless or funny? Put an X before those items. Explain the reasons for your opinions and views.

1. _____ In Bangor, Maine (the United States), you can't put money into another car's parking meter—even to help another driver. If you do, you will pay a big fine.

2. _____ In Oslo, Norway, if you break a traffic law, you must pay a fine to the police officer right then. Then you get a receipt (a printed statement of money received).

3. _____ In Warsaw, Poland, it's against the law to do sit-ups or push-ups (kinds of physical exercise) in a bus inside the city.

4. _____ In Kaunas, Lithuania, a person may ride up in an elevator, but he or she must always walk down. Only three exceptions are allowed every day.

5. _____ In Pilsen, the Czech Republic, beer companies can use only ingredients from the state of Bohemia.

6. _____ In England, Sunday shoppers can buy canned dog food, but they can't buy food in cans for people—not even canned milk for babies.

7. _____ In Valencia, Spain, social dance parties are not allowed for young people.

8. _____ In Addis Ababa, Ethiopia, it's illegal for a person to spit on other people on the street. He or she mustn't spit on the bare feet of children, either.

9. _____ In many Mexican communities, it is against the law to walk around outside barefoot (without shoes).

10. _____ In Mexico City, students can keep many kinds of small animals but not scorpions (a member of the spider family) or tarantulas (a kind of spider).

Do you know any interesting or unusual laws from communities around the world? Explain each law and tell its probable purpose. Give your opinion of the regulation too.

PART 3	# Vocabulary and Language Learning Skills

1 **Recognizing Similar Meanings and Meaning Categories.** Here are two good ways to learn new vocabulary quickly: look at the words and phrases with similar meanings together and learn items in meaning categories at the same time. With both methods, the words should be of the same *part of speech*. (The major examples of "parts of speech" are nouns, verbs, adjectives, and adverbs.)

In each of the following groups of words, do the vocabulary items belong together because they have the same or similar meanings? If so, write S for *similar* on the line. Or are the vocabulary items members of the same meaning category or classification? If so, write C on the line and name the possible category. Two items are done as examples.

1. __*C*__ walking / riding a bicycle / taking the bus / driving

2. _____ Oslo, Norway / Tokyo, Japan / Mexico City, Mexico / Valencia, Spain

3. __*S*__ rules / laws / regulations

4. _____ not often / seldom / rarely / infrequently

5. _____ make sense / seem reasonable / have a purpose / be understandable

6. _____ helmet laws / driving permits / fines for jaywalking / the legal driving age

7. _____ northeast / southwest / northwest / southeast

8. _____ move / motion / gesture / use body / language

9. _____ a colon / a semicolon / a comma / a period

For more practice, tell or write more items with similar meanings to the words in some of the groups. And you can tell or list more vocabulary items like the members of the categories.

2 **Recognizing Nouns and Verbs.** A very useful vocabulary-learning method is recognizing parts of speech. Some words can be more than one part of speech. As examples, in the first sentence that follows, the words *motions* and *gestures* are plural nouns; in the second sentence, the same words are verbs.

Two examples of body language are *motions* and *gestures*. A person usually *motions* or *gestures* with the hands, arms, or other body parts.

On the other hand, some words in noun and verb pairs have *different* forms or endings. Here are some examples of related words from Chapter 4.

Noun	**Verb**	**Noun**	**Verb**
movement	move	direction	direct
expression	express	illustration	illustrate

Here are some sentences with two related words—one noun and one verb. In each blank, write the missing word—the noun related to the underlined verb or the verb related to the underlined noun. The first two items are done as examples.

1. As a frequent traveler, I like to <u>travel</u> to distant places. My main rule for
   _____*travel*_____ is not to carry a map.

2. My <u>preference</u> is to ask for directions. What method of getting around do
   you _____*prefer*_____?

3. Usually, residents like to <u>direct</u> tourists to various places; they give
   _____s in different ways.

4. An example of a street direction is "<u>Turn</u> left." This means "Make a left
   _____."

5. Many people want to <u>reside</u> on the Pacific coast of California;
   _____s of this area usually go places by car.

6. Some <u>measure</u>s of distance are miles, kilometers, and city blocks; but
   people in Southern California usually _____ distance in
   time (minutes).

7. To direct tourists, Greek people often <u>motion</u> or <u>gesture</u>; these
   _____s and _____s are illustrations of
   body language.

8. How do people <u>express</u> themselves without words? They <u>move</u> their hands.
   Facial _____s and body _____s are
   effective ways to communicate meaning.

9. Everywhere in the world, a few people <u>murder</u>, <u>rob</u>, and so on. Two
   examples of serious crimes are _____ and
   _____.

10. There are local laws against <u>smoking</u> and <u>drinking</u> in some communities;
    even so, some teenagers want to _____ and
    _____.

For more practice, tell or write more nouns from Chapters 1 to 4. Which nouns have related verb forms? What are they? Also, you can tell or write some verbs with their related noun forms. (You can check your guesses in a dictionary.)

3   **Real-Life Reading: Community Services and Signs.**   Real-life reading material is not only helpful for language learning. It also gives useful information. For example, telephone books give the names, addresses, and telephone numbers of places in the community. And signs everywhere give directions, give rules, and so on—not only in words but also in pictures.

Here are pages from the community services part of a local telephone book and on the next page are pictures of signs in that community. Which words and phrases do you know? Underline them. Which words are new or difficult for you? Circle them. In groups or in class, try to figure out the meanings of the circled words. You can give the parts of speech; you can suggest definitions, words or phrases with similar meanings, examples, categories, and so on. Remember—the *exact* meaning may not be important. Often, the general sense is enough.

Finally, in your own words, give the general meaning or purpose of each of the pieces of real-life information.

Community Services

A   AIDS/HIV

Aid for AIDS..213-656-1107
AIDS Education & Prevention Center..213-636-6296
AIDS Epidemiology Program..............213-351-8196
AIDS Project Los Angeles (APLA)........800-922-2437
Or..213-876-2437
Multilingual...800-922-2438
Spanish...800-400-7432

B   ALCOHOL & DRUG ABUSE

Adult Children of Alcoholics (ACA)......818-342-9885
Al-Anon...213-387-3158
Spanish...310-948-2190

C   CHAMBERS OF COMMERCE

Beverly Hills...310-271-8126
Brentwood..310-476-4573
Century City...310-553-2222
Culver City...310-287-3850

D   COUNSELING

California Self-Help Center
Statewide referrals to support groups.........800-222-5465
Family Service
Los Angeles...213-381-3626
Los Angeles Free Clinic.........................213-653-1990

E   DEPARTMENT OF MOTOR VEHICLES

Culver City 11400 W Washington Blvd.....310-271-4585
Hollywood 803 N Cole Ave.....................213-744-2000
1600 Vine St..213-461-6257
Santa Monica 2235 Colorado Ave..........310-271-4585

F   COMMUNITY COLLEGES

Los Angeles City College
855 N Vermont Ave, Los Angeles............... 213-953-4000
TDD...213-351-8196

Santa Monica College
1900 Pico Blvd, Santa Monica................... 310-450-5150
TDD...310-452-9273

West Los Angeles College
4800 Freshman Dr, Culver City..................800-400-7432

G   HOUSING

California State Dept. of Fair Employment & Housing
.... 213-897-1997
TDD...213-897-2840
InfoLine-Information & Referrals For Emergency
Assistance..213-686-0950

H   IMMIGRANT & REFUGEE SERVICES

Immigration Legal Assistance Project..213-485-1872
U.S. Immigration & Naturalization Service
Information & Forms..................................213-894-2119
Or...800-755-0777

I   LEGAL SERVICES

American Civil Liberties Union-ACLU..231-977-9500
Bet Tzedek Legal Services....................213-939-0506
Los Angeles County Public Defender...310-491-6361
Malibu...310-317-1348
Santa Monica...213-653-1990

J   LIBRARIES

Brentwood - Bookmobile.......................310-575-8016
Culver City - 4975 Overland Ave.............310-559-1676
Malibu
Main 23519 W Civic Center Way...............310-456-6438

For more practice, make questions with some of the words and phrases like this.

What kind of help can you get at the _____?

Where might you see a sign with the words _____?

You can answer the questions with information from this telephone book page and these signs or from others.

4 **More Real-Life Reading.** Here are some kinds of reading material common in cities and communities. Check (✔) the kinds available to you. Bring some examples to class, or copy the words from signs. Write down the important vocabulary items. Give simple definitions of the words and phrases. Talk about the point of each piece of material.

■ _____ the front pages of a local telephone book

■ _____ the yellow (business) pages of a local telephone book

■ _____ signs on the street and on stores and public buildings

■ _____ signs inside stores and public buildings

■ _____ community or city street maps

■ _____ area or state or national road maps

■ _____ free brochures and information sheets from public places

■ _____ community Internet pages

■ _____ other _____

PART 4 # Personal Stories and Humor

1 The following paragraphs titled "Community Preferences" give various thoughts, ideas, and opinions about places to live and visit. Follow these steps for the stories.

1. Read them quickly. Summarize the main ideas.
2. Answer your instructor's questions about the stories, or ask and answer questions of your own.
3. Give your opinions of the ideas in the stories.
4. Tell or write your own story about a community, a city, or a local area.

Community Preferences

California? It's superlative—the most and the best! It includes the highest point in the continental United States, Mt. Whitney in the Sierra Nevada Mountains—14,496 feet high. It has the lowest point too, in Death Valley, at 280 feet below sea level. The highest and deepest lakes are in the state, along with the tallest and oldest trees. The people grow the best vegetables and fruits; they produce the best cheese and wine. The population (number of people) is the largest of all the fifty U.S. states, even larger than that of some countries. The biggest Chinese community in the Western world is in San Francisco; more Mexicans live in the Los Angeles area than in any other place outside of Mexico. And California gets the most tourists and other travelers from other places. On the

beach in my community, I meet a lot of visitors. What do they say about my wonderful city and state? They say it has the heaviest traffic, the worst smog (bad air), the most extreme weather, the strangest residents, the least culture, and the like.

Addis Ababa, Ethiopia—now *that's* a great place to live! The industrialized capital of our country has modern tall buildings, schools of music and art, a good university, nice museums, and facilities for international meetings; even so, there are lots of natural open spaces and trees, and the climate is perfect—warm and sunny in the daytime and cool and comfortable at night. For me, the happiest, most interesting place is the big open market, the *mercato*; it adds the most to our big, happy community! The eating places in town are inexpensive, and Ethiopian food is the best: we love the wide variety of nutritious fish, chicken, and meat dishes—as well as the vegetables cooked in hot-pepper sauce. We use a special kind of bread and our hands for eating and enjoy long, relaxed meals and delicious coffee with family and friends. So what do visitors have to complain about? They say the desert areas are too hot, dry, and empty. They tell us they don't feel safe or comfortable. They criticize our business activities and regulations, our laws, our customs, and on and on and on.

I travel a lot all over the world, and many travelers visit my homeland too. I live in Iceland, an island country in the North Atlantic Ocean. Tourists come here by plane or boat. They stay in warm, comfortable hotels. They love the beautiful natural places, like the high, snowy mountains and volcanos, the glaciers (rivers or fields of ice), the hot springs (water from under the earth), and the high desert flatlands with no buildings or landmarks for kilometers around. They enjoy skiing, hiking (walking in natural areas), fishing, and other great sports. They learn about our rich history, literature, and culture. They attend wonderful summer festivals and public celebrations. They eat our food—a large variety of dishes to choose from: shark meat, whale steaks, all kinds of fish prepared in unusual ways, sheep parts, dairy desserts, and so on. We even serve a hot alcoholic drink made from potatoes. Even so, our visitors complain and complain. What's their problem? They don't like our high prices!

The Humor of Community

2 There are picture postcards of places in many cities, towns, communities, and areas of the world. Most of these postcards show beautiful scenes or interesting tourist attractions, but some of the cards are humorous. Some are like one-picture cartoons with words. Here are some funny postcards from various places. Discuss your answers to these questions.

1. What place is each postcard from or about? How do you know?
2. What is the point or joke of each cartoon picture? (Explain the humor.)
3. What kind of funny postcard might you create about your own community, town, city, or country? Describe or draw your ideas.

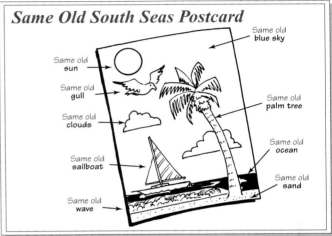

Video Activities: A Homeless Shelter

Before You Watch.   Discuss these questions in a group.

1. Are there homeless people in your town? Tell what you know about their lives. For example, where do they get food? Where do they sleep?
2. Who should help homeless people: their families? the community? the government?
3. Why do some people become homeless?

Watch.   Discuss these questions in a group.

1. Why does Oceanside need a homeless shelter?
2. What does the proposed shelter look like?
3. What is the woman in the hat trying to do?

Watch Again.   Fill in the blanks.

1. There are _____ homeless people in Oceanside.
2. However, now there are only _____ shelter beds.
3. The Oceanside City Council will give _____ dollars for the new shelter.
4. The new shelter will have _____ beds.
5. The new shelter will be for single men and women and couples. Families will stay in _____.
6. The city needs to raise money, and it is also asking people in the community to _____.

After You Watch.

1. Fill in the missing adjective endings on the following words.
    1. port_____
    2. remov_____
    3. home_____
    4. ambiti_____
    5. interest_____

2. Fill in the blanks in the following sentences with the words above.
    1. The old shelter had beds for only 58 _____ people.
    2. People who are _____ in volunteering should call this number.
    3. The new shelter will be _____ and _____.
    4. The city's plan to build a new shelter is very _____.

Chapter 5

Home

IN THIS CHAPTER

What comes to mind when you think of a family? If your idea of a family is a mother, a father, and two children (a boy and a girl), the information in the first reading selection, "A Short History of the Changing Family," may surprise you. In the second selection, "Time with the Family—Past and Present," you will read and give your opinions about family time in the past, present, and future. Finally, you will read stories about two very different housing situations.

PART 1

A Short History of the Changing Family

Before You Read

1 Discuss the pictures in small groups.

1. Where and when does each scene take place? What are the people doing?
2. How are these scenes similar to situations in your family, community, or country? How are they different?
3. How do you think family life is changing these days? How might it change in the future?

2 Think about the answers to these questions. The reading selection answers them.

1. What is the difference between an extended family and a nuclear family?
2. What are some kinds of families in the world today?
3. Why and how did the structure of the family change in the twentieth century?
4. How were the 1930s and 1940s difficult years for most families?
5. How did people's ideas about marriage and family change after World War II?
6. What are the most common family forms around the world today?

3 **Vocabulary Preview.** Here are some vocabulary items from the first reading. You can learn them now or come back to them later.

Nouns	Verbs	Adjectives	Phrases
the millennium	consist of	biological	a social institution
cousins	return	adopted	a common ancestor
relatives	rise	divorced	the extended family
partnerships	decline	widowed	the nuclear family
couples	face	perfect	foster families
thousands	support	childless	heads of households
millions	take in	traditional	for life
divorces	adopt		on their own
war			loosely related
widows			
history			
certainty			

Read

4 Read the following material quickly. Then read the explanations and do the exercises after the reading.

A Short History of the Changing Family

[A] Like the community, the family is a *social institution*. Long ago, human beings lived in loosely-related groups. Each group had a common ancestor (a family member from the distant past). But for over a millennium (a thousand years), there have been two main types of families in the world: the extended form and the nuclear form. The extended family may include grandparents, parents, and children (and sometimes aunts, uncles, and cousins)—in other words, relatives living in the same house or close together on the same street or in the same area. In contrast, the nuclear family consists of only parents and their biological or adopted children. Because of the industrialization in the nineteenth century, the nuclear family became the most common family structure.

[B]   Today there are many different kinds of families around the globe. Some people live in traditional families—that is to say, a stay-at-home mother, a working father, and their own biological children. Others live in two-paycheck families—that is, both parents work outside the home. There are many single-parent families; in other words, only a mother *or* a father lives with the children. Still others have adoptive or foster families (i.e., adults take care of children not biologically theirs) or blended families—in other words, divorced or widowed men and women marry again and live with the children from their previous, or earlier, marriages. There are also same-sex partnerships—with or without children, childless marriages, unmarried live-in relationships, and so on.

[C]   What caused the structure of the family to change? In the early 1900s in the United States the divorce rate (i.e., the percent of legal endings compared to the number of marriages) began to rise, and the birthrate (i.e., the number of births per 100 or 1000 people) began to decline; in other words, couples stayed married for fewer years, and they had fewer children. Women often chose to get an education and take jobs outside the home. Decades later, the same changes began to happen in other industrialized countries. Today, they are happening in many of the developing nations of the world as well.

[D]   The decades of the 1930s and 1940s were difficult years in the industrialized world. Many families faced serious financial problems because the heads of households lost their jobs. During World War II (1939–1945), millions of women had to take care of their homes and their children alone. Because so many men were at war, thousands of these "war widows"—that is to say, women whose husbands were away at war—had to go to work outside the home. Most women worked long hours at hard jobs. There weren't many "perfect families."

[E]   During the next decade (a period of ten years), the situation changed in many places. There were fewer divorces, and people married at a younger age and had more children than in the previous generation. Men made enough money to support the family, so a mother seldom worked outside the home when her children were small. Children began living at home longer—that is, until an older age, usually after high school or even college. The traditional family was returning in the United States, it seemed—as in many other countries.

[F]   In the years between 1960 or so and the end of the twentieth century, however, there were many new changes in the structure of the family around the globe. From the 1960s to the 1970s, the divorce rate greatly increased and the birthrate fell by half. The number of single-parent families rose, and the number of couples living together without marriage went up even more.

[G]   Many people today would like the traditional two-parent family back—that is to say, they want a man and a woman to marry for life; they also think the man should support the family and the woman should stay home with the children. However, few families now fall into this category. In fact, if more women decide to have children on their own, the single-parent household may become more typical than the traditional family in many countries. Also, unmarried couples may decide to have more children—or they might take in foster children or adopt. And because people are staying single and living longer (often as widows), there may be more one-person households. On the other hand, some people believe similar events happen again and again in history: if this is true, people may go back to the traditional extended or nuclear family of the past. Others think the only certainty in history is change: in other words, the structure of the future family could begin to change faster and faster—and in more and more ways.

After You Read

5 **Recognizing Paragraphs in Time Order (History).**   Readings about history (true events or happenings from the past) usually begin with introductory material; these one or two paragraphs may tell the most important ideas and points of the whole selection. The several paragraphs after that may tell about various *periods* of history—probably in time order. The last paragraph or paragraphs may give information about the present or thoughts after the future.

In the reading "A Short History of the Changing Family," there is a capital letter next to each of the seven paragraphs. After its letter, finish the specific topic of each paragraph. Some items are done as examples.

A. definitions of _____

B. the _____ around the globe

C. reasons for *present changes in the structure of the family* _____

D. the typical family *in the 1930s and 1940s* _____

E. the typical family _____

F. _____ between 1960 and the end of the twentieth century

G. How might family structure _____?

6 Which phrase best tells the topic or subject of the whole reading "A Short History of the Changing Family"? Circle its letter. Give the reasons for your answer.

a. the advantages of the traditional family form over single-parent or adoptive relationships

b. the effects of World War II on jobs, home, and children in the future

c. reasons for divorce in a changing global community of live-in couples

d. changes in the structure of the nuclear family from the twentieth century to the future

7 **Understanding the Main Idea.**   What is a simple method to get and tell the point of reading material? You can ask one question about the information in each paragraph—and then a general question about the point of the whole reading. A one- or two-sentence answer to each question gives the main idea.

For each of the paragraph topics from the reading "A Short History of the Changing Family," complete a different question about the information. (Write the necessary words on the lines.) Two items are done as an example.

A. _*What are the definitions*_____ of the two main types of families?

B. _____ the different kinds of families around the globe today?

C. _____ changes in the structure of the family?

D. _*What happened to*_____ families in industrialized countries in the 1930s and 1940s?

E. _____ families in the United States in the next decade?

F. In general, how did families change _____ ?

G. _____ in the future?

In what different ways _____
in the twentieth and twenty-first centuries?

8 In order, here are some false sentences about the information in paragraphs A–G of the reading. The possible statement of the point of the *whole* reading is not right, either. Change the eight wrong sentences to true statements of the point. Then use them as correct answers to the eight questions in Exercise 7.

1. The *nuclear family* is the same as the *extended family:* it consists of many relatives (grandparents, parents, children, cousins, etc.) living in the same house.

2. There is only one kind of family on planet Earth today: it is the traditional nuclear family.

3. In the early 1990s in the United States (and later in other countries), the divorce rate went down and the birthrate began to rise; couples were staying married longer and having more children.

4. Before and during World War II, families faced few financial problems in the industrialized world, so women didn't have to work outside the home. Families were perfect.

5. After the war, family structure changed back in the other direction: there were more divorces and fewer stay-at-home mothers; children began to leave home earlier.

6. From the 1960s on, there were few new changes in the structure of the family around the globe.

7. People don't want the traditional two-parent nuclear family—with a working father and a mother at home; however, this structure will probably come back and all other family forms will disappear from the earth.

In the twentieth century, there weren't any changes in the structure of the typical family; in the next century, there won't be any changes either.

9 **Using Punctuation and Phrase Clues.** Short definitions of new vocabulary items, words with similar meanings, and explanations of meaning sometimes appear between or after certain punctuation marks such as parentheses ( ), dashes (—), or commas (,). They might also be in another sentence part after a semicolon (;) or a colon (:). The phrases *in other words, that is to say,* or the abbreviation *i.e. (that is)* can also be clues to the meaning of vocabulary. So can other words in the sentence or paragraph.

Example: The family is a social institution; in other words, it is an organization with a purpose inside a human community—that is, among the people living together in a certain area. (A definition of a *social institution* is "an organization with a purpose within a community." The word *community* can mean "people living together in a certain area.")

A hyphen (-) between word parts is another punctuation clue to meaning. *Multiword adjectives* before nouns are usually hyphenated. An example in the previous sentence is the phrase *multiword adjectives*; it means "adjectives that consist of more than one word."

On the lines, finish the explanations of the words from the reading material. (The letters in parentheses are the letters of the paragraphs.) One item is done as an example.

loosely related groups: (A) _groups of people that are not close relatives_

_____

an ancestor: (A) a family member _____

_____

the extended family: (A) relatives _____

_____

the nuclear family: (A) a living group with only _____

_____

a stay-at-home mother: (B) a mother that _____

_____

single-parent families: (B) families with only _____

_____

blended families: (B) family groups with _____

_____

the divorce rate: (C) the percent of _____

_____

war widows: (D) women whose _____

_____

a decade: (E) a time period of _____

For more practice, look for and explain other vocabulary items with meaning clues, such as *a social institution, a millennium, family structure, two-paycheck families, adoptive or foster families, previous, same-sex partnerships, the birthrate, one-person households,* and others.

10 **Recognizing Time Details (Facts).**   In readings about history, there are often time details. These facts tell when things happened. Some examples of past-time phrases are years such as *1860* or *the year 2000*; centuries, decades or time periods like *the eighteenth century, the early 1930s,* or *the years between 1990 and 2001.* A hyphen (-) between points of time usually means *to,* as in *1925–1955.* Time details also appear with phrases like *long ago, since the beginning of the millennium, for a century, between the 1960s and the end of the 1900s,* and many others.

In Column A are some of the important events in the history of family forms. Match them with the time phrases in Column B, and write the correct letters a–h on the lines.

Column A

1. _____ Many families had money problems, so more women began to work outside the home.

2. _____ There have been two main types of families: the extended and the nuclear.

3. _____ Industrialization made the nuclear family the most common form.

4. _____ Many new family forms became common, such as single parenthood and unmarried couples living together.

5. _____ Because women began to get education and work, the divorce rate rose and the birthrate fell in the United States.

6. _____ People lived in loosely related groups, not in small family units.

7. _____ Men supported the family, and women stayed home to take care of the children. There were fewer divorces.

8. _____ There are and will continue to be many different family structures: "traditional" two-parent families, families with two working parents, single-parent families, adoptive or foster families, blended families, and so on.

Column B

a. over a millennium ago

b. since the year 1000 or so

c. in the nineteenth century

d. in the early 1900s

e. in the 1930s and 1940s

f. in the decade after World War II in the United States

g. from the 1960s to the end of the twentieth century

h. today and in the future

For more practice, you can turn back to the Before You Read section on page 78 and answer the questions in your own words.

Discussing the Reading

11 In small groups, talk about your answers to the following questions. Then tell the class the most interesting information and ideas.

1. What is the most common family structure in your community or culture?

2. In your opinion, what caused so many changes in the structure of the family after the middle of the twentieth century? Explain your answers.

3. In your opinion, how and why might the structure of the family change in the twenty-first century?

PART 2	# Time with the Family— Past and Present

Before You Read

1 **Vocabulary Preview.**   Here are some vocabulary items from the next reading selection. You can learn them now or come back to them later.

Nouns		Verbs	Adjectives	Phrases
a straw mat	the farm	get up	crowded	a lord and master
a cottage	generations	push aside	next-door	take breaks
goats	a matter	laugh	modern	fall in love
fires	the neighborhood	date		get married
a castle	neighbors	arrange for		either way
a village	custody	get		follow the rules
taxes	a waiter	improve		row houses
the past				the front steps
				take care of

Read

2 **Knowing Time and Place in History.**   Readings about history give information about certain periods of time: each paragraph might be about a different year, a period of years, a decade, a century, or even a millennium. It can describe important events or changes in one or more countries or cultures—or global happenings or developments. Readers can figure out the time and place in history through *skimming*—that is, by reading the material quickly for a purpose.

Following are four paragraphs with the general title of "Time with the Family— Past and Present." Quickly skim the information. Before each of these topic phrases, write the paragraph letter, A, B, C, or D.

_____ The Traditional Japanese Family in the 1900s

_____ The Twentieth Century Community Where I Grew Up

_____ A Simple Family in England—Around the Year 1200

_____ Difficulties of Typical Family Changes in Today's World

Now read each paragraph quickly a second time. Following the material are three possible main-idea statements. In your opinion, which sentence or sentences best express the point of each paragraph? Circle the number 1, 2, or 3. Then give the reasons for your choices.

Time with the Family—Past and Present

[A] The sun was rising. A woman got up from a straw mat on the floor of her simple two-room family cottage. Her husband and their four children were still asleep on the mat. (There *were* five other children: the couple gave two of them to a family with too few workers; the other three died long ago.) The woman pushed aside the family goats. When she started the fire for cooking, the man and the children got up. While the daughter helped with the housework, the sons went outside to work in the fields with their father. They could see a castle, not far away. The family lived under the protection of the lord and master of the castle. They weren't his slaves or servants, but they paid him taxes. There was no schooling, so they couldn't read or write or get jobs in cities. During the long workday, they took breaks only for meals. Occasionally, they went to the village center, where they laughed and talked and played games. At night, people of the community got together around big fires; they told stories about the past. Most families used to live this way in England over eight hundred years ago.

1. At the beginning of the last millennium, most families lived much simpler lives than their lords and masters. They worked on the land and in the household; they had only a little time for social life and enjoyment.

2. In England in the year 1200, families used to live in castles: the daughters of lords used to do the housework, and their sons used to work in the fields with the common people.

3. In the Americas of the thirteenth century, families didn't need lords and masters for protection because they paid no taxes. They lived in extended family groups in the cities.

[B]   In the first half of the twentieth century, the Japanese family was much more "traditional" than the typical American family. Young people didn't even use to date; in other words, they didn't go out together as couples. Instead, their parents arranged their marriages. Maybe they fell in love after they got married, and maybe they didn't. Either way, the wife had children and stayed home with them while the husband supported the family financially. He rarely helped in the household; he seldom spent time with the children. He used to make all the rules, and then his family followed them. When they got older, the children had to work on the farm or in the family business. Often, the husband and wife and their children lived in an extended family situation—three generations in the same crowded house. Because marriage was not an individual matter, family life didn't use to be much fun. It was hard work.

1. All over the world, the twentieth century meant dating and falling in love at an early age. It also meant equal relationships in work, finances, parenting, and decision making.

2. Fathers are more important than mothers in family life because they support their wives and children; they also begin businesses and buy houses for their parents and grandparents.

3. Until late into the twentieth century, Japanese parents used to arrange their children's marriages. Some lived in the same house with the following generations; the men of the household made all the money and all the rules.

[C]   Where I grew up, the community on our street was like an extended family. There was no space between our row houses, and they all had front steps. All the children in the neighborhood used to play ball on those steps; on the warmest evenings, the neighbors used to sit outside on the steps to talk. For these reasons, even at an early age I knew about everyone's family forms and situations. For instance, our next-door neighbors were two women with an adopted son. To the left lived an older couple, married over forty years; they took care of their grandchildren. Two families lived in the same house across the street: a single mother with her ten-year-old daughter and an unmarried couple with a small baby. Next to them lived a successful businesswoman. She was married, but she didn't live with her husband because he had a better job and a new life in another country. Now I'm married and live with my family in another neighborhood. Even so, I will never forget the families of my community when I was young.

1. Some neighborhoods are better than others because the row houses are close together, so people can help each other when they have time.
2. Because of the close relationships formed on our front steps, I knew and remember the families of my neighborhood where I grew up. They had various structures.
3. Older couples should take care of young babies, and unmarried couples shouldn't have children. Also, husbands and wives shouldn't live in the same house.

[D]   A few years ago, a young woman left her family, married again, and moved far away with her new husband. For this reason, a thirty-six-year-old divorced father has custody of his two children, eleven and eight years old. He usually has to work weekends as a waiter, so he can't spend much time with his son and daughter. Even so, he still takes them to movies when possible. On his days off from work, he goes to a local community college. He's studying to improve his job skills so he can make more money for his family; at night he does his homework at the same table as the children. But who takes care of them when their father is working or going to school? His "extended family"—his mother, other relatives, and his girlfriend—help out as much as they can. The children used to go to the college child-care center; now they sometimes stay and play at the community sports center. Because this hard-working father loves his family very much, he believes their lives will get better and better.

1. Usually, women leave their families for financial reasons; fathers want to stay with their children and take care of them.
2. Life can be hard for today's divorced and single-parent families, but together—with the help of relatives and communities—they can improve their lives.
3. Day-care centers and community sports facilities are better for children than parents because they allow people time for study and work.

After You Read

3   **Learning to Summarize.**   How can you summarize information about history? If there is a *trend* in the history—a clear development or a change, begin with that general point. Then *paraphrase* (restate in other words) the important events and facts (the supporting details) that are part of that trend. Here are possible paraphrases for important vocabulary from the reading "Time with the Family—Past and Present."

> tradition: customs from the past, old rules and habits, ways that have existed a long time
>
> typical: most common, not unusual, serving as an example
>
> the first half of the twentieth century: the earlier part of the 1900s, from about 1900 to 1950
>
> date: go out together as couples, spend time together alone, get to know each other

And here is the possible short, paraphrased summary of the information from Paragraph A.

> In contrast to the lords in their castles, the common families of England in the last millennium led simple lives. Nuclear families lived with their animals in small, crowded cottages; members worked hard on the farms and in their households. There were many children, but some died young. Without schooling, people couldn't improve their lives financially. Even so, they had some fun in the community.

Work in groups of four. Choose a different paragraph from the reading selection "Time with the Family—Past and Present." Read it carefully. Begin with the topic or title. Summarize the main idea and important details. Then tell or read your summary to your group.

Discussing the Reading

4   In small groups, talk about your answers to these questions. Then tell the class the most interesting information or ideas.

1. In your view, were the families of long ago healthier or happier than modern families? Why or why not?

2. In your opinion, which cultures had or have the most "traditional" family forms? Explain the reasons for your answer.

3. When and where did you grow up? At that time and in that place, were families or neighborhoods different from today? Give examples.

4. Do you think the life of today's typical family is difficult? If so, in what ways? If not, why not?

Talk It Over

What are your *predictions* (ideas about what will happen) for the future of the typical family around the globe? In your opinion, which of the following present trends will increase, or become more common? Put a *plus sign* (+) on the lines before those sentences. Which of the trends will decrease, or become less common? Put a *minus sign* (−) before those predictions.

Which of the trends do you think will be *good* for people in the twenty-first century? Circle the numbers of those items. In small groups, give your answers. Explain the reasons for your predictions and views.

1. _____ Family groups will become smaller and smaller—maybe only one parent living with one or two children.

2. _____ People are going to live in large groups of relatives or friends, with all ages in the house.

3. _____ When the rate of divorces increases to almost 100 percent (%), people won't want to marry legally anymore. Instead, couples will just live together—or apart.

4. _____ Marriage between one man and one woman might still be the most common family structure, but people are going to marry many times in their lives. Most families will be "blended," so few children will grow up with both biological parents.

5. _____ Couples will have children much later in life: the average age of first-time parents will be forty. There will be many multiple births, births of more than three babies at one time.

6. _____ Single or divorced people, unmarried couples, or same-sex partnerships will become foster parents to children without families, or they will adopt babies from other countries.

7. _____ Small children might spend more time in day-care centers and schools than at home. Instead of their biological parents, babysitters or relatives may care for them.

8. _____ Couples can still have children of their own, but they may choose their features before birth: their sex, color, health, and so on. Science will make this possible.

9. _____ People are going to live much longer, so they will not only have grandchildren; there will also be great-grandchildren, great-great grandchildren, and so on. All these generations will live in the same houses or neighborhoods.

10. _____ Older people are not going to live in the same communities as families with children. Because they will be busy with their own lives and friends, they won't have time for the younger generation.

Do you have any predictions of your own about the future of the family around the world? Give your ideas. Explain why you think these events or trends might happen.

| PART 3 | # Vocabulary and Language Learning Skills |

1   **Recognizing Similar and Opposite Meanings.**   For most vocabulary items, there are words with the same or similar meanings. For some items, there are also words with *opposite* meanings—that is, completely different, or contrasting, definitions. Another way to explain and learn new vocabulary quickly is to learn both words with similar meanings and words with opposite meanings.

In each of the following pairs of words or phrases, do the vocabulary items have the same or similar meanings? If so, write *S* for *similar* on the line. Or do the vocabulary items have *opposite* meanings? If so, write *O* on the line. Two items are done as examples.

1.   _S_   on the other hand / in contrast

2.   _O_   even so / for this reason

3.   _____   but / however

4.   _____   traditional / modern

5.   _____   the structure / the form

6.   _____   marriage / divorce

7.   _____   single-parent families / extended families

8.   _____   the birthrate / the percent of deaths

9.   _____   declined / went down, or decreased

10.   _____   industrialized countries / developing nations

11.   _____   previous or past / future or following

12.   _____   returned / came back

13.   _____   change (different developments) / variation

14.   _____   advantages / useful or helpful features

15.   _____   appear (come into view) / disappear

16.   _____   stay-at-home mothers / two-income working families

17.   _____   a social institution / community organization

18.   _____   have custody of / be responsible for (take care of)

19.   _____   a lord and master / slaves or servants

20.   _____   the neighborhood / the whole world or planet

For more practice, choose some other words from Chapters 1 to 5 and tell or write similar or opposite meanings.

2 **Recognizing Nouns and Adjectives.** A very useful vocabulary-learning method is recognizing parts of speech. Some words can be more than one part of speech. As examples, in the sentences that follow, the words *family, community,* and *ancestor* are nouns; the words *familiar, common,* and *ancestral* are adjectives related to those nouns:

The *family* is a basic institution *familiar* to all of us. Families usually live in a *community.* Family members have *common ancestors* and may have *ancestral* traditions.

Here are some sentences with related words—nouns and adjectives—on the topic of the reading material of Chapter 5. Within each pair of parentheses ( ), circle the correct word form. Then write the missing words in the chart that follows. Some of the items are done as examples.

1. Like the ((community) / common), the ((family) / familiar) is a
   (society / (social)) institution.

2. Long ago, (humanity / human) beings lived in loosely (relatives / related) groups with a common (ancestor / ancestral).

3. In (China / Chinese) in the early part of the 1000s, heads of households gave ownership of their (property / proper) to their children in (equality / equal) parts.

4. In contrast to China, (Europe / European) lords gave their land only to their first-born sons; because of this (custom / customary), their families became rich and (power / powerful).

5. Usually, only the oldest sons owned the family farmland, so the (youth / younger) children moved to cities; where (education / educated) and jobs were available.

6. No longer did men and women enter into (arrangement / arranged) (marriages / married); instead, couples became partners by (choice / chosen).

7. In most of (history / historical), the (nucleus / nuclear) family form became the most (frequency / frequent) living-group arrangement.

8. The main (reason / reasonable) for the (decrease / decreased) in the size of most families was (economy / economic) necessity, or need.

9. In other words, (globe / global) (industrialization / industrialized) was a major cause of the (universe / universal) changes in family size and form.

10. With so many one-parent families in the (modernization / modern) world, social (institutions / institutional) may be more in charge of the (protection / protective) of children than their biological mothers or fathers.

Noun	Related Adjective	Noun	Related Adjective
community	common	power	powerful
family			young
society			educated
humanity			arranged
ancestors			married
China			chosen
property			nuclear
equality			frequent
Europe			reasonable
customs			decreased

For more practice, tell or write more nouns from Chapters 1 to 5. Which nouns have related adjective forms? What are they? Also, tell or write some adjectives with their related noun forms. (You can check your words in a dictionary.)

3 **Real-Life Reading: Classified Ads.** Another kind of real-life reading with useful information and vocabulary is the classified ads of newspapers or magazines. The word *ads* is the short form of *advertisements.* Advertisements are notices (pieces of information for the public) about jobs, housing, things for sale, and other categories of information. There are several kinds of ads about family and community matters.

Following are some kinds of classified ads from local newspapers and magazines for families and parents. Here are the categories of the ads. To match each ad with its classification, write each number 1–5 in two of the boxes after the item letters.

1. Birth Announcements
2. Child-Care Services
3. Housing
4. For Sale
5. Death Notices

Which words and phrases do you know? Underline them. Which words are new or difficult for you? Circle them. In groups or in class, try to figure out the meanings of the circled words. You can tell the parts of speech; you can suggest words or phrases with similar or opposite meanings, examples or categories, and so on. (Remember—the *exact* meaning may not be important. Often, the general sense is enough.) Finally, in your own words, tell the general meaning or purpose of each of the pieces of real-life information.

A.

Birth Announcements

BORN April 15. Justin Nicholas Smith. 6 Pounds, 4 Ounces. Proud Parents: Tom & Susan Smith.

B.

Services

• PLAYLAND DAY CARE •
Ages 1-3. Learning and Fun All in One. Music, Art, and More. Healthful Hot Meals & Snacks. Call 555-8538 and Ask for Maria.

C.

APT. UNF.-CITY-WEST   7550

GRT. LOC. $750 Apartment for Rent. Unfurnished. 3 Bedrooms, 2 Baths. New Carpets and Drapes. Stove, Refrigerator. Great Location for Shopping and Parks. Call First Family Realty at 555-5745

D.

HOUSES FOR SALE   6540

• BIG FAMILY HOUSE FOR SALE •
Great Value as a Fixer-Upper. Big Back Yard with Garden. Close to Good Schools and Daycare Center. Priced for Quick Sale—or Make Us a Reasonable Offer! Talk to the Owners at 999 Poplar Drive.

E.

Services

CENTURY CITY KID'S CLUB
BEAUTIFUL HOME with 3 Outdoor Play Areas. Programs for Preschoolers and After-School Care. Also, Baby Sitting available Evenings and Weekends.
License Number 5493871803   (212) 555-8327

F.

GARAGE SALES   1250

• BIG GARAGE AND YARD SALE! •
SATURDAY & SUNDAY 9 a.m to 3 p.m. Three Families are Moving Out of the Area. GREAT Bargains on Furniture, Household Items, Clothing, Books, Toys, Etc. All Available at 6677 Oak Street.

G.

MISC. SALES   1252

FOR SALE AT GREAT PRICES!
Baby and Children's Furniture (Beds, Tables, Chairs, Etc.) Clothing, Toys—Everything for the Loving Family or Daycare Center. Come See These Wonderful Values at 9876 Orchard Ave.

H.

Obituaries

KATO, Hiroshi, 85, Passed Away on November 5, 2000. Funeral Services were held on Nov. 12 at Eternal Life Cemetery.

I.

Announcements

BIRTH ANNOUNCEMENT— A FAMILY EVENT
Find Out about Our Newest Family Addition—a New Home Business. Natural Baby Food Products Prepared with Skill and Tender Loving Care. Available by Mail Order. See Our Web Page:
naturalbaby@babymart.com

J.

Obituaries

HART, Jessica, 92, Beloved Wife of the Late M.T. Hart, Mother of Joan Hart and Betty Sloan, Grandmother and Great- Grandmother, Author of "The Natural Way to Health." Memorial Service to be Announced.

For more practice, ask questions like these about each of the ads or real ads from a newspaper or magazine.

1. What does this ad announce or offer?
2. What kind of people placed this ad? For what purpose?
3. What kind of people might answer this ad? Why?

4 More Real-Life Reading. Here are some kinds of reading material common in the classified sections and other advertising of newspapers and magazines. Check (✔) the kinds available to you. Bring some examples to class, or copy the words from the ads. Write down the important vocabulary items. Give simple definitions of the words and phrases. Talk about the point of each type of notice.

- ■ _____ jobs offered
- ■ _____ jobs wanted
- ■ _____ businesses wanted or for sale
- ■ _____ apartment rentals
- ■ _____ housing for sale
- ■ _____ home and family services
- ■ _____ birth announcements
- ■ _____ children's services or child care
- ■ _____ family activities and fun
- ■ _____ engagements and weddings
- ■ _____ divorce attorneys and family legal services
- ■ _____ personals
- ■ _____ death notices / funeral announcements
- ■ _____ other _____

PART 4 Personal Stories and Humor

1 The following two readings describe two very different family housing situations. Follow these steps for the stories.

1. Read them quickly. Summarize the main ideas.
2. Answer your instructor's questions about the stories, or ask and answer questions of your own.
3. Give your opinions of the ideas in the stories.
4. Tell or write your own story about a housing or family-living situation.

Our New Home

My family and I lived in a rented apartment until last spring. We weren't happy there because the building was crowded and noisy, and the manager didn't use to fix things. We decided to move. But most available apartments in this city were even worse, and the rent was higher. So we started to look for a house to buy.

It was very difficult to find a house! Homes in quiet, beautiful neighborhoods were too expensive. We found a few inexpensive houses, but the areas were dangerous. Prices in all areas seemed to go up every day, and we needed to find a place fast. For these reasons, we were beginning to get nervous.

Finally, my husband and I found a small house in a neighborhood that wasn't bad. The problem was the house itself. It was advertised as a real "fixer-upper." That meant it was ugly. It need paint. The wallpaper was horrible; there were scenes of deserts and jungles all over the bedroom walls! The carpet was in terrible condition, and it was *orange*. The porch and roof needed repairs. The "garden" consisted of dirt, weeds, and a few half-dead plants with insects all over them. When our kids first saw their new home, they burst into tears. I understood that. I wanted to cry too.

Well, the four of us made a decision to share the work and spend our summer vacation on the house. We cleaned up the yard and painted the house. We fixed the porch and the front steps and the roof. We removed the ugly wallpaper and carpet. We planted trees and grass. Day by day, this horrible little house was beginning to feel like *home*. Now we're happy here. The kids are content—except for one thing. It's their job to cut the grass every weekend.

No Home At All

My father died when I was three years old, and I didn't have a happy childhood. I left home when I was sixteen. My sister and mother moved to another state, so I never talk to them anymore. I'm forty years old now, and I live on the streets.

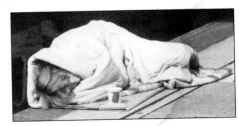

I used to be married, but my wife divorced me because of my alcohol problem. I lost my job and never found another one. After a while, I didn't have any money for rent, so I lost my apartment too. Now I sleep outside in quiet areas of the city. People call me "the Can Man" because I collect empty cans and bottles early in the morning. I sell the cans and bottles and buy food and other things with the money.

About a year ago, I decided to write a book about the experiences of a homeless man. My English isn't very good, so I needed to take some English courses. After I saved enough money, I registered for a creative writing course at the local community college. Now I write during the day and study more English at night. If my book is good, I may not be homeless for much longer. I don't need a fancy home, but I miss sleeping in a bed with a roof over my head.

The Humor of the Family

2 Humor comes in many forms, such as cartoon stories, one-frame cartoons with or without words, or even picture postcards. But the joke doesn't always include the illustrations. The point of the humor may be in the words alone, even in the things people say to others. In other words, conversations between family members and other people can be funny.

   Here are some humorous conversations between family members. Discuss your answers to these questions.

1. Who is talking? What is the relationship of the people in the picture? (Are they married, relatives, friends, etc.?)
2. What is the conversation about? What does each person say to the other? (You can read the lines aloud.)
3. Whose line contains the joke of the conversation? What is the point of the humor? Why do you think so?
4. Do you think the conversation is funny? Why or why not?
5. Does the conversation remind you of funny talk in your own family or home life? Give specific examples.

Conversation 1

Husband: What's the matter, Dear? You look exhausted!

Wife: Yeah, I am. I work in the morning, get the kids from school, take care of them, do the housework—I just can't do it all!

Husband: Yeah, I know what you mean. But you're a good worker, a wonderful wife, and a terrific mother. You can't expect to be great at all three all at the same time!

Wife: Whew. I'm so glad you understand. Then I won't be a great wife anymore.

Conversation 2

Babysitter: O.K. guys, we went outside and played a game. We watched TV. We had a snack. We went for a walk. I told you a story. What do you want to do next?

Kids: We don't know.

Babysitter: Your mom said, "I'll only be gone an hour." And we have fifty minutes left.

Conversation 3

Teen-Age

Daughter: Mom, Kevin's parents are out of town. Can he come over for dinner?

Mother: Well, I don't know, honey. I'm making a special meal, and we're five people already. I'm not sure there will be enough food for your boyfriend too.

Daughter: That's O.K., Mom. I'll just go over to his house and cook for him.

Mother: Of course Kevin can join us!

Conversation 4

Father: Is something wrong, Son? You look depressed.

Son: (mumbles) Yuwuduntunnerstan.

Father: What was that? I didn't get it. Something about wood? A wooden stand? Or your Friend Woody? Or the neighbor Stan? Is that it? Did something happen to one of them?

Son: FORGET IT!

Father: You know, sometimes I just don't understand.

Conversation 5

Woman 1: Mr. and Mrs. Sanchez! Hello! It's been a long time!

Woman 2: Hello, Mrs. McDonald! It sure has!

Woman 1: How wonderful! Are these your grandchildren?

Woman 2: What grandchildren? These are our children!

Woman 1: Really? But don't you also have a thirty-year-old daughter and a thirty-five-year-old son?

Woman 2: Yes, but like so many young people they're not interested in early marriage. So, these days, if you want grandchildren, you have to make your own.

Video Activities: Dust Mites

Before You Watch.   Discuss these questions in a group.

1. What do you know about asthma? Tell what you know about the causes and the treatment of this condition.
2. Can you guess what a "dust mite" is?
3. How can people reduce the amount of dust in their house?

Watch.

1. Write words to describe Linda Vine's house.
   Clean _____

2. How big do you think dust mites are? _____

3. In Linda Vine's house, you won't find

   a. dust   b. dust mites   c. anything made of cloth

4. Write four things Linda Vine does to control dust mites in her house.

   _____

5. What is an easy way to kill dust mites on bedding?

   _____

Watch Again.   Discuss these questions in a group.

1. The announcer says, "Asthma is part genetic and part environment." What does this mean? Can you think of other medical problems like this?
2. Did you know about dust mites before you saw this video?
3. If you had asthma, would it be difficult for you to change your house like Linda Vine did?

After You Watch.   Read about dust mites online or in an encyclopedia. Report what you read to the class. When everyone is finished reading, sit in groups. Below are questions that people often ask doctors about dust mites. Take turns answering the questions with the information from your paragraphs.

1. What are dust mites?
2. Where do dust mites live?
3. How can I reduce the number of dust mites in my bedroom?
4. What kind of floor should I have?
5. What else can I do?

Chapter 6

Cultures of the World

IN THIS CHAPTER

What does the word *culture* mean to you? In conversation form, the first reading selection, "Cross-Cultural Conversation," gives different views on the meaning and importance of the concept. In the second selection, "Clues to World Cultures," there are examples of typical cultural situations— happenings that led to misunderstanding or communication among members of various cultures. And finally, you will read about personal experiences with culture around the world.

PART 1   Cross-Cultural Conversation

Before You Read

1 Discuss the picture on page 101 in small groups.

1. What does the scene show? What kinds of people are taking part in a group conversation?

2. In your view, from what cultures are the group members? Why do you think so? Look at their clothing, the space between them, their body language, their facial expressions, and so on.

3. What do you think the people are saying about culture?

2 Think about the answers to these questions. The reading selection answers them.

1. What is a "cultural legacy" from the past? What elements might it include?

2. What are some technical or scientific achievements of ancient cultures?

3. In what ways might culture be universal in today's world?

4. In what ways might modern cultures vary around the world?

5. What are some views of the concept or idea of "culture"?

3 **Vocabulary Preview.**   Here are some vocabulary items from the first reading. You can learn them now or come back to them later.

Nouns	Verbs	Adjectives	Adverbs	Phrases
cathedrals	interrupt	proud	loudly	works of art
painters	wave	magnificent	pleasantly	classical music
sculptors	object	world-famous	impolitely	concert halls
museums	invent	first-class		in a loud voice
literature	agree	significant		one another
theaters	irritate	ancient		cultural diversity
discoveries		amazing		and another thing
medicine		enthusiastic		
achievements		pleasant		
religions		unpleasant		
weapons		polite		
a concept		rude		

Read

4 Read the following material quickly. Then read the explanations and do the exercises after the reading.

Cross-Cultural Conversation

[A] "You want to talk about culture?" Alain began the conversation in a proud voice. "The United States is only a few hundred years old. Americans aren't lucky enough to *have* any culture—they have *zero* culture, I say." He made the sign for "nothing" with his hand.

[B] "You are completely correct," interrupted Werner, loudly. He was pointing his finger. "*Old Europe* of the last thousand years—it's easy to tell *that's* where the great culture was! The age of architecture—just look at the magnificent historical cathedrals and castles. Our ancestral art legacy—if you don't know the works of world-famous painters and sculptors from previous centuries, it's *essential* to see them in our excellent museums. And *everyone* has the chance to experience our classical literature and music in first-class theaters and concert halls. I just gave you a logical description of a long and significant cultural history!"

[C] "You call a short millennium a cultural history?" Waving his arms, Kamil was objecting strongly to Werner's views. "The *real* beginning of culture—I mean, *significant civilization*—was in the Middle East and Africa over *five thousand* years ago. Ancient communities not only knew how to create magnificent architecture and art; they also made amazing scientific and technological discoveries. They *invented* things. They figured out how to write and do mathematics; they studied astronomy—the science of the skies, the sun and the planets—and invented the calendar. They even had medicine; it's important to remember that the ancient religions came from that area too. I'm happy to tell you about *their* achievements because they made world civilization possible. *Those* were the civilizations that gave humanity the most meaningful cultural legacy!"

[D] With his hands together and his head down, Jade agreed with Kamil. In a soft but nervous voice, he added, "But the *really* important science and technology began to develop in Asia and the Americas. While the ancient Chinese were building walled cities, they organized the first governments. They invented tools for work and weapons for protection. And the native peoples of the Americas had very, very old civilizations and societies. *That* was ancient traditional culture."

[E] "Ancient culture? That's a contradiction in definitions!" Grinning, Kevin objected in an enthusiastic way. Going against Jade's views, he said, "It's *impossible* for culture to be old or traditional. The *opposite* is true! Culture isn't dead—it's *alive*. Culture is *modern*! Culture is *now*!"

[F] Ken was starting to fall asleep, but suddenly he came alive. "I agree!" he said, interrupting Kevin in a forceful way.

[G] "You tell them!" said Kevin, wanting support for his point of view.

[H] "Culture is worldwide—it's universal!" answered Ken in his clear speaking style. He had a wide smile on his face. "I mean, like—take today's food culture. With our global fast food, I have to say, everyone eats the same. And because of the worldwide media—movies, TV, CDs (compact disks), the Internet—everybody knows the same information, plays the same music, enjoys the same stories—even the jokes! And I mean, it's like—people everywhere have a chance to buy the same clothes—all because of advertising. A beautiful young couple in jeans and bright Hawaiian shirts anywhere in the world, eating hamburgers and french fries with their friends from many countries—*finally*, we have a global culture! And *tradition* has nothing to do with it!"

[I] However, Monika was of another opinion. "You want to call modern movies, music, food, and clothes *culture*?" she said, beginning to get irritated. "Culture isn't about the *sameness* of people in communities around the world; it's about their *differences*. Like—it's important for people to *greet* one another in various ways, and they need to use different titles and follow a variety of social rules in their relationships. Some societies are formal, while others are informal, or casual. Some groups are friendly, and others aren't. And another example is the diverse use of language—is it direct or indirect? How do communication styles include motions, gestures, facial expressions, and other body language? And *customs* are so interesting! They're what people of different national groups *do* in their everyday lives and on special occasions like holidays or celebrations. Culture means *cultural diversity*. What makes life amusing? It's the *variety* of cultures around the world, its contradictions and opposites!"

[J] "Why are you talking so much?" interrupted Alain, impolitely.

[K] "Yeah, and why don't you understand what culture is?" said Werner in a loud voice.

[L] "And another thing—what's your problem with ancient civilizations and tradition?" disagreed Kamil with an unpleasant expression on his face. He liked to contradict Monika in a rude way.

[M] "And why do you always have a *different* view of things?" asked Kevin and Brandon. They weren't smiling either, and they wanted to talk a lot more.

After You Read

5 **Recognizing Conversation in Paragraph Form.** In a selection that explains, the information appears in paragraphs—with each paragraph about a different topic within the wider subject of the whole reading. Explanatory material can appear in other forms, however. For instance, opinions and views on a topic can be in the form of a conversation—with the words of each speaker between quotation marks (" ") in a different paragraph.

In the reading "Cross-Cultural Conversations," the speakers talk about different definitions or elements (features) of the concept (idea) of "culture." For each section of the reading, check (✔) the topic.

1. A, B

   _____ the long cultural legacy of the arts in European history

   _____ the importance of international education through the centuries

2. C, D

   _____ humanity's scientific and technological discoveries and achievements

   _____ the business practices of cultural groups in Africa and the Americas

3. E–H

_____ the differences among ancient cultures on various continents

_____ the cultural sameness and similarities among modern peoples

4. I

_____ cultural diversity—how groups vary in their styles and customs

_____ attitudes toward nature in a variety of times and places

5. J–M

_____ definitions of the word *society*—according to various world cultures

_____ different cultural ways of discussing ideas and telling opinions

Which phrase best tells the topic or subject of the whole reading "Cross-Cultural Conversation"? Circle its letter. Give the reasons for your answer.

a. the relationships among human beings in a variety of family structures and forms

b. education, food, community, family, and other subjects of interest to young people

c. various opinions about the meaning and importance of the concept of "culture"

d. variety in contrast to sameness in the global community of the Internet

6 **Understanding the Point.**   Following are some false statements about the points of the reading selection "Cross-Cultural Conversation." Make true statements by changing the underlined words. No. 5 is about the whole reading. The first item is done as an example.

1. Some people believe that a country with a ~~short~~ *long* history has more of a

cultural legacy than _old_ countries—especially in its ~~communication styles~~
~~and body language.~~ *young*   *technology and religion*

2. For other thinkers, civilization <u>didn't include</u> old architecture and art; it also

meant human <u>opinions and statements</u> in mathematics, astronomy, medicine,

weapons, city building, and the like.

3. Young people around the world <u>don't want</u> to think about food, media,

music, or clothes as culture because those things are <u>ancient</u>, and <u>nobody</u>

seems to like the same kinds.

4. According to others, diversity is <u>less significant than</u> sameness in

discussions about culture; such speakers say that people should <u>decrease</u>

<u>and forget about</u> their differences.

5. People from various <u>cathedrals and castles</u> around the world have <u>exactly the same</u> views on the meaning and importance of the concept "culture." In fact, it's common for them to express their ideas in <u>similar</u> ways.

7   **Figuring Out New Vocabulary from Context.**   Only occasionally does reading material give clear explanations of vocabulary items that are new or difficult for language learners; there aren't always punctuation or phrase clues to meaning either. Even so, readers may not have to look in the dictionary to understand important words and phrases. Instead, they can *figure out* their general meaning from the context.

    In the reading "Cross-Cultural Conversation," the speakers talk about two kinds of culture. One meaning of *culture* is "a society's achievements in the arts, science, or government." Werner has that meaning in mind when he talks about the cathedrals, castles, and museums of Europe. Another meaning of *culture* is "the values, beliefs, and customs of a society." Monika has that meaning in mind when she talks about greetings, titles, and social rules.

    Here are some sentences with important vocabulary from the reading selection. From the context, answer the questions about the <u>underlined</u> items. Then circle the letter of the explanation that seems the most logical in the context.

1. Some examples of the <u>architecture</u> of old Europe are the magnificent cathedrals and castles. The design and building styles of modern <u>architecture</u> are excellent too.

   What are some examples of old *architecture*?

   _____

   What are some excellent features of modern *architecture*?

   _____

   What does the noun *architecture* mean in these sentences?
   a. the form and plan of buildings and other structures
   b. the art and science of designing the study of classical literature
   c. people that study the culture of old Europe and other societies

2. Perhaps the real beginning of <u>civilization</u>—with its scientific and technological discoveries and inventions—was in the Middle East and Africa. Over five thousand years ago, ancient <u>civilizations</u> has astronomy, mathematics, medicine, government, and so on.

   Where and when did *civilization* begin?

   _____

   What kinds of things did ancient *civilizations* have?

   _____

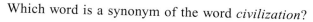

Which word is a synonym of the word *civilization*?

a. astronomy

b. technology

c. culture

3. The cultural <u>legacy</u> of ancient Chinese and Indian peoples included walled cities, the first governments, tools for work, and weapons for protection. Modern peoples built on this <u>legacy</u>.

Does a *legacy* come from the past, the present, or the future?

_____

What kinds of things might a *legacy* include?

_____

What is a possible explanation of the word *legacy*?

a. a gift of money that somebody gives to another person

b. ideas and achievements passed from earlier generations to modern society

c. the state or condition of being legal; not against the law

4. "For me, the idea of ancient culture creates a <u>contradiction</u> in definitions," said Kevin, going against Jade's views. "Only modern things can be part of culture. Of course, people that like classical art and music will <u>contradict</u> me."

According to Kevin, what kinds of things are part of culture?

_____

Do people that like classical art and music agree with him?

_____

Do Kevin and Jade have the same or very different opinions?

_____

What might the noun *contradiction* and the verb *contradict* mean?

a. (noun) the opposition of two opinions; (verb) to say that someone's ideas are wrong

b. (noun) the short forms of two words together; (verb) to put words together

c. (noun) wearing a Hawaiian shirt in an ancient culture; (verb) to eat hamburgers with french fries

5. Because of the worldwide <u>media</u>—movies, TV, CDs, the Internet, newspapers, magazines—everybody knows the same information, plays the same music, and enjoys the same jokes.

What are some examples of "the worldwide media"?

_____

What do *the media* give to people around the world?

_____

How might you define the phrase *the media*?

    a. events that appear in the daily news and that everyone knows about

    b. the tradition of being in the middle—not on the extremes of possible views

    c. the combination of visual, sound, and printed ways to send ideas around the world

For more practice, in the reading material look for and figure out the general meanings of other vocabulary items, such as *in a proud voice, logical, significant, magnificent, essential, amazing, invented, astronomy, tools and weapons, enthusiastic, going against, alive, a wide smile, greet, diverse, cultural diversity, an unpleasant expression,* and so on. For each item, explain the reasoning for your guesses.

8 **Recognizing the Details of Opinions.** Clearly, the speakers in the "Cross-Cultural Conversation" have diverse opinions and views about the value and importance of their various concepts of culture. Some words in their speeches are in *italics*; this special kind of slanted print can mean the speakers think the words are important to their point, so they say them more strongly than other words. An exclamation point, a punctuation mark that looks like this (!), also shows strong emphasis.

According to their opinions, what do the speakers in the "Cross-Cultural Conversation" value within their concepts of culture? Circle the letters of *all* the correct answers to each question.

1. Alain and Werner felt that the age of a culture added to the value of its fine arts. Which elements (parts) of culture were essential to them?

    a. fast food and junk food

    b. old painting and sculpture

    c. literature and classical music

    d. human feelings and emotions

    e. the architecture of buildings and structures

    f. things in museums, theater plays, and concerts

2. Kamil and Jade most valued the ancient civilizations of the Middle East, Africa, and the Americas. What things did they include in "a cultural legacy"?

    a. international business

    b. magnificent architecture and art

    c. scientific discoveries and invention

    d. writing and mathematics

    e. the study of astronomy

    f. protected cities and government structure

3. Kevin and Brandon are happy that modern culture is worldwide and similar all over the planet. Which features did they find the most important?

 a. ancient religions

 b. the historical structure of the family

 c. food from global chains

 d. Indian rock tools and weapons

 e. the media of movies, TV, and the Web

 f. advertising for clothes and other things

4. Monika preferred cultural diversity to sameness. What things did she include in her concept of culture?

 a. greetings, including titles and names

 b. relationships and other social rules

 c. formality in contrast to informality

 d. directness and indirectness in language

 e. body language and movements

 f. everyday and special occasion customs

5. In what ways did the group members discuss their ideas and opinions with one another?

 a. proudly and with emphasis

 b. strongly and forcefully

 c. in a loud or a soft voice

 d. grinning or smiling—or not

 e. with a clear speaking style

 f. agreeing or disagreeing

For more practice, turn back to the Before You Read section on page 100 and answer the questions.

Discussing the Reading

 9

In small groups, talk about your answers to the following questions. Then tell the class the most interesting information and ideas.

1. In your view of the concept of culture, which elements are essential—or very important? Why?

2. According to your experience, in what ways are world cultures similar or alike? Which features are different? Explain your views.

3. Which is better for humanity and the future of the world—one global culture or cultural diversity all over the planet? Explain your reasoning or logic.

PART 2	# Clues to World Cultures

Before You Read

1 **Vocabulary Preview.**   Here are some vocabulary items from the next reading selection. You can learn them now or come back to them later.

Nouns	Verbs	Adjectives	Adverbs	Phrases
a pharmacy	step	patient	impatiently	wait your turn
a pharmacist	serve	insulted	backwards	clean your plate
customers	burst	insulting		pay attention to
attention	ignore	delicious		stand in line
service	expect	successful		thumbs up
pain	beg	mean		
a bite	hitchhike	afraid		
guests	shout	unwelcome		
hosts				

Read

2 A lot of reading material on the topic of world cultures includes descriptions of cultural situations. These very short stories may or may not be people's real experiences; they tell what happened to create cross-cultural misunderstanding or learning. The stories present useful information for better communication between people from various cultural backgrounds; using logic, readers can figure out differences from the "clues to culture" in the material. Most reading of this kind is about topics such as the following:

_____ greetings and introductions; meeting new people

_____ visiting a family at home; eating and drinking with people from other cultures

_____ body language—gestures, hand movements, and facial expressions

_____ concepts of time and timing—doing things in a certain order or at the same time

_____ formality and informality, directness and indirectness in communication

_____ ideas about individual and group responsibility and rights

Following are three short stories with the general title of "Clues to World Cultures." On the lines before *three* of the topics listed above, write the story letters A, B, and C. (There are no stories about the other three topics in this part of the chapter.)

    On your second reading of each story, look for "culture clues"—pieces of information that may suggest differences between members of two cultural groups. These possible differences in customs, attitudes, beliefs, and the like are the *point* of the material. Following each paragraph are some questions about the "cross-cultural meaning" of the experience. Circle the letter of the best (the most logical) answer—a, b, or c. Then give your answers and the reasons for them.

Clues to World Cultures

[A]   An Irish woman was visiting tourist places in a Latin American city when she got a terrible headache. She knew what medicine she needed, so she stepped into a local pharmacy. The pharmacist was waiting on another customer when she came in. The Irish woman patiently waited her turn. While she was standing there, two other customers came in, then another, and then three more. Each time, the pharmacist turned his attention to the new people. He did not greet the Irish woman; he never said, "I'll be with you in a minute."

After about twenty minutes, the woman couldn't stand the pain in her head any longer. "Hey, I've been here a long time," she said loudly, very annoyed and insulted. "Why is everyone ignoring me? I need service too!" she shouted rudely (impolitely).

1. Why didn't the pharmacist pay attention to the Irish woman when she came into his store?
    a. He didn't know her, and he didn't like her looks.
    b. She didn't greet him or ask for attention; she just stood there quietly.
    c. He was probably not waiting on a customer at all—just talking to a friend.

2. Why was the Irish customer irritated, angry, or hurt?
    a. She had a terrible headache; her pain reduced her patience.
    b. She expected the pharmacist to greet her and wait on her in turn (in order).
    c. She didn't want to buy medicine; it was too expensive at the pharmacy.

3. What is the cultural point of the story?
    a. In some cultures, people wait their turn for greetings and attention, but in others, they ask for these things in some clear way.
    b. In stores in all countries, people need to be patient: they have to stand quietly in line and wait for service—often for a long time.
    c. Pain is different in various parts of the world; some people can stand it better than others.

[B]   A Middle-Eastern businessman and his brother invited an American guest to their family home for dinner. The American got there on time and enjoyed the interesting conversation, the coffee, and the attention. But as time passed, he got very, very hungry. Finally he asked in an impatient voice, "So when do we eat?"

"Finally you are hungry!" answered one of his hosts. "We were waiting for you to say you were ready to eat."

At the dinner table everything was delicious, and the American guest ate quickly. He emptied his plate, and his hosts' wives put more food on it. As soon as he cleaned his plate a second time, the women served him more. After several plates of food, he could eat no more: he was going to burst! "Please, please, please—don't give me any more food," he begged them. "I can't eat another bite!"

"Then why didn't you leave any food on the plate?" asked the other host, surprised. "We were amazed at how much you were eating!"

1. Why did the host family serve dinner so late?
   a. They always eat dinner at a late hour because they fast (don't eat) all day.
   b. The wives were working in the kitchen: dinner wasn't ready yet.
   c. In their culture, it is the right of dinner guests to decide when to begin the meal.

2. Why did the American guest eat more food than he wanted?
   a. He was very, very hungry because there was no food in his house and he never went to restaurants.
   b. His hosts' wives kept putting food on his plate; he didn't want to leave food or seem impolite, so he ate it all.
   c. In the dinner conversation, his hosts talked and talked; he didn't get a chance to answer, so he paid attention only to the food.

3. What is the cultural point of the story?
   a. In some cultures, polite hosts wait for their guests to ask for dinner; then they serve them food every time their plates are empty.
   b. All over the world, dinner guests should eat a lot; if they leave anything on their plates, their hosts will think they don't like the food.
   c. In some cultures, guests eat more than their hosts; in others, it is impolite to eat a lot at other people's houses.

[C] A group of international students were attending college in Europe. They had a long time between semesters for travel, so they decided to hitchhike as far as they could in other countries. In many places, they were successful: they put their thumbs out or pointed them backwards and smiled; friendly drivers stopped. As soon as the first traveler got a "yes" answer from a driver, he motioned with his hand or fingers for his friends to come—or he held both thumbs up in an "O.K." sign or made a circle with the thumb and the next finger of one hand. The young tourists saved money, saw a lot of the countryside, and had interesting conversations and experiences.

On the other hand, in Greece and Turkey, the visitors were not so lucky. Few drivers stopped to give them rides; instead, most people ignored them. Others gave them mean looks from their cars: they seemed almost insulted that the visitors were begging for rides. A few drivers shouted terrible words at the travelers; two even got out of their truck and started a fight. The students felt confused, afraid, and unwelcome; after a few days they took the bus back to the countries where they were studying.

1. Why did the young travelers get rides successfully in many places in Europe?

   a. Drivers knew they were trying to "thumb rides" because they recognized the meanings of their hand gestures.

   b. All the travelers were good-looking young men, and the drivers that stopped were single women.

   c. Most people knew the students had money; they expected payment for the rides in their cars and trucks.

2. Why weren't the student tourists so lucky in Greece and Turkey?

   a. In those countries there are laws against hitchhiking, so drivers aren't allowed to give rides to travelers.

   b. In certain places the custom is to ask for rides with printed signs: the signs should tell the place the travelers want to go.

   c. The "hitchhiking" thumb gesture has an insulting meaning in those cultures: drivers thought the young people were being rude and disrespectful.

3. What is the cultural point of the story?

   a. Hand gestures are rude because they are kinds of body language: visitors to other cultures should always ask for things with words.

   b. Travelers should hitchhike only in their home cultures: drivers are afraid to give rides to foreigners.

   c. The same gestures (hand positions and movements) can have very different meanings in various cultures—even opposite meanings.

After You Read

3   **Learning to Summarize.**   How can you summarize a very short story with a point? The shortest way is to begin with the meaning or message of the story in a sentence or two. Then retell the story as an example of the point.

   Work in groups of four. Choose a story from the reading selection "Clues to World Cultures." Read it carefully. Begin with cultural point or "message" of the material. Paraphrase or retell the events of the story in your own words. Then tell or read your summary to your group.

Discussing the Reading

4   In small groups, talk about your answers to these questions. Then tell the class the most interesting information or ideas.

1. In your community, city, or country, do people pay attention to others one at a time or all at the same time? Who gets attention first—the people already in conversation or the new people?

2. At dinner parties in your culture, what are some of the "rules" or customs? How do hosts offer or serve food? How do guests ask for food—or ask for more?

3. What are some hand, finger, or thumb positions or movements in your culture? What do they mean—and do they have the same meanings in all situations? Do people from other communities or countries use the same gestures in the same ways? Explain.

4. What is a "cross-cultural situation"? What kinds of things might cause misunderstanding between members of two different cultures?

Talk It Over

Here are some statements about cultural attitudes, customs, and so on. In your opinion or experience, which sentences are true for typical situations in your social group, your community, your native country, or your culture? Check (✔) those items and explain your choices. Where do you think the other statements might be true? Why do you think so?

1. _____ To greet each other, people bow the head or bend the body forward. This body movement shows respect. Shaking hands or kissing and hugging are not common forms of greeting.

2. _____ Young people usually dress informally. Even for business or special occasions, they can wear comfortable clothes, like jeans and bright Hawaiian shirts.

3. _____ Families invite guests to their homes for dinner parties; they prepare special meals. They rarely meet guests in restaurants.

4. _____ Guests come on time for dinner parties, but hosts don't usually serve food right away. Instead, people enjoy drinks and conversation for a long time before the meal.

5. _____ People give gifts of money for special occasions, like birthdays, weddings, and holidays. They bring food or wine gifts to dinner parties.

6. _____ On social occasions, people smile a lot. They give compliments; that is, they say nice things to others about their clothes, their appearance, their houses, and so on.

7. _____ On the street and in public places like stores, people are not usually very polite; they try to be first and to get what they want. They may shout or use rude gestures.

8. _____ In classes at schools and colleges, students try to be first to answer questions. They tell their ideas and say their opinions on many topics. They may contradict the teacher.

9. _____ The individual is more important than the group or the community. Each person is responsible for his or her own needs, achievements, and success.

10. _____ Time is very important in society because time means money; most people are in a hurry all the time.

Do you have any statements of your own about cultural customs, habits, attitudes, and actions? Give your ideas. Others can give their opinions about your sentences. They can name the cultures where your statements are most often true.

PART 3

Vocabulary and Language Learning Skills

1   **Recognizing Nouns, Verbs, and Adjectives.**   If you don't know the meaning of a new vocabulary item, it helps to figure out the part of speech it is. Is the word a noun (a person, place, thing, or concept)? Is it a verb—a word for an action or a condition? Maybe the word is an adjective; in other words, its function might be to describe a noun or pronoun. One way to tell the part of speech of an item is to recognize its function or purpose in the sentence—what does the word *do* or *serve as*? Another is to figure out what question the item answers. Here is a summary of these clues to parts of speech.

Part of Speech	Function or Purpose	Question the Word Answers	Examples
A noun	serves as the subject of the sentence is the object or complement of a verb or the object of a preposition	Who? (What person?) What? (What thing, place, or concept?)	<u>Kevin</u> writes long <u>letters</u> to a good <u>friend</u> in <u>France</u>.
A verb	names an action, an activity, or a condition (a state of being)	What does the subject of the sentence do?	Kevin <u>writes</u> long letters to a good friend in France.
An adjective	describes a noun or pronoun	How is it?	Kevin writes <u>long</u> letters to a <u>good</u> friend in France.

In the blanks of the sentences on the left, write the missing noun, verb, and adjective from the parts of speech chart. Then give the parts of speech of the words. The first item is done as an example.

1. Are you _____*correct*_____ (adjective) in your concept of culture? Can you _____*correct*_____ (verb) your previous ideas? Can you make necessary _____*corrections*_____ (noun)?

Noun	Verb	Adjective
corrections	correct	correct

2. Can you _Verb_ ~~describe~~ a
   typical cross-cultural situation?
   In your _Noun description_, use
   as many _adj descriptive_ words
   as you can.

Noun	Verb	Adjective
description	describe	descriptive

3. To attract tourists, cities advertise
   the _Noun_ of their
   architecture. They say that the
   buildings _Verb_ in
   their beauty. They talk about the
   adj artwork too.

Noun	Verb	Adjective
excellence	excel	excellent

4. Are you an _adj_
   traveler? Do you like to
   _V_ the customs and
   habits of people in other cultures?
   Do you enjoy new
   _N_?

Noun	Verb	Adjective
experiences	experience	experienced

5. One definition of the word
   Noun is "a high level
   of culture. Does a good education
   adj verb people? Does it
   make them more
   adj adj?

Noun	Verb	Adjective
civilization	civilize	civilized

6. When did ancient civilizations
   _V_ the calendar?
   Which _adj_ people
   figured it out? What were some
   of their other _N_?

Noun	Verb	Adjective
inventions	invent	inventive

7. People of the same cultural background don't always _____ ✓ _____ on the values of society. Even _____ adj _____ people aren't in _____ N _____ all the time.

Noun	Verb	Adjective
agreement	agree	agreeable

8. Every _____ N _____ (group of people of the same culture) has _____ adj _____ problems to solve. It also has to _____ ✓ _____ its young people.

Noun	Verb	Adjective
society	socialize	social

9. Sometimes two cultural values seem to _____ ✓ _____ each other. For instance, individual achievement may be _____ adj _____ to the interests of families. It may create _____ N _____ .

Noun	Verb	Adjective
contradictions	contradict	contradictory

10. When did global advertising begin to _____ ✓ _____ through the Internet? The _____ N _____ of the World Wide Web is a significant achievement all over the globe, including in _____ adj _____ nations.

Noun	Verb	Adjective
development	develop	developing

2 **Using Adverbs of Manner.** In vocabulary learning, the four most important parts of speech are nouns, verbs, adjectives, and adverbs. That's because there are many more of these kinds of words than the "function parts of speech," such as prepositions and pronouns. Vocabulary items that include these parts of speech also "carry the meaning" of most sentences.

Adverbs are parts of speech that answer the question "how?" or "when?" or "where?" "Adverbs of manner" tell *how* or *in what way* something happens. Most often, adverbs of manner are closely related to adjectives; they usually end in the letters *–ly.* For example, the adverb *easily* means "in an easy way." *Loudly* is an adverb of manner with the meaning "in a loud voice."

Here are some sentences with two related words—one adjective and one adverb of manner. In each blank, write the missing word—the adjective related to the underlined adverb or the adverb related to the underlined adjective. The first item is done as an example.

1. A <u>proud</u> Frenchman began the conversation about culture ___proudly___.

2. A German student answered him in a ___loud___ & clear voice. He spoke <u>loudly</u> and clearly.

3. An American member of the group had an <u>easy</u> way about her. She answered questions ___easily___.

4. A Middle-Eastern woman said she found ancient civilizations <u>amazing</u>. As an example, she added, "___amazily___, they studied astronomy thousands of years ago."

5. An Iranian man stated his opinions ___agreely___; the group agreed he had an <u>agreeable</u> personality.

6. "The ___scientific___ mind looks at problems and situations <u>scientifically</u>," said someone from a well-developed Asian culture.

7. "But ___human___ beings don't always act <u>humanly</u> toward one another," objected a Canadian social worker.

8. "I'm afraid I have to disagree with you," a nice African man answered <u>politely</u>. "According to the rules of their culture, most people try to be ___polite___."

9. In a <u>soft</u> voice, a young Chinese student said his opinion; but he said it too ___softly___ for the others to hear.

10. Finally, the most <u>forceful</u> member of the group ended the discussion ___forcefully___.

For more practice, tell or write more nouns, verb, adjectives, and adverbs from Chapters 1 to 6. Which words have related forms that are the same or other parts of speech? What are they? You can check your predictions in a dictionary. Can you use them in sentences that show their meanings?

3   **Real-Life Reading: Calendar Notices and Announcements.**   In addition to classified ads, many kinds of real-life reading material contain other kinds of advertising. A lot of this advertising is for products and services, but some of it is for cultural events and meetings. These notices and announcements (pieces of public information for the community) often appear in the "Calendar" section of local newspapers and magazines. Sometimes, they are listed in the order of their dates (days of the week and times). In other instances, they are organized according to the *kind* of event or happening, such as the following:

1. Sports
2. Music
3. Movies
4. Plays or Performances
5. Literary readings

6. Lectures and panel discussions
7. Art and architecture
8. Cultural festivals
9. Travel packages

Some copies of calendar notices and announcements from local newspapers and magazines are shown on page 119. To match each piece of information with its classification, write the numbers 1–9 in the boxes after the item letters.

Which words and phrases do you know? Underline them. Which words are new or difficult for you? Circle them. In groups or in class, try to figure out the meanings of the circled words. You can tell the parts of speech; you can suggest words or phrases with similar or opposite meanings, examples or categories, and so on. Remember—the *exact* meaning may not be important. Often, the general sense is enough.

Finally in your own words, give the general meaning or purpose of each of the pieces of real-life information.

For more practice, ask questions like these about each of the ads, notices, or announcements in Exercise 3. Or use real information from the calendar section of a newspaper or magazine.

1. What does this piece of information announce or offer?
2. What kind of people or place put this notice in the newspaper? For what purpose?
3. What kind of people might go to these events? Why?

4   **More Real-Life Reading.**   Here are some kinds of reading material about cultural events in the community. Check (✔) the kinds available to you. Bring some examples to class, or copy the words from the notices or announcements. Write down the important vocabulary items. With simple definitions, tell the meanings of the words and phrases. Talk about the point of each piece of material.

- ■ _____ posters (displayed in the community) for special events
- ■ _____ brochures and fliers for performances, concerts, exhibits, and the like
- ■ _____ catalogs and postcards from different kinds of museums
- ■ _____ photos of famous tourist attractions (in books, magazines, etc.)
- ■ _____ travel ads, including descriptions of packaged tours
- ■ _____ the calendar sections of local newspapers, including free community papers
- ■ _____ other _____

A.

OUTDOOR EVENT

"GOING THE DISTANCE FOR OUR COMMUNITY"

The Third Annual International Walk and Run Benefits Local People with Disabilities.

Celebrate our Diversity and Help!

Entry fee $30, $10 for Kids.
Begins at 9:00 a.m. on Saturday, April 28, Sunland Park.

B.

FESTIVALS

ASIAN PACIFIC HERITAGE MONTH

The Yearly Festival Begins at Noon on Tuesday and Continues the Whole Month of May. There are Cultural Exhibits, Dance and Song Performances, Tai Chi and Cooking Demonstrations, Travel Talks, *and Much, Much More.* For more Information, Call State University Student Union at 555-8888.

C.

Community Events

CULTURAL

COMMUNITY MEETING ON DIVERSITY

Matters of Cultural Similarities and Differences Discussed by Members of Jewish, Moslem, Christian, Latino, Asian, African-American, Women's, Disabled, and Gay Communities. Lecture and Class Schedules. Come meet with us and learn to understand. *FREE.* 7 p.m. Tuesday at Global City College, 1500 East-West Drive in Northridge.

D.

TRAVEL

GLOBAL TRAVEL

TRAVEL BARGAINS TO FOREIGN COUNTRIES AND CULTURES!

Cross the Equator and Meet Indian Peoples on an Amazing Amazon River Cruise! See the Magnificent Cathedrals and Castles of Old Europe! Enjoy Traditional Classical Music and Dance Concerts in Beautiful Russia! Eat Your Way Around the Planet on Our International Cooking Trip! *Over One Hundred Low-Cost Tours.* For the Best in Education and Experience in World Cultures, come to the

Wonderful World Travel Store

123 Wilshire Boulevard

E.

Events

CULTURAL

WORLDWIDE BOOKSTORE

PRESENTS POETRY AND SHORT STORY READINGS

by a Multicultural Literary Group. Jerru Assefa reads from "Growing Up in an African Village." Maureen McWay tells her "Luck-of-the-Irish Life Lessons." Great Surprises are waiting for you at 5891 Gifford Lane in Littleton. Monday through Thursday 2-3 and 7-8 p.m.

F.

THEATER

AGAMEMNON: Ancient Classic Greek Tragedy— with a modern International Attitude. Space, Time, History, and Culture—It's all in this Magnificent Live Play for the 21st Century. Bring the Family. Starts Saturday, May 5 at the Actors Theater. 7:30 and 9:30 Performances. Weekend Matinees. Call for Reservations and Tickets.

G.

CINEMA

FOUR FABULOUS FOREIGN FILMS—
All in One Fantastically Fun Film Festival!

See **LIFE IS LIVABLE,** by Famous Italian Director Marcello Marvolini, **THE GREAT EGG WAR,** with Hugh Gulliver, **ALI! ALI!** *(A German Movie with Turkish Actors),* and **MY HOUSE IS YOUR HOUSE,** an exploration of cultural identity.

Showings at Movie Houses around the City. See Film Section of this Calendar.

H.

EXHIBITS

PHARAOHS OF THE SUN

is a special exhibit of ancient architecture (photos and models) and art objects from the Valley of the Nile River—millenniums in the past. All on display at the City Art Museum, along with our regular collections of paintings— Four Centuries of the Classic European Masters.

I.

Entertainment

HARD ROCKIN' CAFE   FREE Weeknight Shows! Tuesday, **April 24:** Nieve, the latest Latin American Sound. Wednesday, **April 25:** Ata Ito & His Japanese Country Music Boys. Thursday, **April 26:** Hawaiian Heads—a Flowery Island Concert. *Doors open 7:00 p.m., Shows start at 8:30.* 7000 Lancaster Lane in Westwood Village

PART 4	# Personal Stories and Humor

1 The following readings describe two very different experiences with life in a "foreign" culture. Follow these steps for the stories.

1. Read them quickly. Summarize the main ideas.
2. Answer your instructor's questions about the stories, or ask and answer questions of your own.
3. Give your opinions of the ideas in the stories.
4. Tell or write your own story about a cross-cultural experience.

The Excitement of a Foreign Culture

World travel? Cross-cultural experience? Cultural diversity? I can't get enough of it all! For me, anything foreign—that is, anything different from the customs and culture of the neighborhood where I grew up—is exciting!

In high school I was an exchange student on the beautiful island of Sumatra. I lived in the private home of an Indonesian family. The mother of the family used to get up very early, wash clothes by hand, and cook the same kinds of food every day. We almost always had dried salt fish and vegetables. It was a hard life, but I found out a lot about the culture. For example, I learned never to eat and walk at the same time, and I didn't use my left hand in public. I'll never forget that wonderful time.

Then as an undergraduate student I went to an international university in Switzerland. All the students lived in language-and-culture "villages." There was a French village, an Italian village, a German village, and so on. All of our professors and teaching assistants were natives of that culture, and we even spoke the language with our classmates from other places. Every day and all the time, we experienced *real life* in a foreign country.

Now I am a "culture expert." As a graduate student abroad, I am studying international business and law.

The Confusion of Multiculturalism

Global culture? Multiculturalism? It's a confusing way of life! I want to be of *one* culture, and I want the same for my children.

When I arrived in Vancouver, Canada, from Trinidad, I was eighteen years old and alone. About a year later, I went back to my South American island homeland to visit my parents. Within days, I realized I was a completely different person. Even after so short a time, my old friends from childhood seemed like strangers. Old places seemed like old places. Already Trinidad—with its ways, its views, its culture and customs—was disappearing in my heart. It was becoming only the place where I grew up. My emotions and feelings were in my new home, my new life, and my new culture.

But Canada values multiculturalism. Trying to be friendly, the neighbors in my community often asked me, "So what nationality are you?"

"Canadian," I used to answer.

"No—really." Where did your family come from? What's your cultural background?

Not long ago, my daughter's teacher asked the children of her first-grade class, "Where did your family come from?"

My daughter told the class, "My father was born in Trinidad into an East Indian family. Now he is Canadian. My mother was born in Quebec, and I was born in Montreal."

"Oh," said the teacher, brightly. "So you're from a West Indian family!"

My five-year-old child came home from school that day confused and depressed.

The Humor of World Cultures

2   Other than cartoon stories, one-frame cartoons, picture postcards, and funny conversations, what are some other forms of humor? One common kind is an *anecdote* or *joke*—a very short story with a humorous point called the punch line.

On the topic of world cultures, many jokes contain ethnic humor. With these kinds of stories, people laugh at common personality features or customs that seem "typical" of their own or others' cultural backgrounds or groups. However, in certain situations some people might object to ethnic jokes or find them insulting. Usually, they are not meant that way; their purpose if just to make light of cultural differences.

Here are some humorous anecdotes on the subject of culture. Some come from true experiences. Others are made-up jokes for amusement only. Discuss your answers to these questions:

1. Who are the people in each anecdote or joke? Where are they? What do they do and say?
2. Whose line contains the joke of the conversation? What is the cultural point of the humor? Why do you think so?
3. Do you think the story is funny? Why or why not?
4. Does the story remind you of a similar anecdote or joke about the same or another culture? Tell your joke if you want to. (Make sure it is not insulting to any of your listeners.)

Joke A

A couple went traveling in India. Of course, they visited the Taj Mahal. Amazed at the beauty of the architecture, the man stood in front of it while his wife took his picture—with the magnificent building in the background. When they got home, they made a large print of the photo, framed it, and hung it in the middle of their living room wall. A short time later, a relative visited the couple with their ten-year-old son. "Hey, when did you guys go to DisneyWorld?" asked the enthusiastic boy.

Joke B

Two South Americans were bragging about the beautiful mountain scenery in their homelands. They were both trying to outdo the other guy's description of the magnificence of nature in their native countries.

"Mount Galan is so big and so high," said the Argentinian, "that you can climb to the top and shout 'Señor Gomez,' and the echo won't repeat 'Señor Gomez' for two minutes." The Peruvian thinks for a moment. Then he brags, "That's nothing. You climb the highest mountain in my country, shout 'Señor Gomez,' and the echo doesn't come back for *three* minutes. And it says, 'Which Señor Gomez do you want?'"

Joke C

A young Scottish guy decided to try life in Australia. He found an apartment on a quiet street and moved in. After a week, his mother called from Glasgow. "How are you doing, Sonny Boy?" she asked.

"I'm fine," he answered. "But there are some really strange people living in these apartments. One woman cries all day long, and another lies on her floor and makes sounds of pain. And there is a guy next door to me who hits his head on the wall all the time."

"Well, my Laddie," worried his mother, "I don't want *you* to go around with people like that."

"Oh," said the young man. "I don't, Mom. No, I just stay inside my apartment all day and night, playing my bagpipes."

Video Activities: Chinese New Year

Before You Watch.   Discuss these questions in a group.

1. Have you ever seen a Chinese New Year celebration? Describe this experience.
2. Talk about your New Year celebration last year. Where were you? Who was with you? How did you celebrate? Was it a happy time for you?

Watch.   Write answers to these questions.

1. In which season is the Chinese New Year? _____
2. Who is the blond woman? _____
3. Which Chinese customs did you see in the video? _____
_____

Watch Again.

1. How is the man going to celebrate the Chinese New Year? Place a check next to the things he says.

    _____ Eat   _____ See dancing

    _____ Drink alcohol   _____ Light firecrackers

    _____ Buy gifts for his children

2. Complete this sentence: "Some men are doing the Red Lion Dance. They dance for _____. If the _____ likes the dance, he gives them _____ envelopes with lucky _____ inside."

3. Why do people light firecrackers on the New Year?

4. The New Year celebrations will continue for _____ days.

After You Watch.   There are many words for describing noises. In the video, you learned that the noise of firecrackers is called a "bang." Below are some more "noise words." With the help of a dictionary, match them with the items on the right that make that noise.

Noise Word

1. _____ boom
2. _____ crash
3. _____ cry
4. _____ jangle
5. _____ purr
6. _____ ring
7. _____ roar
8. _____ slam
9. _____ splash
10. _____ squeak
11. _____ squawk

Thing

a. a door closing loudly
b. a baby
c. a lion or a waterfall
d. a car accident
e. a chicken
f. something falling into water
g. keys
h. a happy cat
i. a bell
j. thunder
k. a metal object that needs oil (like the hinges of an old door)

Chapter 7

Health

IN THIS CHAPTER

What age do you think of as "old"? Sixty? Seventy? Eighty? The first reading selection, "The Secrets of a Very Long Life," is about some places of the world where eighty-year-olds still have many years ahead of them. In the second reading selection, "Claims to Amazing Health," you will learn about some exciting technological changes and trends in modern medicine. Finally, you will read about someone's experiences with smoking—and what that person has learned about health.

| PART 1 | # The Secrets of a Very Long Life |

Before You Read

1 Discuss the picture in small groups.

1. Who are the two people? What are they doing?
2. Describe the lifestyle of the elderly couple. What do they probably do all day? What do they probably eat?
3. Do you know any very old people? How is their lifestyle similar to the lifestyle of the people in the picture? How is it different?

2 Think about the answers to these questions. The reading selection answers them.

1. What places in the world are famous for people who live a very long time?
2. Describe the advantages and benefits of the environment in these places.
3. What kind of diet do people in these places have?
4. What might be some secrets of an unusually long life?

rural life
countryside

3   **Vocabulary Preview.**   Here are some vocabulary items from the first reading. You can learn them now or come back to them later.

Nouns	Verbs	Connectors	Other Phrases
secrets	consume	moreover	public health experts
the altitude	prevent	furthermore	solve a mystery
teeth	cure	in addition	birth records
eyesight	theorize	as a result	a full head of hair
flowers		however	make an effort
wildlife		therefore	
apricots		thus	
an average		nevertheless	
herbs			
preservatives			
stress			
theories			

Read

4   Read the following material quickly. Then read the explanations and do the exercises after the reading.

The Secrets of a Very Long Life

[A]   There are several places in the world that are famous for people who live a very long time. These places are usually in mountainous areas, far away from modern cities. Even so, doctors, scientists, and public health specialists often travel to these regions to solve the mystery of a long, healthy life; in this way, the experts hope to bring to the modern world the secrets of longevity.

[B]   Hunza is at a very high altitude in the Himalayan Mountains of Asia. There, many people over one hundred years of age are still in good physical health. Additionally, men of ninety are new fathers, and women of fifty still have babies. What are the reasons for this good health? Scientists believe that the people of Hunza have these three main advantages or benefits: (1) a healthful unpolluted environment with clean air and water; (2) a simple diet high in vitamins, fiber, and nutrition but low in fat, cholesterol, sugar, and unnatural chemicals; and (3) physical work and other activities, usually in the fields or with animals.

[C]   People in the Caucasus Mountains in Russia are also famous for their longevity. Official birth records were not available, but the community says a woman called Tsurba lived until age 160. Similarly, a man called Shirali probably lived until 168; moreover, his widow was 120 years old. In general, the people not only live a long time, but they also live *well*. In other words, they are almost never sick. Furthermore, when they die, they not only have their own teeth but also a full head of hair, and good eyesight too. Vilcabamba, Ecuador, is another area famous for the longevity of its inhabitants. This mountain region—like Hunza and the Caucasus—is also at a very high altitude, far away from cities. In Vilcabamba, too, there is very little serious disease. One reason for the good health of the people might be the clean, beautiful environment; another advantage is the moderate climate. The temperature is about 70º Fahrenheit all year long; furthermore, the wind always comes from the same direction. In addition, the water comes from mountain streams and is high in minerals: perhaps as a result of this valuable resource, the region is rich in flowers, fruits, vegetables, and wildlife.

[D]   In some ways, the diets of the inhabitants in the three regions are quite different. Hunzukuts eat mainly raw vegetables, fruit (especially apricots), and *chapatis*—a kind of pancake; they eat meat only a few times a year. In contrast, the Caucasian diet consists mainly of milk, cheese, vegetables, fruit, and meat; also, most people there drink the local red wine daily. In Vilcabamba, people eat only a small amount of meat each week; their diet consists mostly of grain, corn, beans, potatoes, and fruit. Even so, experts found one surprising fact in the mountains of Ecuador: Most people there, even the very old, consume a lot of coffee, drink large amounts of alcohol, and smoke forty to sixty cigarettes daily!

[E]   However, the typical diets of the three areas are similar in three general ways: (1) The fruits and vegetables are all natural; that is, they contain no preservatives or other chemicals. (2) Furthermore, the population uses traditional herbs and medicines to prevent and cure disease. (3) The inhabitants consume fewer calories than people do in other parts of the world. A typical North American eats and drinks an average of 3300 calories every day, while a typical inhabitant of these mountainous areas takes in between 1700 and 2000 calories.

[F]   Inhabitants in the three regions have more in common than their mountain environment, their distance from modern cities, and their low-calorie natural diets. Because they live in the countryside and are mostly farmers, their lives are physically hard and extremely active. Therefore, they do not need to make a special effort to exercise. In addition, the population does not seem to have the stress of fast city work and recreation; as a result, people's lives are relatively free from worry—and therefore, illness or other health problems. Thus, some experts believe that physical movement and a stress-free environment might be the two most important secrets of longevity. An additional health advantage of life in these long-lived communities may be the extended family structure: the group takes care of its members from birth to death.

[G]   Nevertheless, some doctors theorize that members of especially long-lived populations have only one thing in common: they don't have valid official government birth records. These health scientists think there is a natural limit to the length of human life; in their theories, it is impossible to reach an age of more than 110 years or so. Therefore, they say, claims of unusual longevity in certain groups are probably false.

After You Read

5   **Recognizing Outline Form.**   Many reading selections follow the structure of an "outline." The outline is the plan of the material: it shows the relationship of the topics and ideas. The main, or most general, parts of the reading can appear after numbers like this: I, II, III, IV. The main topics can appear under these parts after capital letters. Sometimes each topic has details after numbers. Here is an example:

The Good Health of the Hunzukuts

I. Examples
 A. Unusual longevity
 B. New fathers at ninety
 C. Giving birth at fifty

II. Reasons
 A. An unpolluted environment
  1. Clean air
  2. Clean water
 B. A simple nutritious diet
  1. High in vitamins
  2. High-fiber
  3. Low in fat and cholesterol
  4. Not much sugar
  5. Without chemicals
 C. Physical Work and Activity
  1. In the fields
  2. With animals

On the lines, answer the following questions about the sample outline. (The letters and numbers in parentheses indicate lines of the outline.)

1. What is the main topic of the outline? (the title) _____
   _____ *Good Health of the Hunzukuts* _____

2. What is item I of the outline? _____ *Examples* _____
   What do the following capital letters A, B, and C introduce? *Unusual longevity*
   the topics of outline + items / *new father at 90 /*
   have baby at 50 /

3. How many main reasons (II) are there for the good health of the people of
   Hunza? (A, B, C) _____ *three* _____
   What are the reasons? *An unpolluted environment*
   A simple nutritious
   physical work and activity

4. What are two characteristics or elements of an unpolluted environment (A)?

(1, 2) _clean air_

clean water

5. How many characteristics of a simple nutritious diet (B) are there in the outline? (1–5) _5_

What are points 1, 3, and 5? _natural_

6. "In the fields" and "with animals" (2, 3) are two details of what reason for good health? (C) _physical work & activity_

On the lines, write the missing points in the following outline, according to the reading selection "The Secrets of a Very Long Life." You can choose from the phrases in the box. In the parentheses, write the letter of the paragraph that tells about the topic.

The Secrets of a Very Long Life

I. Places where people live a long time
    A. Hunza (in the Himalayan Mountains)   (B)
    B. _Caucasus (in Russia)_   (C)
    C. _Vilcabamba (in Ecuador)_   (C)

II. Diets of the three regions
    A. Differences   (D)
        1. _Hunza diet: raw vegetables, fruit and chapatis, meat_
        2. Caucasian diet: milk, cheese, vegetables, fruit, meat, red wine
        3. _grain, corn, beans, potatoes and fruit_
    B. Similarities   (5)
        1. Natural food
        2. _traditional herbs & medicines_
        3. _Consume fewer calories_

III. Other possible causes of unusual longevity   (F)
    A. Hard physical activity   (F)
    B. _free from worry_
    C. _extended family structure_

IV. Disbelief in claims of unusual longevity   (G)
    A. _valid official government birth record._
    B. A natural limit to human life

> Hunzikut diet: raw vegetables, fruit, *chapatis*
> The Caucasians in Russia
> Fewer calories
> Stress-free lives
> Vilcabamba, Ecuador
> Ecuadorian diet: grain, vegetables, fruit, coffee, alcohol, cigarettes
> No valid birth certificates
> Extended family structure
> Traditional herbs as medicine

Now circle the number of the main (the most general) topic of the reading.

1. places in the world where people live a long time
2. some possible secrets of the mystery of longevity
3. a comparison of the health of people in the Caucasus Mountains and Ecuador
4. the typical diet of the inhabitants of mountain regions

6   Understanding the Point.   Finish the possible main-idea question about the reading selection "The Secrets of a Very Long Life." In the paragraph that follows, change the underlined words so that the paragraph answers the question.

Main-Idea Question: Why do people in some areas of the world _____
_____?

According to health specialists that <u>have</u> longevity, there are <u>no</u> possible reasons for a <u>short</u> and <u>unhealthy</u> life. The first requirement might be a high level of hard <u>mental</u> work and activity <u>without</u> freedom from modern worries. Second, the physical environment makes <u>no</u> difference: people seem to live longer in a <u>low desert or jungle</u> region with <u>a changing</u> climate of <u>very hot and very cold</u> air temperatures. And finally, diet <u>doesn't matter</u>: long-lived people seem to eat mostly foods high in <u>fat, cholesterol, and sugar</u> but low in <u>vitamins and nutrition</u>.

7   Figuring Out New Vocabulary.   As language learners and readers develop their logical reasoning skills—and as their vocabulary knowledge grows, it gets easier to figure out the approximate meaning of new words and phrases from context clues. There may not be any definitions, words with similar or opposite meanings, or illustrations of meaning in the same sentence or paragraph; punctuation clues might not help. Even so, the message or meaning of the *material* may lead to useful guesses about the meaning of unfamiliar or difficult vocabulary.

Here are some sentences with vocabulary from the reading selection. From the context, answer the questions about the items. Then use logic to figure out a definition of each word. Circle the letter of the explanation that is closest to yours.

1. To discover the secrets of <u>longevity</u>, health specialists are studying people that reach ages well over one hundred. These <u>long-lived</u> individuals enjoy good health all their lives too.

Who is trying to find out about *longevity?*

_____

Why might these scientists want to know such "secrets"?

_____

Who are these researchers studying?

_____

What does the noun *longevity* mean?
   a.   health researchers
   b.   a hundred different ages
   c.   many years between birth and death
   d.   old people in the mountains

What is the meaning of the adjective *long-lived?*
   a.   living a long time
   b.   dying at an early age
   c.   the altitude of the Himalayan Mountains
   d.   having a full head of hair and healthy teeth

2.   Scientists believe the people of certain high mountain regions have the
     benefit of a healthful <u>environment</u> with clean air and water and <u>moderate</u>
     temperatures—not very hot or very cold.

What two things can an *environment* have?

_____

Where might an *environment* be?

_____

What is an *environment* in this sentence?
   a.   clean air and water
   b.   a healthful place in the desert
   c.   unnatural or extreme atmospheric conditions
   d.   the conditions of a place that influence people

What kinds of temperatures are not *moderate?*

_____

What is the meaning of the adjective *moderate?*
   a.   very hot and very cold
   b.   not extreme; in the middle
   c.   related to the air and water of a region
   d.   of the modern world

3. A woman named Tsurba and a man named Shirali were among the long-lived <u>inhabitants</u> of the Caucasus Mountain region of Russia. Other people that <u>inhabit</u> the area don't seem to get sick often either.

Were Tsurba and Shirali *inhabitants* of or visitors to the mountains?

_____

Are *inhabitants* people, places, things, or actions?

_____

What are the *inhabitants* of a place?
  a. people that work there
  b. people that live there in summer
  c. people that study the environment in that region
  d. hardworking, physically active farmers

What is the meaning of the verb *inhabit?*
  a. to make an action difficult
  b. to work during the day in a place
  c. to have scientific interests in common
  d. to live in (a region or area)

4. A healthful environment includes <u>unpolluted</u> clean water; the water might come from high mountain <u>streams</u> and contain a lot of minerals.

If an environment has clean water, is the water *polluted?*

_____

What do high mountains *streams* bring to a healthful environment?

_____

What is high in minerals?

_____

What does the adjective *unpolluted* mean?
  a. dirtying of the earth and air
  b. high in preservatives and chemicals
  c. having a lot of vitamins and minerals
  d. not containing unhealthful substances

What are high mountain *streams?*
  a. small rivers of moving water
  b. regions with little serious disease
  c. widows that keep birth records for communities
  d. to move a lot from one place to another

5. According to some doctors, long-lived <u>populations</u> have only one thing in common: their members don't have <u>valid</u> birth records; because the government didn't write down when these people were born, their <u>claims</u> of unusual longevity are false.

   What do *populations* contain?

   _____

   What are *populations?*
   a. members of government
   b. ideas that are widespread
   c. all of the people living in specific areas
   d. kinds of freedom from worry

   Do *all* health experts believe that certain populations have unusual longevity?

   _____

   What don't these long-lived people have?

   _____

   What does the adjective *valid* mean?
   a. officially legal or accepted
   b. of high value in the community
   c. to prove something is correct
   d. of the region of Vilcabamba

   Do certain populations make *claims* about unusual longevity?

   _____

   Do people in these communities believe the *claims?*

   _____

   What is the meaning of the noun *claims* in this context?
   a. to state something is right and real
   b. attempts to get money that is legally yours
   c. something important about a person
   d. statements of the truth of information

For more practice, look for and figure out the general meanings of other vocabulary items, such as *mountainous, solve the mystery, secrets, benefits, official, widow, teeth, eyesight, rich, wildlife, apricots, chapatis, consume, preservatives, an average, low-calorie, effort, worry, stress, stress-free, theorize, theories,* and so on. For each item, explain the logical reasoning for your guesses at definitions.

8 Recognizing Meaningful Connections.   Punctuation such as a colon (:) before a list often indicates the relationship of the following material to the previous point. Numbers in parentheses within a paragraph, like (1), (2), and so on, come before the separate items. *Connecting words and phrases* also give clues to the relationships among points. The phrase *for instance* means that the following sentence part will give instances, or examples, of a previous statement. There are words that show *addition;* they introduce similar facts or concepts or give additional evidence or arguments. Some connecting words mean that differences, opposites, or contradictions will follow. And still other vocabulary of this kind indicates causes, reasons, or results. Here are some commonly used connecting adverbs and phrases with their general meanings.

Addition or Similarity	Contrast or Contradiction	Causes, Reasons, or Results
and	but	thus
also	while	therefore
too	instead	for this reason
in addition	even so	as a result
additionally	however	because of this
furthermore	nevertheless	
moreover	in contrast	
in the same way	on the other hand	
similarly		

In the reading selection "The Secrets of a Very Long Life," use punctuation clues, numbers in parentheses, and connecting words to help you find the answers to these questions. On the lines, write the answers in your own words.

1. High mountain regions where people live to a very old age are far away from modern cities. For what two reasons might medical scientists and health specialists travel there?

   _____

   _____

2. According to scientists, what are three reasons for the good physical health of the people of Hunza?

   _____

   _____

3. Who were two people similar in their longevity to the Caucasian woman Tsurba?

   _____

   _____

4. In what ways do the people of the Caucasian region live well even in old age?

   _____

   _____

   _____

5. What are four or five healthful elements or features of the environment in Vilcabamba, Ecuador?

_____

_____

_____

6. In what three general ways are the diets of inhabitants of the Hunza, the Caucasus, and Vilcabamba similar?

_____

_____

_____

7. In addition to diet, what are three other possible reasons for the healthy longevity of the populations discussed in the reading?

_____

_____

8. Why don't all doctors believe the longevity claims of these groups of people?

_____

_____

For more practice, turn back to the Before You Read section on page 126 and answer the questions.

Discussing the Reading

9 In small groups, talk about your answers to the following questions. Then tell the class the most interesting information and ideas.

1. Do you believe that the inhabitants of the three regions discussed in the reading selection *really* lived to over 150 years of age? Why or why not?

2. Do you know any very old people? Are they healthy? Do they have any "secrets" to long life? Can you suggest any other things that might lead to a long, healthy old age?

3. Do you hope or plan to live to a very old age? Why or why not? How do you plan to do so?

| **PART 2** | # Claims to Amazing Health |

Before You Read

1   **Vocabulary Preview.**   Here are some vocabulary items from the next reading selection. You can learn them now or come back to them later.

Nouns	Verbs	Adjectives	Connectors	Phrases
advice	improve	proven	as opposed to	Websites
remedies	recommend	accurate	vs. (versus)	take advantage of
cures	color	fraudulent		folk medicine
patients	determine	dishonest		senior citizens
benefits	oppose	accurate		cherry juice
limits		parasitic		birth defects
a physiologist		elderly		
bacteria		sour		
viruses		genetic		
joints				
genes				
geneticists				
characteristics				
combination				
length				

Read

2   **Finding Supporting Reasons.**   With a topic like healthcare or medicine, personal beliefs may contradict proven scientific fact. In fact, a definition of the word *fact* might be "reality as opposed to opinion." Researchers are always bringing new information and experience to the world; therefore, the meaning of the concept "scientific fact vs. (versus) opinion" is always changing. Doctors and other specialists in the fields of health and medicine often have to work with theories that are not yet completely proven; these ideas may turn out to be true (right or real) or false (wrong) with time.

Following are four readings on the general topic of "Claims to Amazing Health." They tell the views of *some* healthcare and medical experts; all of these opinions come from a combination of proven fact *and* personal belief. After you skim each paragraph, circle the number 1, 2, or 3 of an interesting title that also tells the topic. Then read each combination or fact and theory a second time: circle the number of the statement that best tells the point.

Claims to Amazing Health

Which title best expresses the topic of paragraph A?

1. The Value of a Variety of Valid Views
2. Long on Longevity: Free but Fraudulent
3. Internet Help and Hope: Health Benefits vs. Limits

[A]   On the subject of physical health and medical research, there are thousands of amazing Websites (places) on the World Wide Web where people can get information. However, when does the *amount* of available information affect its validity and health benefit? The Internet is greatly influencing people's attitudes about their own healthcare: probably, this worldwide cultural trend improves global health. Because computer users can look up almost any topic of interest to them, they become their own researchers. In the busy modern world, doctors don't always take the time to explain illnesses and possible remedies to their patients; they may not give scientific details in words that are easy to understand, either. For this reason, many hopeful people take advantage of Web resources to find the facts they need for good medical decisions. But are the beliefs of "experts" always completely accurate or real? Are they helpful to *everyone* that needs advice on a specific medical condition? To sell health books or products might the claims that seem the most wonderful even be fraudulent—that is, dishonest or false? Do sick or worried people expect too much when they look for clear, easy answers to difficult health questions or problems on the computer?

Which sentence best states the point of the facts and beliefs in the material?

1. The great amount of medical information (facts and opinions) available on the World Wide Web may improve people's attitudes about health; on the other hand, some claims might be inaccurate or dishonest—and therefore dangerous.
2. To find out the easiest and best ways to solve difficult health problems and cure diseases, everyone should go online—that is, people ought to look up the topics that interest them on the World Wide Web.
3. Doctors are too busy to help their patients, especially the people that are the oldest or the sickest; therefore, these people have to take advantage of the Internet to find cures.

Which title best tells the topic of paragraph B?

1. The Cure for All Cancers: Causes and Cases
2. Theories and Advice from Medical Specialists
3. The Personal Problem of Parasites in Patients

[B]   Many medical specialists have their own theories about illness and health. As an example, a certain California physiologist, who is not a doctor, has written books with the titles *The Cure for All Diseases* and *The Cure for All Cancers*. She says there are only two causes of disease: (1) pollution of the environment and

(2) parasites (harmful plants and animals that feed on living things) inside the human body. To prevent or cure the illnesses that these parasitic bacteria and viruses cause, she offers (tries to sell) two kinds of health products on the Internet and in other places: electronic machines and herbal medicines. The two beneficial effects of these items in humans and animals, this scientist claims, are (1) to clean out the body, freeing it of parasites and (2) to rebuild new healthy living cells. According to her theories, people will feel better and live longer as a result. In addition, other medical experts recommend kinds of natural, nontraditional, or non-Western remedies for modern health disorders such as heart disease, cancer, asthma, nervousness, depression, and so on. Their advice might include (1) special diet plans with added vitamins and minerals, (2) folk medicine, (3) environmental changes, or (4) unusual therapies that patients don't get from traditional doctors.

Which sentence best states the point of the facts and beliefs in the material?

1. In the human body, parasites are dangerous viruses and bacteria; for this reason, everyone must use electronic machines and herbal medicines to fight against them.
2. Nontraditional and non-Western remedies are more effective cures and remedies for health problems than the methods of doctors that offer information over the Internet.
3. Many medical specialists have their own theories about illness and health, including the causes of disease and the beneficial effects of certain products and therapies.

Which title best tells the topic of paragraph C?

1. Colorful Cures for Continuing Care: Natural Food Remedies
2. A Variety of Theories vs. Advice from Medical Experts
3. Family and Folk Falsehoods—Physical Facts and Figures

[C]   In a small-town farm market, hundreds of elderly people drink a glass of sour dark cherry juice every day. These happy senior citizens, some of them over the age of ninety, claim that the natural fruit juice cures—or at least decreases the pain of—their arthritis, a disease of the joints of the aging body. It's a folk remedy, not a proven medical therapy. Nevertheless, science is beginning to figure out why sour cherry juice might work to improve the health of patients with arthritis. The secret is in the substance that gives the cherries their dark red color. It belongs to a classification of natural nutrients that color blueberries, strawberries, plums, and other fruits—and vegetables too. Moreover, these coloring substances may help to prevent serious health disorders like heart disease and cancer. In other words, vitamins and fiber are not the only reasons to eat fruits and vegetables. "To take advantage of natural whole foods," advise nutritionists and health researchers, "think variety and color."

Which sentence best states the point of the facts and beliefs in the material?

1. Color makes people happy, so it improves their health and state of mind; therefore, families should wear colorful clothes at meals with colorful foods.

2. Like vitamins and fiber, the substances in foods that give them color may offer an important health advantage.

3. Dark red foods are the best for nutrition, but bright yellow and green vegetables are more effective for elderly people that have arthritis pain.

Which title best tells the topic of paragraph D?

1. Claims of the Advantages of Genetic Research and Engineering
2. Defects in Gene Structure as Opposed to Insect Damage to Foods
3. Characteristics of Folk Remedies vs. Beliefs of Geneticists

[D]   What are *genes* and why are medical researchers always trying to find out more about them? Genes are part of the center (that is, the *nucleus*) of every living cell; in the form of DNA (deoxyribonucleic acid), this biological genetic material determines the characteristics (features) of every living thing—every plant, animal, and human being—on earth. Medical *geneticists* are scientists that study DNA and genes for many purposes: (1) to learn how living things such as parasites, viruses, and bacteria cause illness; (2) to find the gene or combination of genes that cause certain diseases to pass from parents to their children; (3) to prevent or repair (correct) birth defects; (4) to change gene structure to improve health and increase the length of human life (longevity); and (5) to change the biological characteristics of animals and humans in ways that are beneficial to society. Another use of genetic technology that some scientists support is changing the genes of the food farmers grow. Genetic engineers claim that these differences in DNA structure will increase food production, prevent damage from insects, and improve world health; in contrast, others oppose the use of genetic engineering not only in plants but also in animals and humans.

Which sentence best states the point of the facts and beliefs in the material?

1. Deoxyribonucleic acid is not as beneficial as DNA—the biological material related to genetics—in research on the causes of birth defects.

2. Genetic engineers and other specialists claim that research into the gene structure of living things can improve human health in many ways.

3. Because there is a natural limit to the length of human life, only changes in gene structure can increase longevity in senior citizens that drink cherry juice.

After You Read

3 **Learning to Summarize.**   If a reading selection or paragraph is well organized, you can summarize it very effectively. First, you can figure out the relationship of the points to one another; in other words, you can make a simple outline. Then it will be easy to create a short summary from the items in the outline, in order. Here are examples from Paragraph A of the reading "Claims to Amazing Health."

Outline A

Internet Help and Hope: Benefits vs. Limits

I. Benefits (good features)

    A. Changes in healthcare attitudes

    B. Patients doing their own research

    C. Information in clear language

    D. Better medical decisions

II. Dangers or bad features

    A. Information not always accurate

    B. Need for individual advice

    C. Fraudulent claims for sales purposes

    D. Unrealistic to expect real solutions

Summary A

Benefits vs. Limits of Internet Health Information

On the World Wide Web, computer users can find many medical facts and beliefs. Their availability can improve world health: people may change their attitudes about healthcare when they get information in clear language through their own research. Then they can make better medical decisions. However, the information on the Internet may not always be accurate or helpful to all individuals. There may even be fraudulent claims about products to increase sales. Is it realistic to expect real solutions to difficult health problems from a computer? Maybe it is; maybe it's not.

Work in groups of three. Choose a paragraph B–D from the reading "Claims to Amazing Health." Read it carefully. Complete the outline (organizational plan) for your material. From your outline, summarize the information in as few sentences as possible, paraphrasing the important points in your own words. Then tell or read your summary to your group.

Outline B

Theories and Advice from Medical "Experts"

I. Theories of a California physiologist

    A. _____

        1. Pollution of the environment

        2. _____

    B. Her health products

        1. _____

        2. _____

    C. Beneficial effects of the products

        1. _____

        2. _____

        3. Better and longer lives

II. Other recommended remedies

    A. Special diets with vitamins and minerals

    B. _____

    C. _____

    D. _____

Summary B

Theories and Advice from Medical "Experts"

_____

_____

_____

_____

_____

_____

_____

_____

_____

_____

_____

_____

_____

_____

_____

_____

Outline C
Colorful Cures for Continuing Health

   I. Natural substances that color food

      A. Health benefits

         1. _____

         2. _____

      B. _____

         1. Sour dark cherry juice

         2. _____

         3. _____

Summary C
Colorful Cures for Continuing Health

_____

_____

_____

_____

_____

_____

_____

_____

Outline D
Claims of the Benefits of Genetic Research and Engineering

   I. What genes are

      A. _____

      B. _____

  II. Reasons to study genetic material

      A. To learn about causes of disease

         1. Parasites

         2. _____

         3. _____

      B. _____

      C. _____

      D. _____

         1. To improve health

         2. _____

      E. _____

         1. Animals

         2. _____

      F. To change the genes of food

 III. Opposition to genetic study and change

Summary D
Claims of the Benefits of Genetic Research and Engineering

_____

_____

_____

_____

_____

_____

_____

_____

_____

_____

_____

_____

_____

_____

Discussing the Reading

4   In small groups, talk about your answers to these questions. Then tell the class the most interesting information or ideas.

1. Do—or might—you go to the Internet for information about health and medicine? Why or why not? In your view, what are the benefits and limits of this kind of research?

2. What natural, nontraditional, or non-Western remedies for modern health disorders have you heard about? What do the experts that offer these cures claim? Do you believe their claims? Why or why not?

3. Do you believe that natural chemicals in food, including substances that give color, can decrease pain or help prevent serious disease? Why or why not? If so, which foods do you recommend for these reasons?

4. In your opinion, is genetic research beneficial for global health? How about genetic engineering (changing the gene structure of plants, animals, and humans)? Explain the reasons for your views.

Talk It Over

Many sick or worried people want useful advice about health or medicine; even more "experts" like to recommend beneficial foods and other substances, helpful kinds of activity, other kinds of therapy, or health books and products. Here are some common health problems in the modern world. Check (✔) the situations that you might know or want to know about. Then give advice to help solve the problem or tell your opinions. (You can do your own research, of course.)

1. _____ An international student is homesick for his country; in addition, he worries about his finances and grades. For these reasons, he sleeps a lot but still feels tired; he is also nervous.

2. _____ A young man in a cold northern climate gets depressed during the long, dark winter months. He is irritable and moody. He thinks he has SAD (Seasonal Affective Disorder).

3. _____ During times of forceful winds from the mountains, a Japanese woman seems to have more asthma attacks. She can't breathe very well, and she feels afraid.

4. _____ The members of a family often get colds or the flu (influenza)—not only during the winter but also during changes in the seasons. Occasionally, someone gets pneumonia.

5. _____ A professor is having memory problems. From the Web, she learned that foods with the substance lecithin and B-vitamins can help, so she eats a lot of broccoli, soybeans, and nuts. Even so, she often forgets what she is doing.

6. _____ A brother and sister disagree on the best kinds of foods to eat for good health. He follows a famous high-protein diet plan that allows only certain foods at certain times. She wants to eat what tastes good.

7. _____ A Czech woman serves nutritious salads and other vegetables to her family, but her husband won't eat them. He prefers high-calorie meat and dairy dishes with rich desserts, and he is getting very fat. She is afraid he will die of a heart attack.

8. _____ A young man athlete *feels* strong and healthy, but he is worried about his longevity because of his relatives' diseases. For this reason, he welcomes research into genetic engineering.

9. _____ A seventy-year-old man drinks a lot of coffee and smokes cigarettes; he also enjoys alcoholic drinks. He likes to go walking in his mountain community; however, he is often in pain from his arthritis.

10. _____ A couple is going to have a baby. Because there is a history of genetic defects in several generations of their extended families, they are worried about the child's chances for good health and long life.

PART 3 # Vocabulary and Language Learning Skills

1 **Recognizing Word Endings.**   One way to tell the part of speech of a vocabulary item is to recognize its function or purpose—what does the word *do* in the sentence? (Remember—nouns serve as sentence subjects or objects; verbs name actions; and so on.) Another useful clue to the part of speech of a word is its ending, or *suffix*. Here are a few of the common word endings that may indicate if a word is a noun, an adjective, or an adverb.

Nouns		**Adjectives**		**Adverbs**	
Suffixes	*Examples*	*Suffixes*	*Examples*	*Suffixes*	*Examples*
-ance	ignor<u>ance</u>	-ant	ignor<u>ant</u>	-ly	slow<u>ly</u>
-ence	differ<u>ence</u>s	-ent	differ<u>ent</u>	-ward	back<u>ward</u>
-ity	availabil<u>ity</u>	-able	avail<u>able</u>		
-ment	amuse<u>ment</u>	-ible	respons<u>ible</u>		
-ness	happ<u>iness</u>	-ive	act<u>ive</u>		
-sion	deci<u>sion</u>	-ic(al)	economi<u>cal</u>		
-tion	vaca<u>tion</u>	-ous	fam<u>ous</u>		

Here are some of the important nouns, adjectives, and adverbs (or related words) from the reading selections in Chapters 1 to 7. On the line before each item, indicate the part of speech: write *n* for "noun," *adj.* for "adjective," or *adv.* for "adverb." You might want to <u>underline</u> the ending (suffix) that indicates the part of speech. A few words are done as examples.

1. __n__ abil<u>ity</u>   11. __adj__ change<u>able</u>   21. __n__ requirement<u>s</u>
2. __n__ activ<u>ity</u>   12. __n__ disappear<u>ance</u>   22. __n__ resi<u>dence</u>
3. __adv.__ activ<u>ely</u>   13. __n__ longe<u>vity</u>   23. __adj__ return<u>able</u>
4. __adj.__ act<u>ive</u>   14. __adj__ magnific<u>ent</u>   24. __adj__ sens<u>ible</u>
5. __n__ agreement   15. __adj__ conven<u>ient</u>   25. __adv__ similar<u>ly</u>
6. __adj__ agree<u>able</u>   16. __n__ polite<u>ness</u>   26. __adj__ support<u>ive</u>
7. __adv__ agree<u>ably</u>   17. __n__ prevent<u>ion</u>   27. __n__ televi<u>sion</u>
8. __adj__ biologic<u>al</u>   18. __adj__ prevent<u>ive</u>   28. __adj__ theoretic<u>al</u>
9. __adj__ benefic<u>ial</u>   19. __n__ product<u>ion</u>   29. __adv__ forward
10. __adj__ believ<u>able</u>   20. __adj__ religi<u>ous</u>   30. __adj__ vis<u>ual</u>

For more vocabulary practice with parts of speech that have recognizable suffixes, you can make sentences that illustrate some of the meanings of the words in the preceding list. Do you know any related words—nouns, verbs, adjectives, or adverbs? Which of the words have related forms that are the same or other parts of speech? What are they? (You can check your words in a dictionary.) Can you use your words in sentences that show their meanings?

2   **Choosing Word Forms with Suffixes.**   Here are some sentences with related words—nouns, adjectives, and adverbs—on the topic of the reading material of Chapter 7. Within each pair of parentheses ( ), circle the correct word form. Then write the missing words in the Parts of Speech chart that follows—except for the boxes with Xs. Some of the items are done as examples.

1. Three (mountains /(mountainous)) regions of the globe are (fame /(famous)) for the ((longevity) / long) of their inhabitants. There may be (variety /(various)) reasons for their long lives.

2. According to (science /(scientific)) research, many elderly inhabitants of the Himalayan Mountains are still in good (physics /(physical)) health. One ((reasons)/ reasonable) for their amazing condition might be the low level of ((pollution)/ polluted) in their ((environment)/ environmental).

3. Is a simple, (nature / naturally) ((nutrition)/ nutritious) diet (benefits / beneficial) to human health? Is physical work also ((advantages)/ advantageous)?

4. Farmers in the countryside (usual / usually) lead (action / active) lives—
   that is to say, they fill their days with (activity / actively) and physical
   (move / movement).

5. Official birth records of (special / especially) long-lived people are seldom
   (availability / available). Nevertheless, health specialists are in
   (agreement / agreeable): these amazing people are (general / generally) in
   good health when they die.

6. In some regions, the (types / typical) diet of the inhabitants consists of
   (most / mostly) meat and dairy products; in contrast, other groups consume
   (main / mainly) fruits and vegetables and use (tradition / traditional) herbs
   as medicine.

7. How (importance / important) is the (environment / environmentally) to
   human health? There is some (confusion / confused) about the
   (validity / valid) of the research into the matter.

8. The amount of (availability / available) medical
   (information / informative) on the World Wide Web is amazing. This
   (combination / combined) of proven fact and opinion is changing
   (culture / cultural) attitudes of people about their own healthcare.

9. Some patients are (ignorance / ignorant) of the facts they need to make the
   best (medicine / medical) (decisions / decisive). These people may benefit
   from the (recommendations / recommend) of a number of health experts.

10. Many scientists believe in the (value / valuable) of (genes / genetic)
    research and engineering. They hope they can make (defects / defective)
    genes healthy and prevent (biology / biological) diseases.

Parts of Speech		
Noun	**Adjective**	**Adverb**
advantages	advantageous	X
availability	_____	X
activity	active	_____
biology	_____	biologically
_____	confused	X
culture	_____	culturally
defects	_____	X
decisions	decisive	_____
fame	_____	X
genes	_____	genetically
generalities	_____	_____
humanity	_____	_____
_____	_____	ignorantly
_____	_____	importantly
_____	natural	_____
mountains	_____	X
_____	typical	_____
_____	_____	traditionally

For more vocabulary practice with word endings, try to think of more words (nouns, adjectives, and adverbs) with the suffixes listed on page 144. (You can check your guesses in a dictionary.) Can you use your words in sentences that show their meanings?

3   **Real-Life Reading: Instructions for Health Emergencies.**   Some health or medical conditions can create *emergencies*—sudden, serious happenings that require help right away. For some of these situations, free or low-cost instructions—the steps to take in emergencies—are available in printed form in many places: in doctors' offices and hospitals, in newspapers and magazines, in brochures, and even in the front pages of local telephone books.

Look at the following information from the front section of a telephone book. Which words and phrases do you know? Underline them. Which words are new or difficult for you? Circle them. In groups or in class, use your vocabulary-learning skills to figure out the meanings of the circled words.

Then read the questions about the information, find the answers as fast as you can, and write them on the lines. Compare your answers with those of your classmates.

POISONING

The home is loaded with poisons: Cosmetics, Detergents, Bleaches, Cleaning Solutions, Glue, Lye, Paint, Turpentine, Kerosene, Gasoline and other petroleum products, Alcohol, Aspirin and other medications, and on and on.

1. **Small children are most often the victims of accidental poisoning. If a child has swallowed or is suspected to have swallowed any substance that might be poisonous, assume the worst—TAKE ACTION.**

2. **Call your Poison Control Center. If none is in your area, call your emergency medical rescue squad. Bring suspected item and container with you.**

3. **What you can do if the victim is unconscious:**
   A. Make sure patient is breathing. If not, tilt head back and perform mouth to mouth breathing. DO NOT give anything by mouth. DO NOT attempt to stimulate person. Call emergency rescue squad immediately.

4. **If the victim is vomiting:**
   A. Roll him or her over onto the left side so that the person will not choke on what is brought up.

5. **BE PREPARED. Detemine and verify your Poison Control Center and Fire Department Rescue Squad numbers and keep them near your telephone.**

1. What kind of real-life reading material is this?

   _____

2. What are some examples of poisons?

   _____

3. Who are most often the victims of poisoning?

   _____

4. What are the two important words in step 1?

   _____

   What do they mean?

   _____

5. What is the first necessary action in case of poisoning?

    _____

6. What two places can you call for help in case of poisoning?

    _____

    _____

7. If the patient (victim) is unconscious, you need to find out if he or she is

    _____

8. If not, you have to

    _____

    and _____

9. Can you give an unconscious victim water? _____

10. If the patient is vomiting, you should

    _____

    Why? _____

11. How can you be prepared for an emergency poisoning?

    _____

    _____

12. What questions do you have about this kind of medical emergency?

    _____

    _____

For more vocabulary practice and to get useful information for the steps to take in medical emergencies, ask questions like these about real information from the sources listed in Exercise 4.

   What kind of emergency are these instructions for?

   What are the steps to take in a situation of this kind?

   Are these steps valid and useful in all situations of this type? If not, why not?

4   **More Real-Life Reading.**   Here are some kinds of reading material that may contain instructions for health or medical emergencies, such as drowning, not breathing, serious burns, poisoning, drug overdose, electric shock, heart attack, stroke, choking, severe bleeding, and others. Check (✔) the kinds available to you. Bring some examples to class, or copy the words from the materials. Write down the important vocabulary items. With simple definitions, tell the meanings of the words and phrases. Talk about the point of each piece of material. Summarize the important steps in the instructions.

- ■ _____ first-aid books, publications that give official or expert advice on how to help in medical emergencies until a doctor or ambulance arrives

- ■ _____ brochures, pamphlets, or fliers on emergency situations, available from police and fire departments and other government offices

- ■ _____ publications of the International Red Cross or other organizations that offer help in emergencies

- ■ _____ other _____

Also, in your local telephone directory, find the telephone numbers of the poison control center, the fire department rescue squad, and other places to turn in emergencies. Write them here and in easily visible places in your home.

_____

_____

_____

_____

_____

PART 4   Personal Stories and Humor

1   The following story is about a woman's experience with smoking. Follow these steps for the story.

1. Read it quickly and give the main ideas.
2. Answer your instructor's questions about the story, or ask and answer questions of your own.
3. Make up an ending for the story. Explain why you think the story might end that way.
4. Give your own opinions of the ideas in the story.
5. Tell or write about a health-related situation or problem of your own.

Up in Smoke

I began to smoke when I was in high school. In fact, I remember the evening I was at a girlfriend's house and we were watching a movie—a terribly romantic movie. He (the hero of the movie) was in love, she (his lady) was beautiful, and they were both smoking. My friend had only two cigarettes from a pack in her mother's purse, and she gave one to me. It was my first time.

Soon I was smoking a pack every day. My parents didn't care much. They both smoked, and my older brother did too. My mother told me that smokers don't grow tall, but I was already 5'6" (taller than most of the boys in my class), so I was happy to hear that "fact." In school, the teachers were always telling us reasons not to smoke, but the cigarette advertisements were *so* exciting. The men in the ads were *so* good-looking and so successful, and the women were—well, they were beautiful and worldly.

I read a book called *How to Stop Smoking.* The writer said that smoking wastes time and that cigarettes cost a lot of money. "So what?" I thought. The book didn't say that smoking can take away years of your life. But ten years later, everyone began to hear about the negative effects of cigarette smoke: lung disease, cancer, and heart problems. After that, there was a health warning on every pack of cigarettes. Even so, I didn't pay much attention to the reports and warnings because I felt healthy, and I thought I was taking good care of myself.

Then two events changed my mind. First, I started to cough. I thought it was just a cold, but it didn't get better. Second, my brother got lung cancer. He got sicker and sicker. My brother and I used to smoke cigarettes together over twenty years ago, and we smoked our last cigarettes together the day before he died. I sat with him in his hospital room, and that was the time I decided to quit. "No more cigarettes, ever," I said to myself. However, it was very hard to stop. Nicotine (the poisonous substance in tobacco) is a drug; as a result, cigarettes cause a powerful addiction. I tried several times to quit on my own—without success. I made excuses. I told myself: Smoking helps me keep my figure—that is, I don't gain weight when I smoke. Smoking not only relaxes me but it also helps me think clearly. I'm a free, modern woman. I can smoke when I want to. And I can stop when I want to too.

Finally, I ran out of excuses—I might say my excuses went up in smoke. I joined the Stop Smoking program at the local hospital. It still wasn't easy: for the first two months, I thought about cigarettes all the time. I didn't sleep well. I ate all the time, and I gained twenty-five pounds. I got angry very quickly and easily—not only at important things but also at small ones. I was irritable and nervous, and my hands shook. Then . . . .

The Humor of Health and Medicine

2 According to medical research and experience, laughter is good for the health. When it makes fun of human nature, it fills important human needs. It can decrease tension, irritability, depression, or moodiness. In other words, laughter is "good medicine." An *anecdote* or *joke*—a very short story with a humorous point—is the most common kind of humor in magazines or books and on the Internet. It may or may not include an illustration. Amusing anecdotes are often based on real experiences. Funny jokes are more often made up. The "punch line" (the funny ending) is based on surprise—maybe an unexpected change in events, conversation, or logic.

There are anecdotes and jokes on many subjects. Here are some humorous stories—true or not—on the topics of health or medicine. Discuss your answers to these questions.

1. What—or what kind of people—is the subject of the joke? For example, does the story make fun of doctors' schedules, receptionists, health advice, diets, exercise, or what?

2. What is the "punch line" of the story? How might it surprise people that read or hear the joke?

3. Do you think the story is true? Why or why not? Is it funny to you? Why or why not?

4. Does the story remind you of a similar anecdote or joke about diet, fitness, health, or medicine? Tell your joke if you want to. (Make sure it is not insulting to any of your listeners.)

Joke A

A man was feeling very sick, so he called his doctor's office for an appointment. As usual, he talked to the receptionist—the person that receives visitors and takes telephone calls. "I'm sorry," she told him. "The doctor is very busy, and his calendar of appointments is full. He can't see you for a month."

"But I might be dead by then," complained the patient.

"That's all right," answered the receptionist patiently. "Your wife can call to cancel the appointment, and we won't charge you for the doctor's services."

Joke B

It was a man's 110th birthday, so a reporter came to interview him. "How do you explain your longevity?" she asked. "What is the secret of your amazing health at such an old age?"

"Well, my friends and relatives think I am a health nut," explained the very senior citizen. I've always followed the rules for good health. For instance, I never drank alcohol. I never began to smoke cigarettes. I always eat a healthful diet. I still walk four miles a day and keep active. I'm in bed by 9:00 and sleep at least eight hours a night."

"But I had a relative who did exactly the same things," objected the reporter, "and he died at the age of 65. Why didn't your advice work for him?"

"There's only one thing I can think of," answered the helpful old man, smiling. "He didn't follow the rules long enough."

Joke C

Medical specialists often form "medical groups"—that is, doctors work in the same offices and share the services of one or more receptionists. These workers are told never to recommend one doctor over another. When they make appointments, they simply tell patients who has time available.

One day a woman went into the waiting room of a medical group. In a soft voice, she asked the receptionist, "Can you please tell me who is the best doctor for my medical condition?"

The receptionist's supervisor was listening, and she didn't want to break the rules. Therefore, she answered the patient kindly, "Oh, I'm so sorry, Ma'am, but I can't recommend any of our doctors."

"Well, I guess you know best," said the disappointed woman, as she left the medical group to look for a good doctor.

Video Activities: Marathon Man

Before You Watch.   Discuss these questions in a group.

1. What is a marathon?
2. Do you think you could run in a marathon?
3. Why do some people run or jog? Make a list of reasons.
4. Do you enjoy running? Why or why not?

Watch.   Write answers to these questions.

1. What is Jerry's personal reason for running? _____

    _____

2. Does he enjoy it? _____

3. What does Jerry want to challenge Americans to do? _____

    _____

Watch Again.   Fill in the missing numbers.

1. How many miles is a marathon?
2. How many marathons did Jerry run in 1993?   _____
3. How many marathons does Jerry hope to run in 2000? _____
4. How many days has he run marathons?   _____
5. How fast does Jerry run a marathon?   _____

After You Watch.   In an encyclopedia or on the Internet, read about the first marathon runner. After everyone finishes, answer these questions in groups.

1. What do you know about the first marathon runner?
2. Where did he run?
3. How long is a marathon? Why?

Chapter 8

Entertainment and the Media

PART 1	# How the Visual Media Affect People

Before You Read

1 Discuss the pictures in small groups.

   1. What are the people doing? What are they watching—or ignoring—on the TV screens?

   2. How are the media scenes similar? How are they different?

2 Think about the answers to these questions. The reading selection answers them.

1. In what ways can TV watching be beneficial in people's lives?
2. How might the amount of time spent in front of a media screen have a negative effect on family life?
3. What damage might too much TV viewing of low-quality programming do to the human brain?
4. What are some possible effects of violent movies or TV programs on people's personalities and behavior?
5. Why might frequent TV watchers—including viewers of "trash TV"—become dissatisfied with their own lives?
6. What are some signs of (clues to) possible addiction to the visual media?

3 **Vocabulary Preview.**   Here are some vocabulary items from the first reading selection. You can learn them now or come back to them later.

Nouns	Verbs	Adjectives	Adverbs	Phrases
behavior	reduce	beneficial	passively	the visual media
programming	focus	high-quality		the "tube"
disadvantages	scare	average		solve problems
kids	last	well-educated		a TV screen
concentration	copy	dissatisfied		media stars
images	envy	unlimited		
reactions	shout	envious		
films	refuse			
tension				

Read

4 Read the following material quickly. Then ready the explanations and do the exercises after the reading.

How the Visual Media Affect People

[A] How do television and the other visual media affect the lives of individuals and families around the globe? The media can be very helpful to people (and their children) who carefully choose the movies and shows that they watch. With high-quality programming in various fields of study—science, medicine, nature, history, the arts, and so on—TV and videotapes increase the knowledge of the average *and* the well-educated person; they can also improve thinking ability. Moreover, television benefits elderly people who can't go out often, as well as patients in hospitals and residents of nursing facilities. Additionally, it offers language learners the advantage of "real-life" audiovisual instruction and aural comprehension practice at any time of day or night. And of course, television and video can provide almost everyone with good entertainment—a pleasant way to relax and spend free time at home.

[B]   Nevertheless, there are several serious disadvantages to the visual media. First of all, some people watch the "tube" for more hours in a day than they do anything else. In a large number of homes, TV sets—as many as five or more in a single household—are always on. Instead of spending time taking care of their kids, parents often use the tube as an "electronic baby-sitter." As a result, television and video can easily replace family communication as well as physical activity and other interests.

[C]   Secondly, too much TV—especially programming of low educational value—can reduce people's ability to concentrate or reason. In fact, studies show that after only a minute or two of visual media, a person's mind "relaxes" as it does during light sleep. Another possible effect of television and videotapes on the human brain is poor communication. Children who watch a lot of TV may lose their ability to focus on a subject or an educational activity for more than ten to fifteen minutes. Maybe it is because of the visual media that some kids—and adults too—develop attention deficit disorder (ADD), a modern condition in which people are unable to pay attention, listen well, follow instructions, or remember everyday things.

[D]   A third negative feature of the media is the amount of violence or horror on the screen—both in real events in the news and movies or TV programs. It scares people and gives them terrible nightmares; the fear created by media images and language can last for a long time. On the other hand, frequent viewers of "action programming" get used to its messages: they might begin to believe there is nothing strange or unusual about violent crime, fights, killing, and other terrible events and behavior. Studies show that certain personality types are likely to have strong emotional reactions or dangerous thoughts after some kinds of "entertainment." They may even copy the acts that they see on violent shows—start fires, carry and use weapons, attack people in angry or dangerous ways, and even worse.

[E]   Because of the visual media, some people may become dissatisfied with the reality of their own lives. To these viewers, everyday life does not seem as exciting as the roles actors play in movies or TV dramas. They realize they aren't having as much fun as the stars of comedy shows. Furthermore, average people with normal lives may envy famous media personalities, who seem to get unlimited amounts of money and attention. Also, media watchers might get depressed when they can't take care of situations in real life as well as TV stars seem to. On the screen, they notice, actors solve serious problems in hour or half-hour programs—or in twenty-second commercials.

[F]   Yet another negative feature of modern television is called "trash TV." These daily talk shows bring real people with strange or immoral lives, personalities, or behavior to the screen. Millions of viewers—including children—watch as these "instant stars" tell their most personal secrets, shout out their angry feelings and opinions, and attack one another. TV watchers seem to like the emotional atmosphere and excitement of this kind of programming—as well as the tension of the real but terrible stories on TV "news magazine" shows. What effect does frequent viewing of such programs have on people's lives? It makes television more real than reality, and normal living begins to seem boring.

[G]   Finally, the most negative effect of the tube might be addiction. People often feel a strange and powerful need to watch TV or play a videotape even when they don't enjoy it or have the free time for entertainment. Addiction to a TV or video screen is similar to drug or alcohol dependence: addicts almost never believe they are addicted. Even so, truthful media addicts have to give yes answers to many of these questions:

- Do you immediately turn on the TV set when you arrive home from school or work?
- Do you watch a lot of programming that requires little focus or thinking ability?
- Can you concentrate on another topic or activity for only ten to fifteen minutes at a time?
- Do you enjoy the action and violence of the media more than activity in your own life?
- Do you feel envious of the lives of well-known TV or screen personalities?
- Do you feel closer to the people on TV than to your own family members and friends?
- For you, is TV or video the easiest—and, therefore, the best—form of relaxation or fun?
- Would you refuse to give up your TV viewing for a million dollars?

After You Read

5 **Recognizing Comparison and Contrast.**   Some reading selections are organized according to *comparison* and *contrast*—that is to say, they present two points of view or contrasting opinions on the same topic. Material of this kind may be organized into two parts: in a traditional *outline* of the structure of the material, part I can contain the points on one side of the issue while part II has the contrasting features in it. Capital letters (A, B, C, etc.) may introduce the main points for each view of the subject. Following is an empty outline for the reading "How the Visual Media Affect People." It is divided into two parts: (1) the beneficial features of the topic (the media) and (2) the negative elements. To fill in the outline, follow these instructions. (Some answers are given as examples.)

1. Write these words after the numbers I and II:

   - ADVANTAGES
   - DISADVANTAGES

2. In mixed-up order, here is a list of some possibly positive and negative effects of the visual media, as presented in the reading. After each item, write the letter(s) of the one or two paragraphs (A–G) where the information about that feature appears.

   - Increase people's knowledge and thinking ability   (A)
   - Benefit the elderly and the sick   (A)
   - Take too much time from family life and other activities   (B)
   - Reduce people's ability to concentrate on reason   (C)
   - Scare people or get them used to violence   (D)
   - Provide language learners instruction and practice   (A)
   - Offer good entertainment for free time   (A)
   - Cause dissatisfaction in normal people's lives   (E) and (F)
   - Addict people to TV and video   (G)

3. Then, on the lines after the capital letters in the outline, copy the points on both sides of the issue from the list.

Effects of the Visual Media

I.   Advantages (Positive Features)

     A. _Increase people's Knowledge and thinking ability._

     B. _Benifit the elderly and the sick_

     C. _provide language leaners instruction & practice_

     D. _offer good entertainment for free time._

II. _____

     A.   Take too much time from family life and other activities

     B. _Reduce people's ability to Concentrate or reason_

     C. _scare people or get them used to violence_

     D. _Cause dissatisfaction in normal people's lives_

     E. _Addict people to TV and video_

To tell the main (the most general) topic of the reading, finish this phrase:

some possible _(advantages and disadvantages) effect_ of the visual media in the lives of ordinary people around the world

6   **Understanding the Point.**   Finish the possible main-idea question about the material of the reading selection "How the Visual Media Affect People." In the paragraphs that follow, change the underlined words so that the paragraphs answer the question.

Main-Idea Question: What are some positive and negative features of _____

_____?

Television and other visual media probably influence people's lives in <u>positive but not negative</u> ways. Here are examples of their possible benefits: (1) <u>Low-quality</u> programming in various fields provides education value to <u>only scientists, doctors, naturalists, historians, and artists</u>. (2) Also, elderly and sick people who rarely go out <u>can't ever</u> enjoy TV or videotapes. (3) <u>In contrast</u>, students get <u>no</u> educational benefit from shows in the languages they are trying to learn. (4) Another advantage is that TV can help people to <u>get nervous and tense</u> in their free time at home.   *relax*

     <u>In exactly the same way</u>, there are serious disadvantages to the visual media: (1) An "electronic baby-sitter" is likely to <u>bring children and their parents closer together</u> and <u>increase</u> the amount of time they spend on other activities. (2) Second, too much television may make it <u>easier</u> for the overly relaxed brain to pay attention, concentrate, or reason. (3) Third, violent or horrible TV images and language can give frequent viewers <u>beautiful dreams</u>, making them fearful of <u>technology, medicine, or the arts</u>; or people may begin to think of terrible

ordinary and usual

events or acts as ~~very strange or unusual~~. (4) A fourth possible disadvantage of too much television and video is that people may become ~~too satisfied~~ with the reality of their exciting and fun lives. (5) And finally, the most negative effect of the tube is probably viewer ~~independence~~; TV and video watchers ~~will~~ be able to get away from the media easily; they ~~can never~~ become addicted.

7 **Understanding the Vocabulary of Specific Details.** Often, figuring out the meaning of vocabulary from context goes along with understanding the specific details of reading material. If readers get the general meaning of new or difficult words or phrases on their own, they will usually understand the meaning of the sentences in which they appear; then they can figure out how the details of that information relate to the larger ideas of the material.

The following sentences give details of the possible benefits and disadvantages of the visual media as presented in the reading selection. Some of the possibly new or difficult vocabulary is underlined. Here are the steps to follow for this exercise.

■ In each sentence, circle the letter of the best explanation (a–d) for each <u>under-lined</u> vocabulary item. Explain the reasons for your choices.

■ In the parentheses after each sentence, indicate where the detail might belong in the outline of the reading material below. Write the number and letter of point IA, IB, IC, ID, IIA, IIB, IIC, IID, or IIE.

Effects of the Visual Media
  I.   Advantages: Television and videos
       A. Provide learning in many subjects
       B. Benefit the old and the sick
       C. Help with language instruction
       D. Offer ways to relax
  II. Disadvantages: The media
       A. Take time from family and other activities
       B. Can decrease people's concentration and reasoning abilities
       C. Produce strong or dangerous emotional reactions in people
       D. May create dissatisfaction or boredom in everyday life
       E. Can addict people in negative ways

A few answers are given as examples.

1.   At all hours, the media offer language learners "real-life" audiovisual instruction and practice in <u>aural comprehension</u>. (IC)
     a. the answers to test questions
     b. understanding spoken language
     c. hospital and health information
     d. real-life experience

2. Moreover, television helps elderly people who can't go out often, as well as patients in hospitals and residents of <u>nursing facilities</u>. (   )

   a. homes for doctors and nurses

   b. centers for public entertainment

   c. normal housing for average people

   d. institutions for people unable to care for themselves

3. High-quality TV <u>programming</u>—a good plan of shows about various fields of study—can increase people's knowledge and improve their thinking abilities. (   )

   a. scientific and medical shows

   b. academic lecture courses

   c. choice and organization of programs

   d. movies with good music

4. Television and video provide almost everyone with good <u>entertainment</u>—a pleasant way to relax and spend free time at home. (   )

   a. relaxation through exercise

   b. passive amusement requiring no movement

   c. fun through serious study

   d. freedom from worry and tension

5. Children who watch a lot of TV may lose their ability to <u>concentrate</u> or focus on a subject for very long; sometimes they develop "attention <u>deficit</u> disorder." (   )

   <u>concentrate</u>

   a. direct their attention

   b. reduce or decrease

   c. communicate

   d. improve

   <u>deficit</u>

   a. criticism or anger

   b. lack of money

   c. inability or shortage

   d. difficult confusion

6. Because of the time it consumes, television and video can easily <u>replace</u> family communication as well as physical activity and other interests. (   )

   a. take the place of

   b. go back to

   c. find the location of

   d. contribute to family time

7. Images of violence and <u>horror</u> on the screen scare people, giving them terrible <u>nightmares</u> when they sleep. (   )

<u>horror</u>

   a.   atmospheric conditions

   b.   scary things that produce fear

   c.   dark, stormy weather

   d.   physical disabilities

<u>nightmares</u>

   a.   frightening dreams

   b.   the emotion of depression

   c.   traditional visual images

   d.   personality types

8. The talk shows of "<u>trash TV</u>" make instant "<u>stars</u>" of real people with strange or <u>immoral</u> ideas, who tell their most personal secrets, shout angrily, and attack one another. (   )

<u>trash TV</u>

   a.   valuable programs

   b.   shows without quality

   c.   negative effects

   d.   normal life stories

<u>stars</u>

   a.   movie roles

   b.   news magazines

   c.   media addicts

   d.   famous personalities

<u>immoral</u>

   a.   not having values

   b.   refusing help

   c.   excited

   d.   unusual or common

For more practice, look for and figure out the general meanings of other vocabulary items in the reading, such as *visual, action programs, likely, normal, boring, truthful,* and so on. For each item, explain the logical reasoning for your guesses at definitions. Then use each word or phrase in a sentence that tells an advantage or disadvantage of TV watching. In addition, turn back to the Before You Read section on page 156 and answer the questions.

Discussing the Reading

8   In small groups, talk about your answers to the following questions. Then tell the class the most interesting information and ideas.

1. In your opinion, is it a good use of time to watch TV or videos? If so, for what types of people? If not, why not?

2. In general, do you believe that television improves or damages the brain? Does it increase or reduce learning, logical thinking skills, concentration, memory, and the like? Give reasons for your opinions.

3. In your view, why is there so much violence and horror on the TV screen? What effects do they have on individuals and society? Explain your reasoning.

4. Have you ever watched the talk shows of "trash TV"? If not, why not? If so, what do you think of the people on those shows? Why?

5. Look back at the list of questions about TV addiction on page 159 of the reading. For how many of the questions must you answer yes? Do you believe you are addicted to the visual media? Give reasons for your answers.

PART 2   Media Stories

Before You Read

1 **Vocabulary Preview.**   Here are some vocabulary items from the next reading selection. You can learn them now or come back to them later.

Nouns		Verbs	Adjectives	Phrases
a sequence	an investigator	stab	animated	science fiction
fiction	a skeleton	investigate	musical	get the best of
a series	a murderer	sink	run-down	a rocking chair
an adventure	a hunter	kill	spooky	the shower curtain
a drama	explorers	raise	bloody*	
a comedy	gorillas	capture	shadowy	
an episode	imagination	recover	suspenseful	
plots	a vehicle	transfer	halfway	
an enemy	galaxies	propose	neat	
a bank	a shutdown		optimistic	
temptation	singles			
a motel	roommates			
a swamp	characters			

Read

2 **Classifying Stories and Putting Events in Order.**   Most kinds of programs in the media include stories—sequences of events that are fact or fiction—true or untrue. Like real history (the study of past events), media stories tell what happened, most often in time order. Here are the kinds of stories that most often appear in movies.

_____ adventure or action   _____ science fiction

_____ crime or mystery story   _____ comedy

_____ story based on history   _____ animated cartoon

_____ serious drama   _____ musical

_____ suspense or horror

Following are four story plots—that is, they are present-time descriptions of the actions or events of a real movie or TV show that is or was well known worldwide. On the lines before some of the listed story types, write the paragraph letters A, B, C, and D. (You can write the same letter more than once, but you will not find stories of all nine types.) After you skim each plot description, circle the number 1, 2, or 3 of the movie title or the name of the TV show that—in your opinion or experience—best fits the events.

---

* This is a swear word in British English; it should be used with caution.

Media Stories

In what movie does this sequence of events occur?

1. *Psycho* (a psychological suspense film directed by Alfred Hitchcock in 1960)
2. *The Public Enemy* (a drama about the social forces that cause violent crime)
3. *Gone with the Wind* (a world-famous 1939 American Civil War drama)

[A] Marion, who works in a real estate office, is depressed about her life—especially her unhappy love relationship. Because she is feeling ill, her supervisor lets her leave early; he gives her $40,000 in cash from a house sale to put in the bank on her way home. However, temptation gets the best of the moody young woman. With the cash in an envelope, she packs her bags and drives out of town. On a dark lonely road, a severe thunderstorm forces her to stop at the run-down Bates Motel. There is a spooky old house high on a hill behind the motel, with the form of an old woman in a rocking chair at the window. Norman Bates, the motel owner, is happy to sign in a guest, but his mother shouts at him angrily. After a conversation with Norman, Marion goes to her room. When she is in the shower, the bathroom door opens. In a very famous, very bloody murder scene, the shadowy figure of an old woman pulls aside the shower curtain, and stabs the motel guest to death. Horrified, Norman cleans up the room, puts Marion's body in her car, and pushes the car into the swamp.

Worried about her and the stolen money, Marion's sister, lover, and boss send out a detective, who finally arrives at the Bates Motel. Suspicious of Norman's strange behavior, the investigator goes into the scary house, where the dark shape of an old "woman" at the top of the stairs kills him too—with a long knife. Others come to investigate. After many suspenseful scenes, they discover that Norman's "mother" is a skeleton. The murderer in the old woman's clothes was Norman Bates himself, who has turned more and more into his mother.

In what movie (produced in many versions) do these events happen?

1. *Robinson Crusoe* (an adventure story about a man who lives alone on an island)
2. *A Night to Remember* (the film about the sinking of the ship *Titanic*)
3. *Tarzan, the Ape Man* (the first of a series based on the "Lord of the Jungle" characters)

[B] After a hurricane sinks their ship off the coast of Africa, a British couple finds their way to land with their baby son. However, the parents are killed by a wild animal. A gorilla (the largest of the humanlike monkeys) finds the baby, brings him home to her mate, and raises the helpless human in the jungle. As a result, he grows to adulthood in the natural ape community. Nevertheless, the young man's peaceful life in the jungle soon changes. To study African wildlife in its natural environment, Professor Porter arrives with his daughter Jane and a hunter named Clayton. When the explorers meet the jungle man, at first they think he is "the missing link" (a being halfway between an animal and a human being). Therefore, they are surprised to discover that he is as human as they are. When he begins to feel strange, unfamiliar emotions towards Jane, the man that grew up in the jungle becomes very confused. He wants to be with his own kind but doesn't want to leave the gorilla family that raised him—especially since Clayton sees the apes not as friends but as animals to hunt and kill. When Jane has to leave with her father, the apeman is very sad and upset. Even so, he saves the white people when they are captured, and Jane stays with him in the jungle.

What popular American TV series are these events from?

1. *The Twilight Zone* (amazing stories about the effects of the human imagination)
2. *Superman* (the adventures of a being from another planet with superhuman powers)
3. *Star Trek: The Next Generation* (futuristic adventures of travelers in space)

[C] The star ship *Enterprise* (a flying vehicle that travels to other galaxies at amazing speeds) stops at a space station for repairs. The four Bynars (beings with computerized brains) that are doing maintenance seem worried. Suddenly, they realize the ship is about to explode and order evacuation. Everyone leaves except Picard, the captain, and Riker, the second man in command, who don't hear the alert. After everyone else reaches the starbase (the space station), the problem mysteriously corrects itself, and the ship disappears. As the crew on the starbase try to figure out a way to recover the *Enterprise,* the captain and his helper discover what has happened. They instantly transfer themselves to the bridge, where they find the Bynars unconscious, dying, and asking for help.

The ship reaches Bynarus, the Bynars' planet. Because of an exploded star that destroyed the planet's center computer, Bynarus is dead too. The Bynars needed the *Enterprise* to store the data from the planet during the shutdown time. Picard and Riker manage to get into the Bynarus file and restart the computer. The Bynars come back to life. Undamaged, the ship returns to the starbase.

In what well-known TV series—especially popular with young people—
do these characters play roles?

1. *All in the Family* (a funny show about a working-class man and his
   wife and their daughter and son-in-law—all in the same house)
2. *Friends* (a popular show, known worldwide, about the relationships
   and situations of a group of young singles in New York)
3. *The Brady Bunch* (a series about a widower with three sons who
   marries a widow with three daughters)

[D]   Three men and three women frequently get together at one another's apartments and at a New York cafe. Monica is a restaurant cook who wants everything
in order. Her roommate Rachel is her best friend from high school. Ross, Monica's
older divorced brother, has long been interested in Rachel. Living across the hall
are roommates Chandler, who works in an office, and Joey, who wants to be a
successful actor; Joey loves New York, sports, women, and—most of all—himself. The other main character is Phoebe, a strange and very funny folk singer.

   In one typical episode, after a romantic dinner Chandler is going to ask
Monica to marry him. But Richard, an older man who used to date Monica,
happens to come into the restaurant with his date. Chandler feels so uncomfortable that he doesn't propose that night. So he can surprise her later, he pretends
that he is not interested in marriage at all. The next day, Richard goes to Monica's
workplace to propose. She packs her bags and goes home to her parents—so
she can decide what to do. Chandler goes after her, and she accepts his
marriage proposal. Meanwhile, the other main characters promise to marry one
another if they are still single at age forty.

After You Read

3   **Learning to Summarize.**   A reading selection or paragraph that describes a *plot* (a sequence of events in a story) is most often organized in time order—that is, one event follows another. To prepare to summarize a plot, you might number the main events in the reading material. Then after an introduction to set the scene, you tell the most important things that happened. Here is an example of possible event numbering from plot description A of "Media Stories."

Marion, an employee in a real estate office, is depressed about her life—especially her unhappy love relationship. 1. Because she is feeling ill, her supervisor lets her leave work early; he gives her $40,000 in cash from a house sale to put in the bank on her way home. 2. However, temptation gets the best of the moody young woman. With the cash in an envelope, she packs her bags and drives out of town. 3. On a dark lonely road, a severe thunderstorm forces her to stop at the run-down Bates Motel. There is a spooky old house high on a hill behind the motel, with the form of an old woman in a rocking chair at the window. 4. Norman Bates, the motel owner, is happy to sign in a guest, but his mother shouts at him angrily. 5. After a conversation with Norman, Marion goes to her room.

Work in groups of four. Choose a plot description A–D from the selection "Media Stories." Read it carefully. After a short introduction, list the main events needed to understand the story in as few words as possible. Then tell or read your plot summary to your group.

Discussing the Reading

4   In small groups, talk about your answers to these questions. Then tell the class the most interesting information or ideas.

1.   Of the nine media story types listed in Exercise 2 on page 164, tell which is your favorite, your second favorite, and so on. Give reasons for your preferences.

2.   For several of the kinds of stories, tell the titles of some well-known movies or television series. Working together, how many of each media type can your group name within a time limit?

Choose one of your preferred kinds of media stories. In short form, describe the plot of your favorite story.

Talk It Over

What are your favorites and preferences in the area of media entertainment? On the lines, number your choices 1 through 3 or 4. Then explain the reasons for the order you chose. Compare your choices with those of your classmates.

Media

_____ television
_____ prerecorded videotapes or other computerized forms
_____ feature films in theaters
_____ media on the Internet
_____ radio programs
_____ other kinds of media

Movies

_____ comedies or animated features
_____ romance
_____ action or thrillers
_____ horror or suspense
_____ serious drama
_____ other kinds of movies

TV Series

_____ situation comedies
_____ science fiction
_____ crime or detective shows
_____ law or hospital dramas
_____ soap operas (highly emotional dramas with continuing story lines)
_____ other kinds of series

Other Programming

_____ news or current events
_____ talk shows
_____ quiz shows
_____ educational programs
_____ travel shows
_____ other kinds of programs

Music

_____ classical music
_____ jazz or blues
_____ popular singers and groups
_____ country music or dancing
_____ international folk music
_____ other kinds of music

Other Entertainment

_____ live theater (plays)
_____ cabarets or dinner theater
_____ stand-up comedy clubs
_____ dance clubs or discos
_____ casino gambling
_____ other _____

PART 3   Vocabulary and Language Learning Skills

1 **More Word Endings.** A useful clue to the part of speech of a word is its ending, or *suffix*. To review, the noun suffixes presented in Chapter 7 were *-ance* or *-ence*, *-ity, -ment, -ness,* and *-sion* or *-tion.* The adjective endings were *-ant* or *-ent, -able* or *-ible, -ive, -ous, -ic,* and *-al.* The adverbs ended in *-ly* or *-ward(s).* Below are a few additional word endings that may indicate if a word is a noun, a verb, or an adjective. In parentheses are the general meanings of the suffixes. Examples are included.

Noun Suffixes

-er, -or, -ist (a person or thing that does something)

-ship (having a position or skill)

-hood (a state or time of something)

-ism (a belief or way of doing something)

Examples

daught<u>er</u>, ang<u>er</u>, act<u>or</u>, scient<u>ist</u>

citizen<u>ship</u>, friend<u>ship</u>

child<u>hood</u>, widow<u>hood</u>

critic<u>ism</u>, Buddh<u>ism</u>

Verb Suffixes

-ate, -ify, -ize, -en (to make something be a certain way or change it to that quality)

Examples

cre<u>ate</u>, celebr<u>ate</u>, beaut<u>ify</u>, clar<u>ify</u>,

real<u>ize</u>, critic<u>ize</u>, strength<u>en</u>, wid<u>en</u>

Adjective Suffixes

-al, -ar (relating to something)

-y (full of or covered with something)

-ful (full of)

-less (without something)

-ing (causing a feeling)

-ed (having a feeling)

Examples

equ<u>al</u>, financi<u>al</u>, famili<u>ar</u>, muscul<u>ar</u>

rain<u>y</u>, angr<u>y</u>, mood<u>y</u>

care<u>ful</u>, beauti<u>ful</u>

care<u>less</u>, end<u>less</u>

interest<u>ing</u>, exhaust<u>ing</u>

interest<u>ed</u>, exhaust<u>ed</u>

Here are some of the important nouns, verbs, and adjectives (or related words) from the reading selections before or in Chapter 8. In these words, the suffix (ending) clearly indicates the part of speech—as listed in the chart on page 171. On the line before each item, write *n.* for "noun," *v.* for "verb," or *adj.* for "adjective." You might want to underline the suffix. A few words are done as examples.

1. _n._ chapt**er**
2. _n_ behavior
3. _v._ class**ify**
4. _adj._ addicted
5. _n_ psychologist
6. _v_ simplify
7. _v_ organize
8. _n_ viewer
9. _n_ baby-sitter
10. _adj_ dissatisfied

11. _v_ concentrate
12. _v_ computerize
13. _adj_ unlimited
14. _v_ visualize
15. _adj_ visual
16. _v_ personalize
17. _n_ relationship
18. _n_ emotionalism
19. _adj_ exciting
20. _n_ specialist

21. _adj_ boring
22. _adj_ nuclear
23. _adj_ truthful
24. _n_ childhood
25. _adj_ bloody
26. _adj_ shadowy
27. _v_ investigate
28. _v_ sadden
29. _adj_ natural
30. _n_ adulthood

2   **Word Families.**   Within a word "family" of related forms, some words can be used as more than one part of speech. In addition, there may be two or more nouns with different suffixes: often, one noun names an idea, while a related noun with a different ending is a word for a person—like *psychology* (a field of study) and *psychologist* (a specialist in psychology). Also, there may be related words of the same part of speech with meanings that are a little different from each other. Some examples are *vision* (noun: a mental picture) and *visionary* (noun: a person with clear ideas of the future), *criticize* (verb: to judge negatively) and *critique* (verb: to evaluate the quality of), *classic* (adjective: long important and popular) and *classical* (adjective: based on traditional ideas).

Here are some sentences with related words—nouns, verbs, adjectives, and adverbs—on the topic of the reading material of Chapter 8. Within each pair of parentheses ( ), circle the correct word form out of the three or four choices. Then write the missing words in the chart that follows—except for the boxes with Xs. There may be more than one possible word for some of the boxes—maybe one noun for a person and another for an idea. Some items are done as examples.

1. Which kinds of shows do you (preference /(prefer)/ preferable)? Do they decrease your ability to (concentration /(concentrate)/ concentrated)?

2. Are you (addiction / addict /(addicted)) to television or other (visions / visualize /(visual)) media?

3. Many TV critics and viewers (criticism /(criticize)/ critical) the amount of ((violence)/ violate / violent) in the media.

4. Psychologists worry about the ((behavior)/ behave / well-behaved) of young people that watch a lot of TV during their (children /(childhood)/ childless).

(handwritten margin notes: classic story / classical tradition / come from the past)

adj

5. (Frequency / Frequent / Frequently) TV watchers may become (dissatisfaction / dissatisfy / dissatisfied) with their normal or average lives.

6. They might (envy / enviable / envious / enviously) the lives of TV or screen actors because their lives seem (excitement / excite / excitable / exciting). *adj*

7. "Trash TV" brings (reality / realism / realize / real) people to talk shows— people with behavior that may not be (morality / moralize / moral / morally). *always* *to adj*

8. Are the guests on these shows telling the (truism / truth / true / truthful) about their lives? Are they showing their real (person / personalities / personalize / personal)?

9. Many of the films of the director Alfred Hitchcock are (psychology / psychologists / psycho / psychological) thrillers. They are very (suspense / suspend / suspenseful / suspensively).

10. Hitchcock usually (strengths / strengthens / strong) the (scare / scary / scared) mood of his movies with spooky details. *adj* *cause*

important

Noun	Verb	Adjective	Noun	Verb	Adjective
preference(s)	to prefer	preferred preferable	envy	—	envious
concentration	to concentrate	concentrated	excitement	excite	exciting excited
addiction(s) addict	to addict	addicted	reality realism	realize	real
vision(s)	visualize	visual	morality	moralize	moral
criticism	criticize	critical	truth	X	
violence	X violate	violent	personality personalities	personalize	personal
behavior	behave	(well-)behaved	Phsychology phsychologist	X	psychological
children	X	childish childless	suspense	suspend	suspenseful
frequency	frequent	frequent	strong	Strengthen	strong
dissatisfaction	dissatisfy	dissatisfied	scare	scare	scary / scared

For more vocabulary practice with word endings that indicate parts of speech, try to think of more words (nouns, verbs, and adjectives) with the suffixes listed on page 171. (You can check your guesses in a dictionary.) Can you use your words in sentences that show their meanings?

3 **Real-Life Reading. Entertainment at Home and in the Community.** Real-life reading material includes many kinds of schedules, notices, announcements, and advertising for entertainment—at home and in the community. These pieces of information often appear in the Calendar and other sections of local newspapers and magazines—as well as online. Here are some of the common subjects of this type of material:

1. TV programming (local television show schedules)
2. Radio programming (local radio schedules)
3. Neighborhood movies playing (ads and reviews)
4. Recitals, concerts, and dance performances (performance listings and ads)
5. Live theater (plays of various kinds)
6. Clubs (cabarets, comedy, music, and dance)
7. Other entertainment events (fairs, flea markets, sports events, etc.)
8. Entertainment for sale online (tapes, CDs, videos)

Look at the information on pages 175–176 about kinds of available entertainment. What kind of entertainment is the topic of each piece of material? Choose from the preceding list or use your own words. Then tell the general meaning or purpose of each piece of real-life information.

Which words and phrases do you know? Underline them. Which words are new or difficult for you? Circle them. In groups or in class, use your vocabulary-learning skills to figure out the meanings of the circled words.

4 **More Real-Life Reading.** Here are some kinds of reading material related to entertainment. Check (✔) the kinds available to you. Bring some examples to class, or copy the words from the materials. Write down the important vocabulary items. With simple definitions, tell the meanings of the words and phrases. Talk about the point of each piece of material. Summarize the important information.

- ▪ _____ Charts of locally available TV channels or radio stations
- ▪ _____ Schedules of future TV or radio programming
- ▪ _____ Ads for upcoming TV or radio programs, including special events
- ▪ _____ Movie and video ads and reviews
- ▪ _____ Information on local showings of movies and films
- ▪ _____ Ads and announcements for plays, musical performances, comedy shows, and so on.
- ▪ _____ Schedules of local clubs, coffee houses, and other places that offer live entertainment
- ▪ _____ Internet offerings of entertainment available online
- ▪ _____ Sales, price lists, coupons, and other offers of entertainment on video, DVD, CD, and so on.
- ▪ _____ other _____

a.

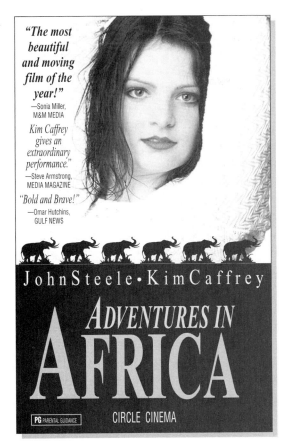

"The most beautiful and moving film of the year!"
—Sonia Miller, M&M MEDIA

"Kim Caffrey gives an extraordinary performance."
—Steve Armstrong, MEDIA MAGAZINE

"Bold and Brave!"
—Omar Hutchins, GULF NEWS

J o h n S t e e l e • K i m C a f f r e y

ADVENTURES IN AFRICA

PG PARENTAL GUIDANCE   CIRCLE CINEMA

b.

CALENDAR	THEATER AND DANCE

W E E K L Y   R E V I E W

ARTS

DAZZLING OUTDOOR DANCE THEATER

Take moms of all ages to a special performance on Mother's Day of "Mysterious Magnetism."

The sounds of the ocean will accompany the drum rhythms, guitar music, and songs of the Diana Davis Dance Company at the Outdoor Arts Cafe, 444 Beach Boulevard. Shows at 4:00 and 7:00 p.m. $20 donation.

c.

TODAY   Morning

(CC) Program is closed-captioned for the hearing impaired

WRAP

Channel **77**

2:00 AM to 6:00 AM	6:00 AM	6:30 AM	7:00 AM	7:30 AM	8:00 AM	8:30 AM
Off air	**Morning Yoga with Lola** Lola teaches the lotus position.	**Early Morning National News** Joe O'Hare and Kuki Chang (CC) **(6:50) Local News Summary** Ramon Wang (CC)	**Good Day People** Muffy welcomes artist Cosmo Dome, singing group The New Plastic Boys, Chef Zito cooks home fries.			

9:00 AM	9:30 AM	10:00 AM	10:30 AM	11:00 AM	11:30 AM	12:00 AM (noon)
Irma Live! When good things happen to bad people, interviews with millionaires who got their money by cheating other people.			**Animal Court** Veterinarian and Judge Honest Days rules on stolen parrot, barking dogs, and poisoned goldfish.		**The World Never Turns** Agnes discovers Betty is her sister, Betty finds out her new boyfriend is her father, Abe; Abe has a midlife crisis.	**Happy News at Noon** Joe and Kuki join Ramon for local and national news and entertainment gossip. (CC)

d.

listen2us.com
AN AFFILIATE OF
PUP-FM
99.6

Find and hear the music you want online.

We have more than 60,000 artists.
Just choose your music and artist and
follow the instructions on your screen.
Rock/Pop, Dance, Country, Oldies, Jazz, Soul,
Rhythm & Blues, World/Reggae, Movie Soundtracks,
Easy Listening, Classical, Religious, and More!

listen2us.com

g.

Whoopie!

CLAUDIA'S COMEDY THEATER

135 N. LaBrea Avenue. Every Friday: an improvised game show and live talk show. Saturday night stand-up comedy. See the hilarious Henrietta Howe and the unheard-of Ursula Adams. $7 cover charge + 2-drink minimums. Performances start at 8:30 p.m.

e.

MOVIES   **HEREAFTER**

R E V I E W

Director Kenji Shizuoka's latest film *Hereafter* celebrates the beauty of life. The story is set between heaven and earth, where psychologists interview the newly dead. Meaningful topics, beautiful images, and heavenly color. Worth seeing!

Showing at the Monica 4-Plex. Sat. Sun. 2 p.m., 5 p.m., 8 p.m.

h.

COUPON
R&R RECORDS
JUST FOR FUN
1/2-OFF Sale

50% off all new records (vinyl only)!
15% off all new CDs!
30% off all used CDs!
Please bring this coupon.

Three days only!!! *Friday, Saturday, Sunday*
rrr@earthlink.net
Open 7 days a week at 12202 Broadpath Lane.

f.

THEATER

FIDDLER ON THE ROOF The best in musical theater—live performances for over 30 years and still going strong! Theodore Bikel stars in Joseph Stein's musical based on the writings of Sholom Aleichem, the classic story of a family with five daughters in czarist Russia.

Long Beach Performing Arts Center, 300 Ocean Wave Way. Fri., Sat., Sun. Weekend Matinees. (555) 436-3361

| **PART 4** | # Personal Stories and Humor |

1   Follow these steps for the three stories about the media.

1. Read them quickly and tell what the main ideas are.
2. Answer your instructor's questions about the stories, or ask and answer questions of your own.
3. Give your own opinions of the ideas in the stories.
4. Tell or write about your own opinions of entertainment in the media.

Views of Entertainment in the Media

My television set is an important piece of equipment for me. I can't get out of the house very often, but my TV brings the whole world to me. From the evening news and the all-news channels, I learn about events in the outside world: politics, the environment, recent changes in technology and medicine, and so on. I like game shows and travel programs, too. Even the talk shows are exciting—all of these strange people telling their life stories and secrets to the whole world! And I love comedies; I think it's important to be able to laugh. I can even watch shows in other languages and "go shopping" by TV. With the major national networks, the educational and cable channels—and the extra sports, movie, science fiction, history, music, and other specialty channels, I have a choice of fifty different programs at the same time! The only programs I don't watch regularly by myself are the children's shows, but when my grandchildren visit me, those are fun too! Maybe I'll get a satellite dish. Then I'll have even more TV choices; and if those aren't enough, I can buy or rent a video, listen to radio programming, and so on. How can I ever feel lonely or bored with so much media?

We used to have a television set in every room of our house. Our eight-year-old son used to spent *hours* each day in front of the "boob tube." He was beginning to get strange ideas about reality from the violence and sex on many programs. He was having nightmares; he was losing interest in school, in creative play, in other children, in his family! We (the

adults) were starting to get confused too. Sometimes we weren't sure what we saw on TV and what we experienced in real life. We stopped inviting our friends and relatives to our home or visiting them; because we weren't communicating with each other either, our marriage was suffering. So was our health; we were getting lazy and becoming old and tired very quickly. So one day we decided to "pull the plug" on our dangerous family addiction. We quit TV "cold turkey"— from that time on, there was no television in our lives! It was a *very* difficult time for all of us. Like most recovering addicts, we had all the signs of withdrawal—feelings of boredom, of loneliness, of emptiness. Our son was always running to the refrigerator to satisfy his need for pleasure. My wife and I went back to smoking, to drinking alcohol, and to some other bad habits. But we finally recovered—and found the perfect solution to our discomfort and emptiness! Now we each have our own computer at home, and we spend all our free time in front of another screen. We are addicted to the Internet.

When I came to this English-speaking country, I didn't speak any of the language. I took classes and studied but it wasn't enough. I wanted to learn faster. I began to watch TV for two hours every day: a half-hour of news, a half-hour comedy program, and a one-hour interview show where people asked and answered a lot of questions. I didn't understand anything at first. But then I discovered some new methods to help me understand: for instance, I watched the news in my native language first and then saw the same news in English. I also watched children's programming—the same show several times in the day; I understood almost everything in those programs. Sometimes I recorded a program on videotape and watched it again and again until I got the main ideas, or the points. I also rent or buy videotapes so I can see the same images and hear the same language as many times as necessary. Now I have some new ideas. For instance, I can get closed-captioned TV for the hearing impaired and use it when I watch certain programs; then I can read the words in English subtitles at the same time I hear them. And I can get videos of movies in my native language and read the English subtitles while I watch and listen—or I can watch films in English while I read the translations in my language. Now I think of TV as one of my best "teachers."

The Humor of the Entertainment Media

2 Specialists in both physical and psychological health agree: laughter is good for the emotions because it fills important human needs. It can even help decrease the effects of withdrawal from addictions. In other words, laughter is good medicine.

There is plenty of humor in the media designed to produce laughter and release tension. *Sitcoms,* or "situation comedies," are television series in which the same characters appear in funny situations in each episode. In addition to the events of the plot, the humor lies in the *one-liners,* very short jokes of one or a few sentences. Similarly, most *stand-up comedy* (one person talking in funny ways in a live or taped performance) includes one-liners.

Here are some very short pieces of humor (one-liners) by some very famous or popular comedians or other personalities. Discuss your answers to these questions:

1. What is the topic of the humor? For example, does the line make fun of the media, of marriage, of human nature in general, or what?

2. Is the line funny to you? Why or why not?

3. Can you think of a short and funny response to any of the lines? Say your lines and see if anyone responds with laughter.

- Today, watching television often means fighting, violence, and bad language—and that is just to decide who gets to hold the remote control. (Donna Gephart)

- It's so simple to be wise. Just think of something stupid to say—and then don't say it. (Sam Levenson)

- I have enough money to last me the rest of my life—if I don't buy anything. (Jackie Mason)

- I went on a diet, stopped drinking and heavy eating—and in fourteen days I lost exactly two weeks. (Joe E. Lewis)

- I don't want to achieve immortality through my work. I want to achieve immortality by not dying. (Woody Allen)

- Marriage is a wonderful institution. But who wants to live in an institution? (Groucho Marx)

- Too bad that all the people that know how to run this country are busy driving taxis and cutting hair. (George Burns)

- A committee is a group that keeps minutes and loses hours. (Milton Berle)

- Television is a medium because it is neither rare nor well done. (Ernie Kovacs)

- When I bore people at a party, they think it is their fault. (Henry Kissinger)

- The secret of a happy marriage remains a secret. (Henny Youngman)

- My wife and I were happy for twenty years. Then we met. (Rodney Dangerfield)

- Never go to bed mad. Stay up and fight. (Phyllis Diller)

Video Activities: Quiz Shows

Before You Watch.

1. Circle the kinds of TV show you like to watch.

    a. comedies   b. dramas   c. quiz shows   d. soap operas

2. Do you like watching quiz shows on TV? Discuss with a partner.

3. Describe your favorite TV quiz show to your partner.

Watch.   Discuss the following questions with your classmates.

1. On all the game shows you saw in the videos, what must contestants do in order to win money?

2. Why do television networks like to make game shows?

3. The contestants on today's game shows are

    a. millionaires   b. ordinary people   c. scholars

Watch Again.   Write T if the statements below are true and F if they are false. Then correct all the false statements.

1. _____ In the U.S., you can watch a game show on TV almost every night of the week.

2. _____ Quiz shows are a new idea.

3. _____ The first game show in America was called "Who Wants to Be a Millionaire?"

4. _____ If a television show is successful, other networks hurry to copy it.

5. _____ Game shows are cheaper to make than sitcoms.

6. _____ In the short term, American TV networks will stop making game shows.

7. _____ The questions on the new "Twenty One" show are called "relatable." This means they are about families.

After You Watch.   Work in groups to play a word game. Your teacher will write words on the board. Each group chooses one word and writes down as many words of similar meaning as they can. The group that comes up with the most words wins.

Chapter 9

Social Life

IN THIS CHAPTER

The readings in this chapter have to do with friendship and other kinds of social relationships. The first two reading selections, "Meeting the Perfect Mate," are a fiction story. They tell about some of the many ways young people meet possible husbands and wives. Finally, you will read about different experiences and opinions related to social life around the world.

PART 1	# Meeting the Perfect Mate

Before You Read

1 Discuss the pictures in small groups.

1. Who are the people?
2. What are they talking about? How are the three people different from one another?
3. Do you agree with any one of them? Why or why not?
4. How do young people in your country often meet their boyfriends/girlfriends?

2 Think about the answers to these questions. The reading selection answers them.

1. What was a common kind of marriage in Korea in the past?
2. How do some young people around the world meet the people who become their boyfriends or girlfriends?
3. What is an advantage to each method (way) of meeting people? What is a disadvantage?

3   **Vocabulary Preview.**   Here are some vocabulary items from the first reading selection. You can learn them now or come back to them later.

Nouns	Verbs	Adjectives	Adverbs
photos	examine	popular	fortunately
mates	interview	potential	
a guy	reply	aggressive	
a search	match	discouraged	
a match	accept		
cyberspace			
cafes			

Read

4   Read the following material quickly. Then read the explanations and do the exercises after the reading.

Meeting the Perfect Mate

For the past month I've been taking a university graduate course called "Social Structure." It's a very popular class. We've been discussing friendship, social life, dating, marriage, and other relationships—through the generations and throughout the world. One of our assignments is to examine the ways that people meet potential husbands and wives. I've been interviewing students on campus all week as part of my study.

First, I talked with my roommate in the dormitory, Sook In, an international student from Korea.

"What's one way to meet a possible mate?" I asked her.

"Well," she said, "one method in my country is to have a matched marriage."

"A what?" I asked. "I know you can match a tie to a shirt—or two socks after you do the laundry. Then they're a match. But people?"

"Sure," she replied. "There aren't many arranged marriages these days, but there were a lot not too long ago. My parents, for example, met each other for the first time on their wedding day. My grandparents chose their children's mates and arranged the wedding."

"Do you mean that they weren't in love? That sounds awful! Weren't they worried?"

"Maybe a little bit," Sook In said, "but they accepted each other. Then, fortunately, they grew to love each other. They've had a good, successful marriage for the past thirty years. This happens in a lot of arranged marriages."

I shook my head. "Amazing!" I said.

The next person that I interviewed was Bill, a guy in my business management class. "I meet a lot of women in dance clubs—at least more than I do on campus," he said. "The environment is exciting and I go every weekend, if possible, to dance or talk or just listen to music."

"That seems great," I said.

"I thought so, too, at first," he said a little sadly. "But on the other hand, very often the women in those places are unfriendly. A lot of men are too aggressive, and as a result the women are very cold. So I tried the Internet—you know, the World Wide Web."

"You meet potential girlfriends on the Web? On your computer?" I asked, even more amazed.

"Yeah, there are plenty of people to communicate with in cyberspace—at home, at cafes, in the library . . . but who knows what is real there and what isn't? Who knows who might be dangerous?" asked Bill, discouraged. It seemed he was talking more to himself than to me. I continued my search for the perfect way to find the perfect mate.

"The Internet? Never!" said Julie, a student who works part-time in the campus bookstore. "I prefer to make new friends at places where people have interests in common. I met my boyfriend at the health club, for example, and it seems that the healthy atmosphere of the gym is continuing into the relationship that I have with him."

"That sounds wonderful," I said.

"Yes," she said, "I guess so. But to be honest, there's one problem with this arrangement."

"What?" I asked.

"The truth is that I really hate to exercise, so I don't want to go to the gym anymore. What's my boyfriend going to think when he finds this out?"

To be continued . . .

After You Read

5 **Recognizing the Structure of Conversations.** Even in conversational form—with the words of each speaker between quotation marks (" "), some reading selections may follow the organization of an outline. The main parts, or topics, can appear after numbers like I, II, III, IV, and so on. The ideas of each part can follow capital letters like A, B, C, and so on.

The following outline shows the organization of the parts (main topics) and important ideas of the reading selection "Meeting the Perfect Mate." First, on the numbered lines, arrange these phrases in the same order as in the reading. Items I and IV are done as examples.

- Arranged marriages
- Meeting people in dance clubs
- Finding friends in cyberspace
- Meeting in health clubs or the gym
- Introduction: Reasons for interviewing people

Next, write the following ideas in sentence form on the correct lettered line under each topic. Be sure to put them in the right order. Items IIA and VB are done as examples.

- I'm studying "Social Structure" in a graduate seminar.
- I'm interviewing people about ways to meet potential mates.
- You can talk or just listen to music.

- Husbands and wives may learn to love each other.
- Mates may meet for the first time on their wedding day.
- The women act unfriendly because a lot of men are too aggressive.
- You can go online at home, in cafes, and in other places.
- People with common interest in physical exercise meet here.
- You don't know what is unreal or dangerous about people you meet on the Web.
- If you're not really interested in exercise, there might be a problem.

Meeting the Perfect Mate

I. _Introduction: reasons for interviewing people_

   A. _I'm studying "social structure" in graduate seminar._

   B. _I'm interview people about ways to meet potential mates._

II. _arranaged married_

   A. _Husband and wives may learn to love each other_

   B. _Mates may meet for the first time on their wedding day_

III. _Meeting people in dance club_

   A. _You can talk or just listen to music._

   B. _The women act unfriendly because a lot of men are too aggressive_

IV. _Finding friends in cyberspace_

   A. _You can go online at home, in cafes, and in other places._

   B. _You don't know what is unreal or dangerous about people_

V. _Meeting in health club or the gym_

   A. _People with common interest in physical exercise meet here_

   B. _If you're not really interested in exercise, there might be a problem._

To tell the main (the most general) idea of the reading, finish this sentence.

There are _____ and disadvantages to the

various ways _____.

6 **Understanding the Main Idea.**   The main idea of the reading selection "Meeting the Perfect Mate" is in the first sentence of the following paragraph, but it is not quite true. Change the underlined words in the topic sentence and the important supporting details that follow so that the paragraph correctly tells the point of the reading. A few items are done as examples.

There are ~~only~~ <u>disadvantages</u> to the various possible ways of meeting potential
advantages and
~~classmates or roommates~~. (1) <u>An advantage of</u> arranged marriages is that mates
mates
may not meet until their wedding day; even so, through the years they may learn
to <u>take graduate courses</u> anyway. (2) At <u>stand-up comedy</u> clubs, you can talk
or just listen to music; on the other hand, <u>the men</u> in such places are often cold
and unfriendly because <u>the children</u> act too aggressive. (3) Meeting people in
cyberspace is <u>inconvenient</u> because computers are <u>nowhere</u>; however, it is
<u>easy</u> to know what is unreal or unsafe about the people online. (4) If you meet
potential dates at a place where you have <u>nothing in common</u>, like the gym, you
can share your interest, but what happens if one person <u>gets interested</u> in the
activity?

7   **Supplying Left-Out Words and References.**   Often a writer leaves out words
because information in other sentences or in another part of the sentence makes them
unnecessary. The reader figures out the missing information from the context.

Examples:

"What's one way to meet a possible husband or wife?" I asked.
   "Well," she said, "one method in my country is to have a matched marriage."
(Method for what? For meeting a possible husband or wife.)

"I know you can match socks. But people?"
(But can you match people?)

In the following sentences there are missing words that readers can figure out from
the context. Which words are understood in these sentences? Write them in the blanks,
as in the examples.

1. "What's one way to meet a possible mate?" I asked my roommate, Sook In.
       "Well," she said, "one method <u>for meeting a possible mate</u> in my
    country is to have a matched marriage."

2. "I know you can match a tie to a shirt—or <u>match</u> two socks,
    too, after you do the laundry. But <u>   </u> people?"

3. "Sure," she replied. "There aren't many arranged marriages these days, but
    there were a lot <u>   </u> not too many
    years ago."

4. "Do you mean that they weren't in love? That sounds awful! Weren't they upset?"

   "Maybe _____ a little bit," Sook In said. "But they've had a successful marriage for thirty years."

5. "I meet a lot of women in nightclubs," Bill said. "At least more _____ than I do on campus. The nightclub environment is exciting. I go _____ every weekend."

Some words refer to ideas that came before them in the reading.

Example:

"My parents have had a good marriage for the past thirty years. This happens in a lot of arranged marriages."

(What does *this* refer to? Having a good marriage.)

In each of the following sentences, circle the words that the underlined word refers to. The first one is done as an example.

1. I've been taking a graduate (seminar) in social structure for the past month. It's a very popular course.

2. "One method is to have a matched marriage," Sook In said. "A who?" I asked.

3. "My grandparents chose their children's mates and arranged their wedding," she explained. "Do you mean they weren't in love?"

4. "I meet a lot of women in dance clubs—at least more than I do on campus," said Bill.

5. "Dance clubs seem great," I said. "I thought so too at first," he said a little sadly.

6. "Yeah, there are plenty of people to communicate with in cyberspace—at home, at cafes, in the library . . . but who knows what is real there and what isn't?"

7. "It seems that the healthy atmosphere in the gym is continuing into our relationship," Julie said. "That sounds wonderful," I said. "Yes," she said. "I guess so."

8. "But the truth is that I hate to exercise. What's he going to do when he finds this out?"

Now turn back to the Before You Read section on page 182 and answer the questions.

Discussing the Reading

8   In small groups, talk about your answers to the following questions. Then tell the class the most interesting information or ideas.

1.   Do you know anyone who had an arranged marriage? Are there arranged marriages in your country or culture? What is your opinion of this way to meet potential mates?

2.   Do you like to communicate with potential friends in cyberspace? How do you do it?

3.   Where might people with common interests usually meet in your community?

PART 2   # Meeting the Perfect Mate (continued)

Before You Read

1   **Vocabulary Preview.**   Here are some vocabulary items from the next reading. You can learn them now or come back to them later.

Nouns		Verbs	Adjectives	Phrases
a dormitory	a lifestyle	fill out	optimistic	to tell the truth
background	the beach	miss		computer dating
height	motorcycling	film		services
feet (')	membership			make a mistake
inches (")	statistics			a personal ad
characteristics	supermarkets			shake your head

Read

2   **Making Inferences.**   The first time readers skim a piece of information, they usually read for *literal* meaning—that is to say, they find out quickly what the material *says*. Beyond the basic meaning of the words, however, they may be able to *infer* (figure out) other ideas or opinions. On a second, more careful, reading they can recognize and understand thoughts that the writer did not state directly.

Read the second half of the reading selection quickly for literal (basic) meaning. Then to better understand the writer's meaning, read the material a second time.

Meeting the Perfect Mate (continued)

"What is the best way to meet the perfect husband or wife? Computer dating services are the answer!" said my friend Sara, who lives down the hall from me in the dormitory. "They provide a great way to meet people! The biggest advantage is that you have a lot in common with the people you meet through a computer. The computer can match you up with someone of your same intelligence, cultural background or religion, age, personality, and so on. If you want, you can meet someone who is famous, exciting, optimistic, healthy, polite—any characteristics that are important to you. You can match your preferences in lifestyle, food, nature, sports, movies, and everything else. And you can ask for a professor, a scientist, a computer specialist, an artist, or . . ."

"Have you had many successful dates so far?" I asked.

"To tell the truth," she said, "not really. I think I made a big mistake when I filled out the application form. I didn't want to miss a wonderful guy because of an answer that was too specific, so I was careful to write very general answers."

"What do you mean?"

"Well, there was a question about height. I said, 'anyone between 3'5" and 7'5".' Then there was a question about recreation. I answered 'yes' to 147 interests, from classic historical architecture to motorcycling. I wrote that I liked tennis, swimming, the beach, the mountains, the desert, health food, junk food, ethnic foods, eating out, cooking, staying home, traveling, the arts, TV comedies, quiz shows, crime dramas, family life, single life, and on and on and on . . . you know, I think that the computer got confused. It hasn't found a date for me since I sent in the application."

"And what about video dating?" asked Sara's roommate, Sandra.

"Dating by video?" I asked. "How is that possible?"

"Well, I haven't done it myself because it's expensive. But I've seen the ads on TV and in the newspaper. You join a video-dating club. They film you as you talk about yourself . . . you know, your background and your interests and things like that. Then you view videotapes of men, and if you want to meet someone, you write his membership number on a computer form. Then he sees your video, and if he likes what he sees on the screen . . . you arrange to meet!"

"Hmm . . .," I answered. "More television in your life."

"Well, you could place a personal ad," Sandra continued.

"In the newspaper?"

"Sure. A friend of mine did that. He wanted to get married, so he figured it out by statistics. He decided that out of every ten women, he liked one. And out of every ten women he liked, he might fall in love with one. Therefore, to get married, he just needed to meet one hundred women."

"Did it work?" I asked.

There was no answer.

Last, I interviewed a guy in the cafeteria.

"Supermarkets," he told me.

"You're kidding," I said.

"No, I'm serious. I meet a lot of potential dates over the frozen pizzas in the convenience-food section. Also, it's easy to make small talk over the cabbage and broccoli in the produce section. We discuss chemicals and nutrition and food prices. Sometimes this leads to a very romantic date."

I slowly shook my head: it is strange . . . very strange. I didn't respond because I didn't want to be impolite.

That evening, I talked with my roommate, Sook In.

"You know," I said. "I think maybe your parents and grandparents had a pretty good idea. A matched marriage is beginning to seem more and more attractive to me."

After You Read

3 Often a reading gives information from which the reader can infer (figure out) other information. Write an X on the line in front of the ideas that the author stated (clearly said) or implied (suggested) in the reading. Write an O before the ideas that the writer did not state or imply. Look back at the reading selection if necessary.

1. __X__ The writer's friend Sara is a student.

2. __O__ There is a computer dating service in the dormitory.

3. _____ Sara thinks that computer dating has many advantages.

4. _____ A computer application asks questions about height, interests, and other things, and the computer uses the information to match people for dates.

5. _____ Sara wants to have a date with a doctor who doesn't eat meat.

6. _____ Sara had a lot of success with computer dating so far.

7. _____ If you join a video-dating club, you meet people on network TV.

8. _____ In video dating, two people can arrange to get together if they like each other's videotapes.

9. _____ To place a personal ad, you write about yourself and pay the newspaper to print the information.

10. _____ Dating and mating may be a matter of statistics.

11. _____ The student that the writer interviewed in the cafeteria likes computer dating services and video clubs too.

12. _____ He makes small talk with potential dates in stores.

13. _____ On dates, he likes to eat pizza with broccoli and cabbage salad.

14. _____ The writer doesn't think that it is a good idea to date people you meet in the supermarket.

15. _____ The writer didn't tell her opinion to the guy in the cafeteria.

16. _____ She thinks that arranged marriages may have some advantages after all.

4 **Learning to Summarize.** The story in Parts 1 and 2, "Meeting the Perfect Mate," is fiction, but it contains real information about possible ways to meet potential husbands and wives in many societies of today's world. One way to summarize the story is to tell the advantages and disadvantages of each of the possible ways to meet people.

Work in groups. Each student completes one or more of the following items. Then put your sentences together in a summary.

1. The writer has been interviewing people about friendship, marriage, and other relationships. She found out that the mates in arranged marriages

    _____

    _____.

2. The advantages of meeting people at dance clubs are that _____

    _____.

    The disadvantages are that _____

    _____.

3. It's easy to "meet" people online. On the other hand, it can be a problem if

    _____

    _____.

4. Some people make new friends at places where _____

    _____, such as a gym. But there might be a problem if _____

    _____.

5. An advantage of computer dating is that _____

    _____.

    But if you _____

    the computer might not _____.

6. In a video-dating club, _____.

    If you place a personal ad in a newspaper, you can meet _____

    _____.

7. Some people think the supermarket is a good place to meet potential dates

    because _____

    _____.

8. After interviewing many people about a possible way to meet potential mates, the writer decided _____

    _____.

Discussing the Reading

5   In small groups, talk about your answers to these questions. Then tell the class the most interesting information or ideas.

1. Do you sometimes make conversation with people in places where you have interests in common? Do these people ever become your friends?

2. Do you have video and/or computer dating services in your country? What do you think of this way to find dates?

3. Where do you usually meet the people who become your friends? Where or how did or do you meet potential boyfriends or girlfriends?

Talk It Over

Proverbs are old, short, well-known sayings about human nature and life. Here are some well-known English-language proverbs about social life, friendships, and love relationships. First, match the proverbs on the left with their meanings (the paraphrases) on the right. Write the letters on the lines. Then for each proverb, discuss your answers to these questions.

1. Do you agree with the "wisdom" of the proverb? Why or why not? Give some examples from your own experience.

2. Is there a proverb with a similar meaning in your native language? If so, translate it into English for the class and explain it.

3. Do you know any proverbs with an approximately opposite meaning (in English or in any language)? If so, tell about them.

Proverbs

1. _____ Love makes the world go 'round.

2. _____ Absence makes the heart grow fonder.

3. _____ All's fair in love and war.

4. _____ Better to love and lose than never to love at all.

5. _____ Love is blind.

6. _____ Any friend of yours is a friend of mine.

7. _____ A friend in need is a friend indeed.

8. _____ The best of friends must part.

9. _____ A woman without a man is like a fish without water.

10. _____ The course of true love never did run smooth.

Meanings

a. If you don't see someone for a while, you will miss that person.

b. In love relationships, anything is possible.

c. Love motivates people all over the globe.

d. Even after it ends, a failed relationship is better than no relationship at all.

e. When you are in love, you don't see the faults of the other person.

f. In times of need, you find out who your real friends are.

g. No friendship can last forever.

h. Women need men in their lives.

i. If you like someone, I will like that person too.

j. There will always be hard times in a real love relationship.

| **PART 3** | # Vocabulary and Language Learning Skills |

1 Recognizing Negative Prefixes. A *suffix* (an ending added to a word) often indicates its *part of speech*—that is, if it is a noun, a verb, an adjective, and so on. Some suffixes have general meanings. In contrast, a *prefix* (a part added to the beginning of a word) does not show the part of speech; however, a prefix usually changes the *meaning* of the word it is attached to.

These are some common prefixes that add negative meanings to words; that is to say, these word beginnings change a word to its opposite.

dis-   il-   im-   in-   non-   un-

Examples:

During our trip, we discussed our <u>dis</u>satisfaction with our relationship. He was <u>im</u>polite, and I was <u>in</u>direct. Even so, the talk was so important and interesting that the miles seemed to <u>dis</u>appear.

(In the words *dissatisfaction, impolite,* and *indirect,* the prefixes *dis-, im-, and in-* add a negative meaning. The same letters are not negative prefixes in the words *discussed, important,* and *interesting.*)

Notice that the prefix *im-* appears most often before the letters *b, m,* or *p.* Words beginning with the letter *l* may take the prefix *il-.* The most common negative prefix is *un-.*

Which of these words from Chapter 1 to 9 contain a prefix with a negative meaning? Underline those prefixes. Put X on the lines before the words without negative meanings. Use a dictionary if you need help.

1.	_X_	discussion	16. ____	independence
2.	____	disease	17. ____	indirectness
3.	____	dishonesty	18. _X_	individual
4.	____	disrespect	19. _X_	industrialization
5.	_X_	distance	20. ____	informal
6.	____	illegal	21. _X_	international
7.	____	illogical	22. ____	nonsense
8.	_X_	illustration	23. ____	nontraditional
9.	_X_	images	24. ____	non-Western
10.	_X_	immediately	25. _X_	understanding
11.	____	immoral	26. _X_	universal
12.	____	immortality	27. ____	unlimited
13.	____	impatience	28. ____	unrelated
14.	____	impolite	29. ____	unusually
15.	____	inability	30. ____	unwelcome

From your own knowledge of the vocabulary in this book, write the missing negative prefix (*dis-, il-, im-, in-, non-, un-*) in each blank, as in the example. Then you can check your answers in the dictionary.

1. _dis_ appearance
2. _dis_ advantage
3. _il_ legality
4. _im_ mortality
5. _im_ politeness

6. _in_ effective
7. _in_ consistent
8. _non_ sense
9. _non_ violent
10. _non_ specific

11. _un_ healthy
12. _un_ natural
13. _un_ certain
14. _un_ common
15. _un_ pleasant

2   To change the meaning of the following paragraph to its opposite, write the contrasting word (a word with the opposite meaning) over all the underlined items, as in the examples. Be careful: not all words with opposite meanings include negative prefixes—or any prefixes at all.

Some people looking for ~~impossible~~ (possible) husbands and wives try ~~unnatural~~ (natural) methods. For instance, they might find it <u>difficult</u> to make small talk with people that look <u>unfriendly</u> or <u>depressed</u> in the produce section of the supermarket, where they are choosing <u>packaged</u> or <u>prepared</u> fruits and vegetables. Or they might have a conversation at a <u>slow</u>-food restaurant, where they <u>dislike</u> eating hamburgers, french fries, or other items with <u>high</u> nutritional value. In a <u>similar</u> way, a computer service is <u>incapable</u> of matching singles with <u>married</u> people that are very much <u>unlike</u> them; men and women that get together in this <u>inconvenient</u> way often share many interests. A video-dating center may be <u>unhelpful</u> as well; meeting people on the Internet has benefits, but it can have <u>advantages</u> too. In any case, <u>many</u> ways of meeting people can be <u>unsuccessful</u> all the time.

For more vocabulary practice with the words that begin with prefixes, identify the parts of speech of the items in Exercises 1–3 of Part 3. Can you use these words in sentences that show their meanings?

In the readings of this chapter, you can find other words with prefixes, such as *interviewing, international, unfriendly,* and so on. Remember—only *some* words begin with prefixes. You can also look for words that can take negative prefixes, such as *perfect* (+ ***im-*** = *imperfect*), *matched* (+ ***un-*** = *unmatched*), or *fortunately* (+ ***un-*** = *unfortunately*). Can you explain the meanings of these words or use them in sentences appropriately?

3   Real-Life Reading: Personal Ads.   In newspapers, magazines, and many other places, including the Internet, there are many kinds of advertisements—ads about jobs, housing, items for sale, community events, travel, and so on. People place ads when they are looking for certain things; similarly, to meet people that might become potential mates, some singles take out personal ads. Here are some ads of this kind; they are based on real ads placed in reading material around the world. If many of the ads seem funny, it's because they were meant to be amusing to attract interest.

Which words and phrases are new or difficult for you? Circle them and work together to figure out their general meanings. Then try to match the women's ads with the ads by men that you think they should meet. Which ad placers should not get together? Explain the reasons behind your matchmaking decisions.

P E R S O N A L S   MEN SEEKING WOMEN

1.   **MALE**   Retired senior citizen wants female companion 70+ for comparing health conditions and illnesses, complaining, and sitting around watching a lot of television. Under 30 is also OK.

2.   **RELIGIOUS MALE**   I am a serious student of religion. I plan to devote my life to God. I go to church every week and pray three times a day. I am looking for a fun-loving girl to share an exciting life in the fast lane.

3.   **CHRISTIAN MALE**   34, very successful, smart, independent, and self-made. Looking for a wife whose father will hire me.

4.   **SINGLE MALE**   I am an unmarried businessman with no shocking family secrets, no terrible past, no horrible life experiences, and no personality. So call me some time.

5.   **DIVORCED MALE**   As a divorced Jewish man, I need someone who will do these things with me: keep kosher, attend synagogue, observe the Sabbath, celebrate all the Jewish holidays, and attend bar mitzvahs and other life events. Religion not important.

6.   **MALE**   My favorite foods are sushi, soybean burgers, water bugs in spicy hot-pepper sauce, and tiramisu. My main interests are unusual laws about jaywalking, twelfth-century Ethiopian literature, biometereology, and eternal life or immortality. Also, I like to go barefoot in elevators with electric carpets, warm my feet with a Japanese kotatsu, and collect art objects of the Egyptian pharaohs. Seeking a like-minded soul mate to live with me in a fixer-upper castle in the Sahara Desert. No weirdos or other strange individuals, please.

P E R S O N A L S   WOMEN SEEKING MEN

a.   **FEMALE**   75-year old grandmother, no money, no house, seeks handsome, strong male under the age of 35. Object: marriage. I can dream, can't I?

b.   **SINGLE FEMALE**   Attractive and accomplished woman, college graduate, looking for handsome, successful European lord or prince to save me from my parents' house. I don't cook, but I do love to shop.

c.   **FEMINIST**   Faithful Jewish feminist, devoted to women's liberation and female rights, seeking man who will accept my independence and strength—but you probably will not. Oh, just forget it.

d.   **FEMALE**   Worried about the meddling interference of irritating in-laws and other relatives? I am an orphan with no brothers or sisters. Please write me.

e.   **FEMALE**   I am a sensitive multicultural woman you can open your heart to. share your innermost thoughts and deepest secrets. Trust and confide in me. I'll understand your insecurities. No talkative fat guys, please.

f.   **EDUCATED FEMALE**   Israeli professor, 41, with eighteen years of teaching behind me. Looking for a Latin-American romantic who likes to sit around and speak Spanish.

4   **More Real-Life Reading.**   Here are some kinds of reading material related to social life. Check (✔) the kinds available to you. Bring some examples to class, or copy the words from the materials. Write down the important vocabulary items. Give simple definitions of the words and phrases. Talk about the point of each piece of material. Summarize the important information.

- ■ _____ personal ads in newspapers or magazines or on the Internet
- ■ _____ computer dating service forms with the purpose of matching people
- ■ _____ ads and calendar event announcements of singles' groups or other clubs for people that share common interests
- ■ _____ other _____

PART 4   Personal Stories and Humor

1   Follow these steps for the story about the beginning of a friendship.

1. Read it quickly and tell what the main ideas are.
2. Answer your instructor's questions about the story, or ask and answer questions of your own.
3. Tell your own opinions of the ideas in the story. Give your ideas about how the story will continue—and end.
4. Tell or write about your own experience or ideas about friendship or other social relationships.

The Beginning of a Friendship

Lucy was a shy and frightened little girl when she first stood in front of Mrs. Campbell's third-grade class. It was Monday. "Now, children, we are very lucky today. I would like you to meet Lucy. She and her family just moved here from Guam. She will be in our class for the rest of the year." Pointing to a two-student desk that was empty, the teacher addressed the new student. "You can have that desk over there."

Looking only at the floor and holding her books close to her, Lucy walked over to her desk. However, she stumbled slightly and her books fell on the floor. Some of the kids in the class laughed—because that's the way some kids were. Lucy picked up her books and sat down, alone. The class had an odd number of students, so she was the only one without a desk partner.

When it was time for the first recess, all the kids hurried out of the class-room—all the kids but Lucy, that is. She waited until they were gone, got the snack out of her lunchbox, and walked slowly out to the playground. All the children were laughing, running, and playing. Unnoticed, Lucy made her way

to a big tree, where she sat down on a bench and ate, alone. She watched the others play, but nobody came over to ask her if she wanted to join them.

When lunch time came, the situation was the same. The girls played hopscotch and the boys played ball, and Lucy sat alone on the bench under the big tree. The only thing any of the kids said to her all day was, "Guam? I've never heard of Guam. I'm from America." Lucy was too shy to say anything. The little boy ran off to tell his friends that people from Guam didn't talk. That's the way some kids were.

The next day Lucy told her mom she didn't want to go to school anymore because she didn't have anybody to play with. She wanted to go back to Guam, to her friends. Her mother told her she would make new friends—and to hurry up and get ready. She shoved her lunchbox into her hands and led her out the door. Lucy's second day went just like her first. During recess, she went out to the bench under the big tree to eat her snack. She didn't look up much, but she could hear the sounds of laughter coming from the playground. She was lonely and very homesick. Then, halfway through her apple, she started to cry. Some of the other kids saw her crying, but they didn't ask her what was wrong. They just whispered to one another and pointed at her. Some laughed, because that's the way some kids were.

The third day of the week went pretty much the same—and the fourth day too. Lucy talked to nobody. Nobody talked to her. She sat alone during all the recesses and lunch periods. Then she went home and cried.

Then on Friday something different happened. In the middle of math class, the teacher was called out of the room. When she returned, she had a little boy with her. She said, "Class, this week we are very, very lucky. We have another new student. His name is Henry. Henry, you can take the other seat at that desk, next to Lucy." The little boy came over an put his book bag on Lucy's desk. He looked at her before he sat down, and he smiled. He smiled at her. It was a shy kind of smile, but it was a nice smile. She smiled back.

When lunch time came, Lucy sat on the bench under the big tree eating her peanut butter sandwich. She didn't feel like crying. She was looking for Henry. There he was—playing ball with some boys. Henry made friends quickly, it seemed. Then he looked over at Lucy and saw her looking at him. Shyly, she looked down, but when she looked up again, there was Henry—standing right in front of her, his lunch bag in his hand. "Can I sit on this bench with you?" he asked. She nodded. For a few minutes they didn't talk at all. But right away Lucy new she had a friend. Henry was nice. Some kids were just that way . . .

The Humor of Social Life and Love

2 Proverbs are one-sentence pieces of wisdom collected through the centuries and throughout the world. Comedians, children, and others often base their "one-liners" (very short pieces of humor) on old, well-known proverbs or famous sayings. When they change a few words, usually at the end, the proverb becomes funny.

Here are some changed proverbs by some very famous or popular comedians, children, or others. Discuss your answers to these questions.

1. What was the original proverb? (You can look back at page 192.)

2. What is the specific topic of the humor? For example, does the line make fun of love relationships, friendships, or what?

3. Is the line funny to you? Why or why not?

4. Can you think of any lines (new proverbs) of your own on the topics of social relationships, friendships, or love? Tell your lines and see if anyone responds with laughter.

- Love makes the world . . . grow in population.

- Absence makes the heart . . . go yonder (find other places to go).

- All's fair in love and . . . fighting with your brother.

- Better to love and lose . . . than never to lose at all.

- Love is blind . . . but marriage opens the eyes.

- Any friend of yours is a friend . . . of yours.

- A friend in need is a . . . friend to avoid.

- The best of friends must . . . find their own apartments.

- A woman without a man is like a fish without . . . a bicycle.

- The course of true love . . . won't earn you any college credits.

Video Activities: Online Dating

Before You Watch.   Discuss these questions in a group.

1.   What is a "chat room"? Have you ever visited one?
2.   Do you think the Internet is a useful way to meet new people?
3.   How do you usually meet people?
4.   Do you believe that there is only one man or woman in the world who is exactly "right" for each person?

Watch.   Number the following events in the order that they happened.

_____ Patrick and Vesna chatted online.

_____ They got married.

_____ Patrick came home from work late and couldn't sleep.

_____ Patrick and Vesna got engaged.

_____ Vesna came to Patrick's house.

Watch Again.   Discuss these questions in a group.

1.   Patrick asked Vesna, "What do you look like?" Her answer was "You won't run from me." What did she mean?
2.   Why was it easy for Patrick and Vesna to meet?
3.   How soon after they met did Patrick and Vesna get engaged?
4.   How soon after that did they get married?
5.   What did Patrick and Vesna's friends predict about their relationship?
6.   What do Patrick and Vesna say about one another?
7.   What is the "Romance Network"?

After You Watch.   Read personal ads in an English language newspaper, magazine, or on the Internet. When everyone is finished reading, answer the following questions in groups.

1.   What words can you find regularly in personal ads? Make a list.
2.   How honest do you think personal ads are? Why?
3.   Why do so many people join a dating service or answer a personal ad?

Chapter 10

Customs, Celebrations, and Holidays

IN THIS CHAPTER

Do you know how to be a good guest at a dinner party? When you give a dinner party, do you know how to be a good host? The first reading selection, "A Dinner Party," gives some good advice on how to act in both those situations. In the second reading, "A Traditional Holiday," you will learn about the history of a traditional holiday in some countries of the world—Halloween. The final reading selection, "The Spirit of the Holiday Season," tells two holiday stories—one real and one fiction.

| **PART 1** | # A Dinner Party |

Before You Read

1   Discuss the picture in small groups.

1.   Where is the young man? What is he doing?
2.   Why does he look confused? What is his problem?
3.   What do you think he should do in this situation?
4.   Have you ever had a problem like this? What did you do about it?

2   Think about the answers to these questions. The reading selection answers them.

1.   Who wrote the letters in the reading? Who answered them?
2.   Should you bring something when you go to someone's house for dinner? If so, what?
3.   At what time should you arrive for a dinner party?
4.   What can you do if you don't know which knife, fork, or spoon to use at a formal dinner party?
5.   If you give a dinner party, how can you help your guests feel comfortable?
6.   What are some secrets of a successful dinner party?

3 **Vocabulary Preview.** Here are some vocabulary items from the first reading selection. You can learn them now or come back to them later.

Nouns	Verbs	Adjectives	Adverb	Phrases
an invitation	arrive	honored	perhaps	follow someone's lead
Thanksgiving	thank	grateful		express appreciation
a gift	advise	elaborate		a thank-you note
a present		appreciated		help themselves
chopsticks		appropriate		go back for seconds
hospitality		delayed		
appreciation		stuck		
etiquette		considerate		

4 Read the following material quickly. Then read the explanations and do the exercises after the reading.

A Dinner Party

[A] Dear Etty Kitt:

I am an international student in a small town in the United States. My Chinese-American roommate's family wants me to celebrate Thanksgiving with them—and all their relatives—in their home. I know it's an important holiday, so I felt honored to receive such an invitation. I accepted it gratefully and am looking forward to the occasion, but I am also feeling a little nervous about it. With the cultural diversity and variety of styles and customs in this country, which rules do I follow? I'm worried about making mistakes and looking like a fool.

Should I bring a gift, such as something beautiful for the house? Should I arrive early or exactly on time or a little late? At the dinner table, how can I know which utensils—which fork or spoon or knife, or even chopsticks—to use? How can I let the family know I am grateful for their kindness?

Confused About Customs

[B] Dear Confused:

I suggest bringing a small gift when you go to an elaborate dinner party, but not an expensive present for the house that might not fit. Flowers or a small gift of candy are usually appreciated; a nice bottle of wine is appropriate if you know that the family drinks alcohol.

You should try to arrive on time or five to ten minutes after the time on the invitation. Don't get there early; if you are going to be delayed more than fifteen minutes or so, be sure to let someone know. I advise calling your hosts if you are running late. Do you have a cell phone? If you get lost or are stuck in traffic, it's considerate to call from your car.

At the dinner table, just relax and be yourself. If you're confused about choosing the appropriate eating utensil (fork, spoon, or even chopsticks), just watch the other guests and follow their lead. If you still have no idea of what to do, don't be shy about asking the person next to you; it's better to ask than to be silently uncomfortable or nervous. If you like the food, say so. Of course, you'll thank your hosts for the meal and express your appreciation for their kindness and hospitality. The traditional custom of sending a thank-you card after a formal occasion is no longer expected but will certainly be appreciated.

[C] Dear Miss Kitt:

I'm going to give a dinner party next month for some Canadian visitors. I want my guests to enjoy themselves and feel comfortable. What's the secret of giving a successful party in North American culture?

Worried About Cross-Cultural Etiquette

[D] Dear Worried:

Cook something for dinner that lets you spend time with your visitors. If a guest offers to help you in the kitchen, accept the offer. It often makes people feel more comfortable when they can help or have something to do.

Before serving the meal, while your guests make small talk in the living room, offer them appropriate snacks and drinks. Those who drink alcohol might like liquor or wine, but make sure to provide soft drinks or fruit juice for people who don't. If there are many different things to eat and many guests, you can put the serving dishes out on a long table, where people can help themselves. Then they can easily go back for seconds—and thirds, and they can sit in different places to converse with various people.

Of course, if your family or culture has different social rules and customs for dinner parties, your guests will probably want to learn about them. Perhaps the most important rule of good hospitality in any culture is to be natural. Treat your guests as you want them to treat you when you're in their home—that is, act naturally toward them, and don't try too hard to be correct or overly polite. Make it easy for everyone, including yourself, to have a good time in a pleasant, relaxed atmosphere.

After You Read

5 **Recognizing Question-and-Answer Letter Form.**   Information may appear in the form of personal letters, especially in newspapers but also in other kinds of reading material. Generally, the first letter of each pair asks a question about the topic of the reading; the letter that follows gives an answer, usually information or advice.
    Following is the organization of topics in the reading selection "A Dinner Party." Write in the missing words; choose from the words *guest* or *host*.

1. Letter from a <u>guest</u>, who is going to a dinner party.

2. Answer to the _____.

3. Letter from a _____, who is going to give a dinner party.

4. Answer to the _____.

The following ideas are from the reading. On the line next to each idea, write the letter of the section that the idea is from.

1. __B__ It's a good idea to bring the host or hostess a gift.

2. _____ You should arrive at a party on time or a few minutes late.

3. _____ I'm nervous about accepting an invitation to Thanksgiving dinner.

4. _____ I want my guests to enjoy themselves at a party that I'm going to give.

5. _____ Spend as much time with your guests as possible.

6. _____ When should I arrive at a dinner party?

7. _____ How do I choose the correct knife, fork, or spoon?

8. _____ Offer your guests drinks before dinner.

9. _____ How should I thank my host and hostess?

10. _____ Let your guests serve themselves at dinner.

11. _____ Watch the other guests at the table to find out what to do.

12. _____ Thank the host and hostess after the party; you can also send a note.

Circle the number of the main idea of the reading.

1. Always bring a nice gift when you go to a dinner party.
2. Just watch the guests at a party and follow them, and do not be shy about asking questions.
3. There are no secrets to giving a successful party.
4. If you follow a few cultural rules for dinner parties, everyone can have a good time in a pleasant atmosphere.

6 **Understanding the Main Idea.** The writer of a reading selection does not always state all of his or her ideas in a clear, direct way; instead, he or she may imply or suggest certain facts or personal views. It is left to readers to infer (figure out) what the writer wants to communicate. To do so, they begin to form opinions on the basis of the information and context clues in the material.

For which of the following statements do the letter writers of the reading selection "A Dinner Party" give or suggest information or views? On the lines before those items, write T for true or F for false. In the reading, underline the sentences or parts of sentences that lead you to your answers. Also change the false sentences to make them true statements of the point.

On the lines before the other items (the ideas that the writer did not state or imply), write an O. You can also tell your own opinions about these and the other statements, but make clear that they are your views, not the ideas of the writer.

1. _____ People write letters to Etty Kitt, and she gives advice about social rules and customs.

2. _____ There are no social rules for dinner parties in the United States and Canada.

3. _____ Dinner guests should always bring expensive house gifts to the hosts of the party.

4. _____ Leaving a party on time or a little late is very important; call home if you are running late.

5. _____ Guests that don't know what to do should just follow the lead of others or ask questions.

6. _____ In most cultures, party guests are not expected to express thanks or appreciation for their hosts' hospitality.

7. _____ When you give a party, you should spend all your time in the kitchen to take care of your visitors.

8. _____ Plan on making enough food for your guests to have two or three servings, but don't offer visitors food directly.

9. _____ Because it's important for both guests and hosts to feel comfortable, no one should try *too* hard to be polite.

10. _____ People in the United States and Canada have a lot of dinner parties, but people in other countries don't.

7 Supplying Missing Information.   Sometimes information in other sentences or in another part of a sentence makes certain words or phrases unnecessary. Readers can figure out the missing information from the context. At other times, a writer uses words with similar meanings to previous words to avoid repetition. In these cases, readers figure out from the context which information the new vocabulary refers to.

Examples:

> I am in international student (From where? From another country) in a small town in the United States. My roommate's family wants me to celebrate Thanksgiving with them—and all their relatives—in their home. I know it's an important holiday (Why? Because all the members of an extended family get together), so I felt honored to receive such an invitation (What kind of invitation? An invitation to Thanksgiving dinner in a family's home.)

In the following sentences there are missing words that readers can figure out from the context of the information in the reading "A Dinner Party." Which words are understood or can be added to these sentences? Write them in the blanks, as in the examples.

1. Dear Etty Kitt: As an international student, I gratefully accepted an invitation to Thanksgiving dinner and am looking forward to __the dinner__,

   but I am also feeling a little nervous about __the visit__. Which

   rules for _____ do I follow? I'm asking this question because I feel

   _____.

2. Should I bring _____ to the party? Should I arrive

_____? At the dinner table, which _____

should I use. How can I _____ to my kind hosts?

Confused About Customs

3. Dear Confused: How about flowers, candy, or a bottle of wine? They are

usually _____. In answer to your question

about _____, I suggest not getting there too

early or too late. To show consideration of your hosts' dinner preparations, be

sure to call if you _____.

4. At the formal dinner table, it's better to follow what others do or ask

questions than to _____. And of course, you should

_____ for their kindness and hospitality. Even if a

thank-you note isn't expected, it _____.

5. Dear Ms. Kitt: I want my guests to feel comfortable and enjoy themselves at

a dinner party I am giving. What is the secret of _____?

Worried About Cross-Cultural Etiquette

6. Dear Worried: One advantage of cooking something simple for dinner is that

it _____. A benefit of accepting a guest's

offer to help in the kitchen is that it _____.

7. Be sure to provide guests with snacks and drinks as they

_____ before dinner. There are three

advantages to putting the food out on a separate table: (a) guests can

_____; (b) it's easy for them to go back

for second or third helpings; and (c) _____.

8. Perhaps the most important rule of _____

is to be natural and treat guests as you want to be treated in their homes. In

other words, _____.

Now turn back to the Before You Read section on page 202 and answer the questions.

Discussing the Reading

8 In small groups, talk about your answers to the following questions.

1. In your country, is it a good idea to arrive early, on time, or late for a dinner party? How late is "too late"?

2. Is it the custom in your country to bring a gift to the host or hostess? If so, what kind of gift?

3. Have you ever been to a dinner in a Canadian or American home? How was it similar to dinner parties in your country or culture? How was it different?

4. Look at the picture at the beginning of the chapter. How is the table setting different from one in your country? What do you think each fork, knife, and spoon is used for?

5. In your country, do guests serve themselves or does the host or hostess serve them?

6. What is polite or natural to do at a formal dinner party? What is not polite or natural?

PART 2   # A Traditional Holiday

Before You Read

1 **Vocabulary Preview.**   Here are some vocabulary items from the next reading selection. You can learn them now or come back to them later.

Nouns		Verbs	Phrases
a god	devils	celebrate	hold on (to)
a goddess	gum	rule	dress up (as)
ghosts	mixture	chase	ring doorbells
spirits	costumes		"trick or treat"
saints	disguises		light candles
the harvest	skulls		baked goods
gardens	skeletons		
witches	coffins		
a symbol	graves		
broomsticks	cemeteries		

Read

2 **Making Inferences.**   The first time readers skim a piece of information, they usually read for *literal* meaning—that is to say, they find out quickly what the material says. After this quick reading, they can usually tell the topic of the material and the main idea or point. On a second, more careful reading, readers often infer (recognize and understand) thoughts that the writer did not state directly.

After you read each of the following five paragraphs for literal (basic) meaning, complete the possible title on the line before the material. On the line that follows the information, finish the possible statement of the main idea or point. Then to better understand the writer's meaning, read the material a second time and follow the instructions for the exercise after the reading.

A Traditional Holiday

[A] *Title: The First Halloween*

Hundreds of years before the birth of Christ, the Celts—the inhabitants of parts of France and the British Isles—held a festival at the beginning of every winter for the Lord of the Dead. The Celts believed that this god ruled the world in winter, when he called together the ghosts of dead people. On October 31, people believed these spirits of the dead came back to earth in the forms of animals. They thought that very bad ghosts came back as black cats. At their festival on this day, the Celts used to make big fires to frighten the ghosts and chase them away. This celebration was the beginning of the holiday of Halloween.

Main Idea: _____ in the Celtic culture,

centuries ago in areas of France and the British Isles.

[B] *Title: A Mixture of* _____

The Romans, who ruled the British Isles after the birth of Christ, also held a celebration at the beginning of winter. Because this was harvest time, the Romans brought apples and nuts for the goddess of gardens. Later, the Christians added their customs to those of the Celts and Romans. They had a religious holiday on November 1 for the saints (the unusually good people in Christianity), which they called All Hallows' or All Saints' Day. The evening before this day was All Hallows' Even ("holy evening"); later the name of this October 31 holiday became Halloween.

Main Idea: Through the centuries, Halloween added customs from

_____.

[C] *Title:* _____*: A Symbol of Halloween*

Long ago in Britain, people used to go to wise old women called "witches" to learn about the future. They believed that these witches had the power to tell the future and to use magic words to protect people or change them. There were many beliefs about witches, who are now a symbol of Halloween. For example, people believed witches flew on broomsticks to big, secret meetings, where they ate, sang, and danced. The Christians tried to stop people from believing in witches, but many uneducated people, especially in the countryside, held on to their beliefs.

Main Idea: _____ associated

with witches, a common symbol of Halloween.

[D] *Title: Halloween in* _____

When people came to North America from the British Isles, they brought their Halloween customs with them. Today, Halloween is a night when children dress up in costumes—like ghosts, witches, devils, and so on. They go from house to house in their disguises, ring doorbells, and shout, "Trick or treat!" People give them candy, apples, gum, and nuts, and the children have a good time. But most children have no idea that their holiday has such a long history.

Main Idea: Today in North America, Halloween is _____

_____ .

[E] *Title:* _____ *in Latin American Culture*

Today, Halloween is celebrated—mostly by children—not only in the British Isles and the United States but in other areas of the world as well. Related to this holiday are the "Days of the Dead," a traditional Latin American celebration with a mixture of pre-Hispanic and Roman Catholic customs. In many towns of Mexico, November 1 (All Saints' Day) is a time to remember the "little angels"— babies and children that have died; November 2, or All Souls' Day, is a day in honor of people that died as adults. Neither occasion is meant to be sad or scary; instead, their purpose is to welcome back the souls of the dead. Sweets (candy and baked goods) in the shape of skulls, skeletons, and coffins are available everywhere; families get together at the graves of their relatives in cemeteries, where they light candles, have picnics, make music, and tell stories.

Main Idea: In contrast to Halloween, the Days of the Dead _____

_____

_____ .

After You Read

3 Often a reading selection gives information from which the reader can infer (figure out) other information. Write an X on the line in front of the ideas that the author stated (clearly said) or implied (suggested) in the reading selection. Write an O before the ideas that the writer did not state or imply—even if the ideas are true. Look back at the reading material if necessary.

1. __X__ Halloween began a long time before the birth of Christ.

2. __O__ People today put candles in pumpkins (jack-o'-lanterns) to scare away ghosts.

3. _____ Ideas about ghosts, black cats, and witches are part of the celebration of Halloween.

4. _____ The early Romans were Christians.

5. _____ People associated apples and nuts with Halloween because they were symbols of the harvest in Roman times.

6. _____ One of the origins of Halloween was religious.

7. _____ The belief in witches came from Christianity.

8. _____ Witches could really fly and had the power of magic.

9. _____ Halloween customs came to the United States from Britain.

10. _____ The custom of trick-or-treating in costumes comes from the days of the Celts.

11. _____ If people do not give treats to children on Halloween, they might play tricks; thus, Halloween is a very dangerous holiday.

12. _____ People in many countries of the modern world celebrate Halloween.

13. _____ The "Days of the Dead" in Latin American culture have no relationship to Halloween.

14. _____ All Saints' Day and All Souls' Day are meant to be happy celebrations.

4 **Learning to Summarize.** In a summary, you should paraphrase the important information in as few words as possible. You can leave out the minor details and combine items into a series.

Example:

Some Halloween symbols are ghosts, black cats, jack-o'-lanterns, and witches.

You can combine short sentences with connecting words.

Example:

Because the Celts believed the Lord of the Dead called ghosts together on October 31, they made fires to scare away the ghosts.

Work in groups of five. Each student chooses a different paragraph from the reading "A Traditional Holiday." Summarize the information in your paragraph. Then take turns sharing your summary with your group.

Discussing the Reading

5 In small groups, talk about your answers to the following questions.

1. Have you ever celebrated Halloween? If so, how did you celebrate it?

2. What two colors and other symbols have you noticed at Halloween time? Can you guess what they mean?

3. In your native culture, do you celebrate Halloween or a holiday related to honoring the dead?

4. Do some people in your culture believe in witches or in other people who can tell the future?

Talk It Over

Here are some customs and symbols related to well-known holidays or celebrations around the world. First, to match the clues on the left with the occasions listed on the right, write the letters on the lines. Give the reasons for your choices. Then for each occasion, discuss your answers to these questions.

- Do you or does your family observe this holiday? If so, describe your customs and their meaning. If you can, tell the historical or other reasons for them.
- If you don't celebrate the holiday or occasion, is there a comparable observance in your native culture? Explain.

Column 1

1. _____ This fall religious observance is the most serious day of the year. There is fasting (no eating or drinking). So they can begin the year with a clean heart, people go to the synagogue to pray.

2. _____ This historical occasion is the subject of political disagreement. In 1492, a European explorer arrived with three ships on a Caribbean island. Did he "discover America" or was he a conqueror and murderer of native peoples?

3. _____ In this weeklong celebration, light is a symbol of seven principles: unity, self-determination, social responsibility, economics, purpose, creativity, and faith. Each night the family lights a different candle and talks about the value it represents.

4. _____ During this nine-night observance, children and their families go from house to house with lighted candles to act out the story of Mary and Joseph. Each house turns them away until the last place, where they are welcomed in for a celebration.

5. _____ People throughout the world observe different customs on the last evening of the year. In many places, there are fireworks; people stay up late to celebrate at parties—often with alcohol and noise.

6. _____ On this very old holiday, Christians used to honor a saint on the day of his death. They played games to choose their mates. Now this is the "day of romance"—when people give romantic cards and gifts to their sweethearts and others.

7. _____ On the anniversary of the birth, enlightenment, and death of their spiritual leader, observers of this religion meditate in the temple. During this time, people decorate their homes and there are lights everywhere.

8. _____ In this very spiritual month of fasting (not eating until evening) and self-control, people celebrate this time when the holy Koran was received from an angel.

Column 2

a. Los Posadas, a Mexican tradition in the days before Christmas

b. Yom Kippur, the "Day of Atonement" for observant Jewish people

c. St. Valentine's, celebrated on February 14

d. Kwanzaa, an African American celebration at the end of December

e. Wesak, the holiest day of Buddhism, observed at the full moon of May

f. Columbus Day, observed on October 12 in the United States

g. Ramadan, the ninth month of the Islamic (Moslem) calendar

h. New Year's Eve (December 31) in the Western calendar

| **PART 3** | # Vocabulary and Language Learning Skills |

1 **Recognizing Other Prefixes.** In addition to the negative prefixes *dis-, il-, im-, in-, non-,* and *un-,* there are other common syllables that change or add to the meanings of base words when they are added to the beginning. Here are some of them—with their general meanings and examples.

Prefix	Meaning	Examples
com-, con-, co-, cor-	with; together	compare, contrast, co-worker, correct
contra-	against; in opposition to	contradiction
de-	away from	decline, depression
ex-	out from; no longer	exit, exchange, ex-wife
inter-	between	international
re-	again; back	return, reduce
uni-	one; single	universality

Paying attention to the meaning of the prefix, match the following vocabulary items in Column A with their parts of speech and explanations in Column B. On the next page, match the items in Column C with their opposites in Column D. (Write the letters on the lines after the numbers.)

A. Words With Similar Meanings

Column A

1. _____ collect
2. _____ combination
3. _____ co-workers
4. _____ contradict
5. _____ decline
6. _____ discover
7. _____ exchange
8. _____ immortal
9. _____ interrupt
10. _____ nonsense
11. _____ recover
12. _____ universal

Column B

a. verb: to say the opposite of what someone else says
b. verb: go down in amount
c. verb: bring together in one place
d. verb: give something out to get something else in return
e. noun: different things put together
f. adj: of all people and places everywhere
g. noun: people that work together
h. verb: get something back; get better (healthier)
i. verb: come between others in conversation
j. noun: material that doesn't make sense
k. verb: find out for the first time
l. adj: living or continuing forever

B. Words With Opposite Meanings

Column C		**Column D**
1. _____ correct		a. verb: keep (something) for yourself; not give to others
2. _____ contrast		b. adj: unfree; controlled by others; dependent
3. _____ contribute		c. verb: act alone; not have contact with others
4. _____ disrespect		d. verb: accept; say yes
5. _____ extreme		e. adj: wrong; false
6. _____ impatience		f. noun: politeness; respect
7. _____ independent		g. verb: increase; make larger
8. _____ interact		h. verb: compare to; show similarities
9. _____ nonalcoholic		i. adj: wanted; appreciated
10. _____ reduce		j. noun: patience; ability to wait
11. _____ refuse		k. adj: not moderate; not average
12. _____ unwelcome		l. adj: containing alcohol

C. Below is a list of some common word beginnings, with their general meanings. You can use the prefixes as clues to the meanings of the unfamiliar word choices in the following sentences if they help—and you can look up the words in the dictionary. Within each pair of parentheses ( ), circle the vocabulary item that best fits the meaning of the context.

Prefixes	**Meanings**
a-, ab-	away from
a-, ad-, ap-	to
con-, com-, co-, col-, cor-	with; together
de-	from; away
dif-, dis-	apart; not
e-, ex-	out; former
in-	into; very; not
inter-	between
intro-	inward
mis-	wrong
non-	not
ob-	against
pre-	before
re-	again
un-	not
uni-	one; single

1. Throughout history, people have (considered / reconsidered) the celebration of the new year a (happy / unhappy) (event / prevent) of (new / renew) beginnings. Almost (conversely / universally), people plan to use the occasion to (turn / return) away from old habits and (place / replace) them with new and better ways.

2. The ancient Roman calendar (attained / contained) only ten months. Then the emperor (conduced / introduced) an (improved / reproved) system of time that (included / precluded) two (additional / conditional) months, January and February. Since those days, people in most Western countries have (deserved / observed) the beginning of the new year on the first day of January.

3. The fifteen-day Chinese New York, however, is (different / indifferent). Each year, it begins at the (appearance / disappearance) of the full moon between January 21 and February 19. The first day is a (serious / nonserious) time of prayer and (religious / nonreligious) observance. In contrast, the next two weeks are filled with joyful celebration. When friends and relatives visit one another, they (change / exchange) baskets of fruit and other (presents / resents). There are (frequent / infrequent) parades; the celebration ends with the (exciting / reciting) festival of flowers.

2 **Recognizing Prefixes, Stems, and Suffixes.** To review, a suffix (word ending) often indicates the part of speech of a word; it may also give clues to its general meaning. A prefix (word beginning) may change the meaning of the base word or stem (the main part of a longer word). With some knowledge of what one or more of these three word elements—the prefix, the stem, and the suffix—might mean, readers can figure out new or difficult vocabulary, especially long words with several parts.

In the following paragraphs, use your knowledge of word parts to choose the best and most appropriate missing vocabulary items. Choose from the words below each item, and write them on the appropriate lines.

1. In Iranian _____ on the last Wednesday of the Persian year, big fires are built in _____ places. The fires are supposed to _____ the town or village from the ghosts of the dead—so it can live through this scary and _____ night and awake to a new beginning. The warmth and _____ of the flames _____ people's hope for _____ and _____ in the coming year.

brightness	enlightenment	public	represent
communities	protect	happiness	unlucky

2. A few weeks before the New Year begins, Iranians _____
clean and _____ their homes. As signs of _____,
they make or buy new clothes, bake, and plant seeds. Special
_____ play musical _____ as they dance
through the streets. Their faces are _____ with black, and
they wear red _____. This color _____ the
blood of a dead Iranian prince.

completely	disguised	rearrange	singers
costumes	instruments	renewal	symbolizes

3. The two-week Persian New Year, or Nowruz, begins on the first day of spring
because it celebrates the _____ of nature. The typical
customs of the _____ are _____ with its
spirit. The ceremonies include _____ actions and activities
that date back to _____ times: (1) cleaning of the
_____ (the house and the community), (2) putting out and
_____ fires, and (3) _____ of the normal
order of things with loud parties.

ancient	disruption	observance	relighting
consistent	environment	rebirth	symbolic

For more practice with prefixes and suffixes, divide the items of Exercises 1–3 into
their parts: draw lines between the prefixes and stems and between the stems and
their suffixes. Can you use the words in sentences of your own that show their
meanings? Can you add other prefixes or suffixes to some of the base words to form
new words? Can you explain the meanings of these words or use them in sentences
appropriately? In the readings of this chapter, you can find other words with prefixes
and suffixes, such as *international*, *important*, *gratefully*, *mistakes*, *nervous*, and
others. Can you explain the meanings of these words from the general meanings of
their parts? Can you use them in sentences appropriately?

3 Real-Life Reading: Announcement and Greeting Cards. On special occasions and some holidays around the world, people give or send one another special announcements, greeting cards, or other kinds of printed or written communication. Below are listed the most common kinds of cards that are sent.

For Special Occasions

a. birth announcements

b. birthday cards

c. wedding announcements

d. anniversary cards

e. party invitations

f. thank-you notes

g. get-well cards (for sick people)

h. death announcements

i. sympathy cards

For Holidays

j. New Year's greetings

k. Valentine's Day cards

l. Halloween greetings

m. Thanksgiving greetings

n. Christmas cards

Some copies of announcement and greeting cards and other kinds of material for special occasions and holidays appear on pages 218–219. To match each card with its classification, write a letter from the list above after each item number.

Which words and phrases do you know? Underline them. Which words are new or difficult for you? Circle them. In groups or in class, try to figure out the meanings of the circled words. You can tell the parts of speech; you can suggest prefixes or suffixes for the words, and so on.

Finally, give the general meaning or purpose of each card in your own words.

1. _____

You're Invited

For ___a New Year's Eve party___
Date ___New Year's Eve___
Time ___8:00 p.m.___
Place ___345 N. Elm Road___

R.S.V.P.   B.Y.O.B.

2. _____

Announcing

name ___Breton (Bret) Lee___
arrived ___March 27___
weighing ___8___ lbs ___4___ oz
parents ___Marv and Nancy___

3. _____

Thank You!

Just a little note to say
Thank you very much—
When it comes
To pleasing people,
You have the perfect touch!

4. _____

May your birthday be delightful,
Your very best one yet,
A happy, carefree kind of day
That you won't soon forget—
And may the year that follows
Be bright and happy, too,
And bring the very loveliest
And nicest things to you!

Have a Wonderful Day!

5. _____

*Sorry to hear
of your hospital stay . . .
Hope you're improving
with every new day,
And before long you'll feel
well and happy again—
You'll be in my thoughts
and my wishes till then.*

Hope You're Home Soon!

6. _____

With Our
Sympathy

*In times of sorrow,
when words of comfort
are needed most,
it seems they are
most difficult to say.
May you find comfort in
the thoughts and sympathy
of friends.*

7. _____

HOPE
HALLOWEEN
TREATS YOU
TO LOTS
OF FUN!

8. _____

As we greet the harvest season
in a joyful, grateful way,
Warm wishes go to your home
for a glad Thanksgiving Day,
And may the year that lies ahead
bring happiness and love
And all the special blessings
that you're so deserving of.

4 **More Real-Life Reading.** Here are some kinds of reading material that may contain information or ideas related to celebrations and holidays. Check (✔) the kinds available to you. Bring some examples to class, or copy some of the words from the materials. Write down the important vocabulary items with their meanings and examples. Talk about the purpose of each piece of material. Summarize the important information.

- ■ _____ invitations to holiday parties and celebrations for special life occasions

- ■ _____ holiday and special-event greeting cards

- ■ _____ programs and menus from formal or informal special events

- ■ _____ thank-you notes and other expressions of friendship or appreciation

- ■ _____ holiday decorations that include symbols of the occasions

- ■ _____ other _____

<table>
<tr><td>**PART 4**</td><td></td></tr>
</table>

Personal Stories and Humor

1 Follow these steps for the two stories about the spirit of the winter holiday season.

1. Read each story quickly and retell the main events.
2. Do you think each story is true? (Did it really happen?) Give reasons for your views.
3. What do you think the point of each story is? In your opinion, what is the attitude of each writer about holiday gifts?
4. Tell or write about your own experience during a holiday season or explain your ideas about the "holiday spirit."

The Spirit of the Holiday Season

On the weekend before Christmas my husband and I took his grandmother out to finish her shopping. The first hour in the streets and stores was fun! Gran (our nickname for her) and I were having a great time as my sweet hubby patiently stood around waiting for us. However, as Gran was looking at a shirt in a men's clothing store, a very big man hurried over to where we were standing; he started picking through the shirts.

Gran, a friendly senior who will talk to anyone said, "Lovely shirts, aren't they?"

The man replied, "They sure are! And you're in my way, old lady!" Poor Gran was shocked! I went up to the man and asked him where his manners were. Rudely, he told me to . . . well, you get the idea. He pushed past us and went to pay for his shirts. He didn't let the clerk touch them. "You sales people are so slow!" he complained, but in much ruder language. With his packages in his arms, he left.

It was a strange experience, but it didn't end there. The next day, the same man came into the liquor store where I work. When he came to pay for his purchases, I didn't say anything at first. Nevertheless, he didn't want me to touch his bottles, so I told him—politely—that I couldn't register the prices of his items without holding them near the scanner. In response, he used the worst language I ever heard. I threw him out of the store. He left shouting, "The customer is always right! How dare a salesclerk treat me that way! I'm going to complain to the store manager."

There are some crazy people out there, especially around the holidays.

Adapted from a real experience by Julie Farnborough, UK, 12/20/99, on the Website happychristmas.com.

It was Christmas Eve, and everyone in the Holly household was asleep except Norman. He was too excited to sleep. He was looking forward to the morning, when everyone would open their presents. Norman got out of bed and went downstairs.

The house was full of holiday spirit. The decorated tree was beautiful, especially with the presents all around it. There were decorations everywhere—Santa Claus and angel figures and candles in Christmas plants and much more. Yeah. This was Norman's favorite time of year. He was just filling up a glass of milk when Mrs. Holly stepped into the kitchen. "Norman, what are you doing up?" she said softly.

"I couldn't sleep. Can we open the presents now?"

"Oh, honey. It's only two o'clock in the morning. It's too early to do that yet. Why don't you go back to bed?" He looked at her and nodded his head, reluctantly. She took his hand and they went back upstairs.

He got back under the covers but sleep didn't come easily. He knew that there were wonderful things downstairs to discover. He tossed and turned. It was two-thirty, then three, then four. "Will morning ever come?" he worried. Finally at five o'clock he could stand it no longer. He jumped out of bed.

He ran to the bedroom across the hall and turned on the light. "Merry Christmas! Merry Christmas!" he shouted. "Time for presents! Come on, let's go!" A tired person slowly sat up in bed and rubbed her eyes. She looked at the clock and then back to the figure in the doorway. "Aw, Dad, it's only five in the morning. Can't we just sleep a little more?"

Adapted from a story by Jim Irving, on the Website christmas-tales.com

The Humor of Celebrations and Holidays

2 Before any worldwide—or even local—holiday, there is seasonal humor everywhere, in newspaper cartoons, on joke pages, on the World Wide Web, and in the greeting cards that people send. Of course, some holiday or special-occasion messages are meant to be serious, religious, romantic, or sentimental. On the other hand, on happy holidays people enjoy laughter and fun; therefore, many cards attempt to be funny—through one-line or two-sentence jokes. Usually, the first page of a greeting card starts out serious or ordinary; the "punch-line," or joke, is inside the card.

On the left are some lines, or their beginnings, from the covers of various kinds of greeting cards that are meant to be funny; on the right in mixed-up order are the punch lines—the lines that are supposed to get a laugh. Follow these instructions and answer these questions.

1. Match the two parts of the messages by drawing lines between them. Give the reasons for your choices.

2. What special occasion is the card for? What kind of person sent the card? To what kind of person?

3. Explain the point of the humor. For example, does the punch line make fun of relationships between relatives? Of the hard work of parenting? Of sending out cards too late?

4. Is the joke of each card funny to you? Why or why not?

5. Do you have any favorite greeting card lines—or can you think of any—that are funny? Tell your lines and see if anyone responds with laughter.

Card Covers

- Being a Dad has meant years of hard work, major responsibilities, and endless sacrifice, but look what you got in return . . .

- TO MY SISTER. Because it's your birthday, I want to tell you how I really feel.

- The Christmas season came and went . . .

- I LOVE YOU, I LOVE YOU, I LOVE YOU, I LOVE YOU . . .

- Happy Valentine's Day to my favorite sister . . .

- Another birthday? Because we are mature, reasonable, sophisticated people, there is only one thing to say.

- Happy Mother's Day, MOM! I know you've thought of it a few times, . . .

- Pecsa, my pet codfish, and I want you to get well soon!

Card Interiors

- I feel just fine, thanks.

- . . . on second thought, maybe you shouldn't think too much about that. HAPPY FATHER'S DAY from your "GROAN" CHILDREN

- . . . So what if you're my *only* sister?

- . . . but thanks for not running away!

- You're older than I am, you're older than I am, nyah-nyah, nyah, nyah-nyah.

- You've heard of a get-well cod, haven't you?

- . . . and still no cards has this family sent. So please accept our sentiments on this Day of Presidents (February).

- If you had to look inside this Valentine's Day card to see who sent it, we're in serious trouble. Your hubby forever.

Video Activities: Puerto-Rican Day Parade

Before You Watch.   Discuss these questions in a group.

1. What is a parade?
2. What kinds of things and people can you see in a parade?
3. What do you know about Puerto Rico?

Watch.   Discuss these questions in a group.

1. What does this Puerto Rican Day Parade commemorate?
2. Which of the following things or people were part of the parade?

spectators	a marching band	floats
a fire truck	clowns	police
a queen	flag wavers	the mayor of New York

Watch Again.   Fill in the missing information.

1. Columbus discovered Puerto Rico _____ years ago.
2. The queen says she feels _____ of her people.
3. The kind of music that Tito Puente plays is called _____.
4. _____ people traveled from Puerto Rico to New York for the parade.

After You Watch.   Many English words are both nouns and verbs. The following words were in the video. Find them in the dictionary, then answer the questions.

float   respect   estimate

1. How was each word used in the video?
2. Make two sentences for each word. In one sentence use the verb. In the other sentence use the noun.

Chapter 11

Science and Technology

IN THIS CHAPTER

Do you find the latest developments in science and technology exciting, or do some of the more dramatic advances frighten you? The first reading selection, "Everyday Uses of Technology," discusses how technology influences every aspect of our everyday lives. The second reading, "Controversial Issues in Technology," raises interesting questions about some controversial issues in technology today. Finally, you will read how modern technology fascinates some people—and causes them problems too.

| PART 1 | # Everyday Uses of Technology |

Before You Read

1 Discuss the pictures in small groups.

   1. What area of science and technology might each picture or symbol represent—for example, atomic energy, chemistry, mechanics, and so on?

   2. If you are an expert in one of these subject areas, tell the class a few facts about it.

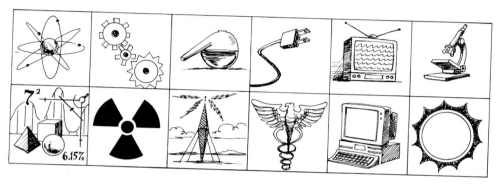

2 Think about the answers to these questions. The reading selection answers them.

   1. What are some controversial issues in science and technology today?

   2. How can using a computer improve someone's social life and ability to communicate?

   3. What are some examples of computer technology in the home?

   4. What are some examples of advances in medical technology?

3 **Vocabulary Preview.**   Here are some vocabulary items from the first reading selection. You can learn them now or come back to them later.

Nouns		Verbs	Adjectives	Adverbs	Phrases
issues	scans	create	controversial	automatically	e.g. (for example)
radiation	surgeons	dial	convicted	photographically	a microwave oven
samples	surgery	collect	separate		the medical sciences
criminals	treatments	distribute	warmed-up		emergency medical
an aspect	a schedule	turn on	electrical		technicians
terminals	an ambulance	turn off	interactive		in the meantime
connections	the hospital	record	high-tech		radioactive tracers
the wish	a patient	program			organ transplants
the body	a victim	advance			
X-rays					

Read

4 Read the following material quickly. Then read the explanation and do the exercises after the reading.

Everyday Uses of Technology

[A] We often hear and read about controversial issues in science and technology. For example, will radiation from electronic equipment negatively change or destroy the environment? Should the DNA samples of convicted criminals be put into a computer data base so investigators can compare it to the DNA of blood at murder scenes? Should medical scientists change gene structures to prevent genetic disease or to create "more perfect" human beings? While people are arguing about these and other controversial subjects, technology continues to influence every aspect of everyday life—the home, health and education, entertainment and communication, and so on.

[B] Some people carry on active social lives with computers—their own or the ones available at terminals in public places like cafés, social centers, libraries, and so on. Communicating with others on electronic bulletin boards or in chat rooms, computer users can get to know people they might never meet in traditional ways. Some look for potential dates or mates by computer: they might place personal ads with photos on the screen or even produce digitized video segments for their Websites. With live online video connections, two people with cameras in their computers can see and talk to each other from separate places.

[C] With modern telephone technology, most people stopped writing letters—especially personal letters and notes. But now, writing to communicate has returned in electronic form, or e-mail, which is a way of sending messages from one computer to another. When a computer is ready to "mail a letter," it dials a server—that is, a central computer that collects and distributes electronic information. Delivery time from the sender to the receiver is no more than a few seconds, even from one country to another. For some computer users, the wish to communicate intelligently or creatively with others makes them want to write better.

[D] Computer technology has also made it possible to run a house electronically. From turning lights on and off on a regular schedule to starting the coffee and cooking the hot cereal, computers are taking care of people at home. Many modern machines (e.g., kitchen appliances) contain computer chips that allow their owners to program them. For instance, you can "instruct" a microwave oven how to cook a certain dish. You can program your electric or gas range, dishwasher, washing machine and dryer, and so on, to "do the housework" on their own. Most entertainment equipment operates with computer technology too: some examples are radios, television sets, VCRs (i.e., videocassette recorders), which can be set up electronically to go on and off, go to certain channels or stations, record specific programs at certain times, and so on. Computers can even start cars automatically so that on cold winter mornings you can get into a warmed-up vehicle and drive off. And of course, the typical U.S. family has a microcomputer (a computer that fits on a table or desk) in their home, which they use for everything from keeping household records and writing letters to playing computer games.

[E]   Largely because of the computer, technology continues to advance in the medical sciences. One example is the use of computer information in an ambulance before a patient even gets to the hospital. Emergency medical technicians can attach small sensors (i.e., devices with cables) to the patient (e.g., a heart-attack victim) to get information about electrical activity in the heart and the brain. By radio and computer, they can send the information to the hospital so that medical specialists can get ready for the patient's arrival. In the meantime, technicians can get advice on how to keep the patient alive. Later, doctors can look into the patient's body in new ways—not only with X-rays but with CAT (computerized axial tomography) scans and DSA (dynamic spatial reconstruction) scans that photographically "slice through" an organ from any or many different angles. Other methods of collecting medical information are based on sound (sonography), temperature (thermography), radio waves, radioactive tracers, tiny cameras that patients swallow, and so on. Technology extends to new surgical procedures as well: for instance, with cameras and lasers (devices that produce very narrow beams of light), surgeons can do heart surgery through tiny holes in the chest; they can do surgery on babies even before they are born.

[F]   Although much of the technology in our everyday lives has positive effects, there are some uses that raise controversial issues and questions. For example, are interactive media (i.e., a combination of television, telephone, and computer) going to control minds, destroy privacy, and cause people to forget about family life and personal relationships? What effects will the genetic engineering of foods (e.g., changing the gene structure of fruits and vegetables) have on people's health? High-tech medical treatments (organ transplants, changing the gene structure, etc.) can increase the longevity of individuals, but can they improve the health and happiness of human beings in general? Only time will tell, but, in the meantime, science and technology will continue to move forward.

After You Read

5   **Review of Outline Organization.**   For an informational reading selection with a lot of facts and details, an outline will probably give the clearest picture of the organization of the material. It will have at least three levels of detail: numbers like I, II, III, and IV for the major divisions; capital letters (A, B, C, etc.) for the main topics in each division; and numbers (1, 2, 3, 4, etc.) for the details of each topic. Even smaller details can follow small letters like a, b, c, d.

Here is one way to organize the information in the reading selection. To complete the outline, write words and phrases for the major divisions of the material, topics, and important details in the blanks. Look back at the reading if necessary. (The letter in parentheses refers to the paragraph that contains the information.)

Everyday Uses of Technology

I. Social lives through electronic bulletin boards (B)

    A. Location of computers

        1. _____

        2. Public places

    B. Advantages

        1. Can meet people you might never meet in traditional ways

      2. _____

         a. _____

         b. Action videos on Websites

         c. _____

II. Communication through e-mail (C)

   A. How it works

      1. _____

      2. _____

   B. Advantage: _____

III. Computerized equipment in homes (D)

   A. Running a house electronically

      1. Kitchen appliances

         a. _____

         b. Gas or electric range

         c. _____

         d. _____

      2. Entertainment equipment

         a. Radios

         b. _____

         c. _____

      3. Cars and other vehicles

      4. _____

IV. _____ (E)

   A. _____

      1. Sensors attached to patient's body to collect information

      2. Information sent to hospital to prepare for arrival

      3. _____

   B. _____

      1. X-rays, CAT scans, and DSA scans

      2. Other informational methods or devices

         a. Sonography (sound)

         b. _____

         c. _____

         d. _____

         e. Tiny cameras in the body

      3. _____

         a. _____

         b. Surgery on unborn babies

Circle the number of the main idea of the reading.

1. Although there are controversial issues, modern science and technology continue to influence every area of life.
2. Radiation offers both benefits and disadvantages to human beings and the environment.
3. To have a good social life, everyone can make new friends with the help of electronic bulletin boards.
4. Computer technology such as e-mail improves people's communication skills.

6 **Understanding the Main Idea.**   In addition to stating information clearly and directly, the writer of a reading selection may imply or suggest certain facts or personal views. Readers infer, or figure out, what the writer wants to communicate on the basis of what they already know, the information in the text, and context clues in the material.

For which of the following statements does the reading selection "Everyday Uses of Technology" give or suggest information or views? On the lines before those items, write an X. Put an O before those items not suggested. In the reading, underline the sentences or parts of sentences that lead you to your answers. Give your own opinions about all the statements, but make it clear that they are your views, not the views of the writer.

1. _____ Because electronic machines are destroying the environment, science and technology cannot advance.

2. _____ Computer technology can help people to meet others, make friends, and get married.

3. _____ Instead of always using the telephone to communicate, some people are sending e-mail messages or looking at and talking to each other on the computer screen.

4. _____ Kitchen appliances of the future will be much more colorful.

5. _____ Modern medical technology can prevent disease, and it can also help save or extend lives.

6. _____ The worst problem caused by modern technology is computer crime.

7 **Special Uses of Punctuation.**   If a word or phrase has a new or special meaning in a specific context, it may be in quotation marks (" ") or italics (a special kind of slanting type).

Example:

When a computer is ready to "mail a letter," it dials a *server.*

(What does "mail a letter" mean? The quotation marks show that in this special context, the phrase means that the computer is going to send a message electronically. A server is a computer that serves a special function.)

Sometimes common, everyday words take on new or special meanings. In a small or old dictionary, you may not find the exact definition you need, but you can often figure out the meaning from the modern context.

Example:

Are there *computer terminals* at the *bus terminal?*

(A *bus* terminal is a starting and ending point for buses. A *computer* terminal, then, must be a starting and ending point for electronic information.)

From the definition of the everyday words or phrases in italics, try to figure out the meaning of the items in quotation marks in their new or special contexts. Then answer the questions. To find the item in context, you can look back at the reading selection; the capital letters in parentheses indicate the paragraphs. You can also check your dictionary to see if it contains the specific definition you need. The first one is done as an example.

1. (A) *Data* is collected information. What might crime investigators do with a "data base" of DNA samples?

   compare the DNA of a crime suspect with it

   Perfect means "with no faults or defects." How might medical science change gene structure to create "more perfect" human beings.

   modify the gene structure to prevent disease

2. (B) A *bulletin board* is a board on the wall on which people put messages. What is an "electronic bulletin board"?

   To *chat* is to talk in a friendly, casual manner. What is a computer "chat room"?

   What can computer users do on electronic bulletin boards and in chat rooms?

3. (B) The *personals* are ads that people place in newspapers or other print media, usually with the purpose of finding potential dates or mates. What are the "personals" on Websites?

   Digitized means "put into electronic instead of physical form." *Video* is "motion pictures." What are "digitized video segments"?

Live means "broadcast at the time; not pre-recorded," and *online* means "controlled by computers." What are "live online video connections"?

_____

To *meet* means to "come together by chance or arrangement." How might computer users "meet" in nontraditional ways?

_____

4. (C) *Mail* refers to the postal system of sending and receiving letters. What is "e-mail"?

_____

A *server* is a person or thing that collects and gives out food. Some computers are "servers" too. What do they do?

_____

How do computers "deliver" information from senders to receivers?

_____

_____

_____

5. (D) *Chips* are small pieces of material. What are "computer chips"?

_____

A *program* is a plan of what someone intends to do. When people "program" a computer, an appliance, or another piece of equipment, what do they do to it?

_____

How might a household that is "programmed" with "computer chips" operate?

_____

_____

_____

6. (E) To *sense* means to "get a feeling about." Medical technicians can attach "sensors" to a patient's body. What do these devices do?

_____

To *slice through* means to "cut into flat pieces." How does photographic equipment such as CAT and DSA "slice through" body organs?

_____

A *procedure* is a way of doing something. What is a "surgical procedure"?

_____

In medical investigation and healthcare, how is science advancing?

_____

_____

_____

_____

_____

7. People *interact* when they have an effect on one another. What do television, telephones, and computers do in "interactive media"?

_____

Engineering is "using scientific principles to design and build structures." What is "genetic engineering"?

_____

The word *tech* is a short form of "technical." What is "high-tech" equipment?

_____

What are some of the controversial issues and questions raised by "interactive media," "genetic engineering," and "high-tech" medical treatments?

_____

_____

_____

_____

_____

Discussing the Reading

8 In small groups, talk about your answers to the following questions.

1. Do you use or have you ever used an electronic bulletin board, a chat room, or e-mail? If so, explain how they work. Give your reactions to your experiences.
2. What electronic or computerized equipment or appliances do you have in your home? How do you use them?
3. Have you even been in an ambulance or a hospital during an emergency? If so, what do you remember or know about modern medical technology?
4. Do you think that computers and interactive media benefit or hurt family life and personal relationships?
5. What is the effect of high-tech medical treatments on the health and happiness of people in general?
6. Should medical scientists change gene structures to create "more perfect" human beings?

| PART 2 | # Controversial Issues in Technology |

Before You Read

1 **Vocabulary Preview.**   Here are some vocabulary items from the next reading selection. You can learn them now or come back to them later.

Nouns	Verbs	Adjectives	Phrases
a warrant	sue	tiny	invasion of privacy
a password	invade	portable	on the part of
a receptionist	suspect	electromagnetic	as things stand
monitoring			electronic surveillance
interference			solve cases
antennas			accident victims

Read

2 **Making Inferences.**   When readers skim information, they usually recognize the topic and the main idea or point; in other words, they find out what the material says literally. On a second, more careful, reading, readers often infer ideas and thoughts that the writer did not state directly.

After you read each of the following four paragraphs for literal (basic) meaning, circle the number of the best (and most interesting) title. Then answer the questions that follow.

Controversial Issues in Technology

1. Who Can Open the E-Mailbox?
2. Secret Passwords and Issues
3. Illegal Warrants for Love Letters
4. What's Mine Is Mine

Letters and phone conversations are private. It is against the law to open someone's mail without permission or to secretly listen in on someone's telephone conversation. Furthermore, the U.S. Electronic Communications Privacy Act of 1986 gave the same privacy protections to people who use e-mail. For instance, without a warrant it is illegal for the police to read the messages that a person has received or sent on a computer. Nevertheless, in several cases employees have complained about invasion of privacy by co-workers or their employer. The law is now clear on this issue: Even though each person has a secret password for his or her e-mail, the company can keep a complete list of these words. Also, an employer has ownership rights to everything employees write during work time because they are using the company computer system. Therefore, as things stand right now, it is probably a good idea for employees to be careful about the e-mail messages they send; a monitored e-mail system may not be the best place for love letters or other private or personal communication.

1. What issue is the paragraph about?

   the privacy of e-mail.

2. What does the law say about his issue?

   Companies may keep password lists and "own" what employees write.

3. What is the main idea of the paragraph?

   The laws about the privacy of e-mail are different from the legal regulations concerning letters and phone conversations.

1. Electronic Crimes Cases
2. The Politeness of Receptionists
3. Surveying Surveillance Issues
4. Fourteen-Year-Old Employee Records

Electronic surveillance, that is, a close watch over someone, is the cause of wide disagreement—depending on the purpose of the surveillance. High-tech surveillance systems can be very useful in solving crime, in finding missing children, in looking for accident victims, and so on. However, detection devices such as tiny microphones, laser sensors, video cameras, and so on, also make electronic surveillance possible in the workplace. In one case, a receptionist with a perfect fourteen-year employment record lost her job because of information collected by the company's computer system. The new monitoring system, which checked on workers' speed and performance, recorded that she was spending about nine minutes "too long" with each visitor or caller. The receptionist, who said she was helping company sales by being friendly to customers, sued her employer in a court of law. She complained that electronic surveillance at work not only causes unnecessary stress but also invades people's privacy.

1. What kind of computer system is the paragraph about?

   _____

2. Why might people complain about this system?

   _____

3. What is the main idea of this paragraph?

   _____

1. Computers with Wing Temperatures   3. The Secrets of Surveillance
2. Electronic Mysteries in the Sky   4. Speedy Airplane Antennas

Since 1990, there have been hundreds of reports of mysterious electronic interference with the communications systems of airplanes. Because important flight information—about directions, plane temperature, wind speed, and so on—has disappeared from pilots' computer screens, they have lost their way. Technicians haven't found certain answers to these mysteries, but some people suspect that the cause may be passengers' use of portable computers, electronic games, CD players, and so on. Modern airplanes have so many sensors, chips, and wires that they are like "computers with wings"; electromagnetic radiation from entertainment equipment may send confusing signals to airplane antennas.

1.   What situation is this paragraph about?

   _____

2.   Why might this situation cause problems?

   _____

3.   What is the main idea of this paragraph?

   _____

1. Attack of the Killer Tomatoes?   3. Vegetable or Fruit
2. Electronic Eating   4. Animal Supermarkets

Through biotechnology, scientists can create new foods in the laboratory. For example, they can change a tomato genetically so the fruit can stay on the plant longer, have more taste, and not get soft quickly. They can put a gene from a vegetable plant into a fruit, or even combine some animal genes with plant genes. But are these new foods safe? And what should the creators and growers have to tell the government, supermarkets, and consumers? Producers claim that genetically engineered products are not much different from traditionally grown foods; nevertheless, some people want to know exactly how scientists changed the DNA material, how many copies of a new gene are in the food, and what problems might come up. For example, will new DNA structures genetically strengthen the bacteria that cause disease? Some people that object to genetically engineered foods call them "Frankenfoods"—after the Frankenstein monster created in the laboratory in the famous horror story.

1.   What kind of technology is this paragraph about?

   _____

2.   What are some people worried about?

   _____

3.   What is the point of this paragraph?

   _____

After You Read

3   Often a reading selection gives information from which the reader can infer (figure out) other information. Write an X on the line in front of the ideas that the author stated (clearly said) or implied (suggested) in the reading selection. Write an O before the ideas that the writer did not state or imply—even if the ideas are true. Look back at the reading material if necessary. You can give your opinions of the statements, but make clear that they are your views.

1. _____   It's illegal to open letters with someone else's name on them without permission.

2. _____   It may or may not be against the law to read someone's e-mail at work.

3. _____   High-tech surveillance systems can include computers, microphones, laser sensors, video cameras, and so on.

4. _____   If you lose your job because of electronic surveillance, you will win your case against your employer.

5. _____   Portable computers, electronic games, CD players, and other electronic equipment may have nothing to do with the mysterious interference in airplane computer systems.

6. _____   There will soon be laws against the use of electronic entertainment equipment inside airplanes.

7. _____   Biochemistry will continue to improve the taste and quality of our food.

8. _____   No one knows the effects of genetically engineered food products on people's health.

4   **Learning to Summarize.**   Work in groups of four. Each student chooses a different paragraph from the reading selection "Controversial Issues in Technology." Summarize the information in your paragraph, beginning with the main idea. Then take turns sharing your summary with your group.

Discussing the Reading

5   In small groups, talk about your answers to the following questions.

1. In what ways might electronic equipment and surveillance devices lead to invasion of privacy? Who should have the right to use this equipment? In what kinds of situations? Should there be limits on its use?

2. Do you usually feel safe when you take a plane? Do you use or approve of the use of electronic entertainment devices in a plane? Why or why not?

3. Should scientists try to improve the taste and appearance of food through genetic engineering? Should they make food last longer? Why or why not?

Talk It Over

In your opinion, which scientific developments or technological inventions have had the most important positive effect on humanity and the planet? In each category, rank the items with numbers: 1 for the most beneficial, 2 for the next most important, and so on. (Some explanations and the years of invention or discovery appear in parentheses.) If you think a development or invention was unimportant and that it *damaged* people or the environment more than it helped, put X on the line. Then explain the reasoning behind your rankings and choices.

1. Personal Items

_____ clothing (500,000 B.C.E.)

_____ money (coins: 10,000 B.C.E.)

_____ paper clips (1900)

_____ hair dryers (1902)

_____ cigarette lighters (1909)

_____ zippers (1914)

_____ ballpoint pens (1938)

_____ bikini bathing suits (1946)

_____ disposable diapers (1946)

_____ credit cards (1950)

2. Household Devices, Appliances

_____ the gas stove (1826)

_____ the refrigerator (1850)

_____ electric lamps (1879)

_____ electric irons (1882)

_____ vacuum cleaners (1907)

_____ the electric washing machine (1907)

_____ air conditioning (1911)

_____ frozen food (1924)

_____ supermarkets (1930)

_____ the microwave oven (1945)

3. Entertainment and Media

_____ microphones (1827)

_____ the phonograph (record players: 1877)

_____ motion pictures (1890)

_____ radio (1895)

_____ television (black-and-white: 1928)

_____ audiocassettes (1962)

_____ home video recorders (VCRs: 1964)

_____ video games (1972)

_____ compact disk players and CDs (1984)

_____ DVDs (digital video disks: 1997)

4. Communications Technology

_____ the printing press (moveable type: 1450)

_____ the telegraph (electrical communication: 1837)

_____ photography (1816)

_____ the telephone (1876)

_____ xerography (copiers: 1938)

_____ weather satellites (1960)

_____ the electric typewriter (1872)

_____ the facsimile machine (fax: 1907)

_____ the microcomputer (1973)

_____ the Internet, or World Wide Web (1992)

5. Transportation

_____ sailing ships (1000 B.C.E.)

_____ submarines (underwater boats: 1779)

_____ locomotives (engines for trains: 1804)

_____ bicycles (1843)

_____ cars (with internal combustion engines: 1884)

_____ motorcycles (1885)

_____ airplanes (with propellers: 1903)

_____ parking meters (1935)

_____ turbo jet planes (1937)

_____ helicopters (1939)

6. Medical Science and Technology

_____ vaccines (injections to protect against disease: 1796)

_____ antibiotics (penicillin: 1928)

_____ the electron microscope (1933)

_____ the discovery of DNA (1953)

_____ laser beams (1958)

_____ heart by-pass surgery (1967)

_____ the first test-tube baby (1978)

_____ surgery on babies before birth (1984)

_____ gene transfer (from one organism to another: 1989)

_____ cloning (producing an adult animal from the DNA of another: 1997)

PART 3 Vocabulary and Language Learning Skills

1 **Understanding Word Use in Context.** The same word or phrase can not only be more than one part of speech; it can also have several or many different meanings in context. Some of these meanings may be similar or related, but others may be very much different from one another. Whether a reader guesses the meaning of new items or looks them up in a dictionary, it is important to choose the appropriate definition or explanation for that specific context. Conversely, writers and speakers should pay attention to appropriate and correct vocabulary use—according to the meaning they want to express.

Following are some simplified dictionary entries. Each entry includes one or more numbered definitions or explanations of the word's meaning in each of its possible parts of speech. Following the definitions are some sentences with underlined vocabulary items from this chapter. To match each underlined word with its meaning in the context, find the appropriate definition in the dictionary entry. In the parentheses after each word, write the part of speech and the number of the appropriate definition (n. = noun; v. = verb; adj. = adjective). The first item is done as an example.

Definitions

issue _n._ 1 a subject or problem that people discuss; 2 a magazine or newspaper for a specific day, week, or month. _v._ to officially make a statement.

sample _n._ 1 a small amount of something that shows what the rest is like; 2 a group of people chosen to give information or opinions.

perfect _adj._ 1 of the best possible quality; 2 exactly right for a specific purpose; 3 without any mistakes. _v._ to make as good as possible.

warrant *v.* 1 to call for or be a good enough reason for. *n.* 1 an official paper that allows the police to do something.

invasion *n.* the forcible entry of an army into another country; 2 an intrusion or violation; 3 **invasion of privacy** a situation in which someone tries to find out about someone's private life, perhaps illegally.

watch *v.* 1 to look at and pay attention to; 2 to be careful about doing something; 3 to take care of or guard someone. *n.* 1 a small portable clock; 2 the act of closely observing.

stress *n.* 1 physical or emotion strain or worry; 2 special attention or importance given to an idea; 3 the physical force or pressure on an object. *v.* 1 to emphasize a statement.

interference *n.* 1 the act of getting involved uninvited; 2 in sports, the illegal act of keeping another player from doing something; 3 the distorted part of broadcast signals; unwanted noise.

chip *n.* 1 a small piece broken off; 2 a thin slice of food; 3 an electronic computer component. *v.* 1 to break off a small piece of something; 2 to become broken.

taste *n.* 1 a feeling (of sweetness, etc.) produced in the mouth by food; 2 a little bit of something to eat or drink; 3 the type of music, art, etc. that someone likes. *v.* 1 to experience the taste of food.

1. In this month's <u>issue</u> (n. 2) of a news magazine, it says that a national science organization has <u>issued</u> (v. 1) a statement about cloning. The news media often present controversial <u>issues</u> (n. 1) in science and technology.

2. Should DNA <u>samples</u> (   ) of convicted criminals be put into a computer data base? In a random <u>sample</u> (   ) of college students, half said yes.

3. Should medical scientists change gene structures in an effort to <u>perfect</u> (   ) human nature? Or is there such a thing as a "<u>perfect</u>" (   ) human being? Many people believe that a newborn baby is <u>perfect</u> (   ) by definition alone.

4. Without a <u>warrant</u> (   ) it is against the law for the police to open a private citizen's mail. To do it lawfully, the situation must be serious enough to <u>warrant</u> (   ) it.

5. Employees sometimes complain about <u>invasion</u> (   ) of privacy by co-workers or their supervisor.

6. Electronic surveillance—that is, a close <u>watch</u> (   ) over people—is becoming more common in the workplace. As employers <u>watch</u> (   ) over workers' speed and productivity, employees are <u>watching</u> (   ) what they are doing.

7. Does electronic monitoring at work cause unnecessary <u>stress</u> (   )? Employers may <u>stress</u> (   ) the need for surveillance for productivity reasons. They put a lot of <u>stress</u> (   ) on money.

8. There have been reports of mysterious electronic <u>interference</u> (   ) with the communications systems of airplanes. Are passengers causing this problem? The pilots do not welcome their <u>interference</u> (   ) with the job they need to do.

9. Modern airplanes have so many sensors, <u>chips</u> (   ), and wires that they are like "computers with wings." Meanwhile, flight attendants serve sandwiches with potato <u>chips</u> (   ) in bags, not in dishes that passengers may <u>chip</u> (   ).

10. Does a genetically changed tomato have a better <u>taste</u> (   ) than a naturally grown one? It might be a matter of <u>taste</u> (   ). You have to <u>taste</u> (   ) these "Frankenfoods" to find out.

2 On the right are some examples of various uses of vocabulary in context underlined. Write the letter of each example on the line after the number of the most appropriate definition in the left column.

1. _____ n. a subject or problem that people discuss

2. _____ v. to taste a food or drink to see what it is like

3. _____ v. to make perfect (of the highest possible quality)

4. _____ v. to enter without permission; to intrude on

5. _____ v. to give protection to; to keep safe

6. _____ n. a bad or hurtful coming in of many people or animals

7. _____ v. to give out or distribute officially

8. _____ n. a device that looks like a television screen and gives computer information

9. _____ adj. of the best possible quality, without disadvantages

10. _____ v. to keep track of systematically, often by machine

11. _____ n. a portable timepiece

a. One hot <u>issue</u> in medical technology that people argue about is gene restructuring.

b. Will geneticists ever <u>perfect</u> the gene structure of fruits and vegetables?

c. An <u>invasion</u> of ants or other insects in the kitchen can be harmful to human health.

d. Have you ever wanted to <u>sample</u> a genetically engineered tomato? You probably already have!

e. Employers feel they need to <u>protect</u> their rights to employee productivity during the workday.

f. Does electronic surveillance <u>invade</u> the rights of people planning to commit crimes?

g. What is the <u>perfect</u> crime monitoring system; that is, what device has no defects or faults?

h. Is a <u>watch</u> that tells time perfectly a high-tech personal device?

i. Governments can <u>issue</u> warnings about the health effects of genetically changed foods.

j. Hospitals can <u>monitor</u> patients' blood pressure with simple machines.

k. A computer screen is also called a <u>monitor</u>.

3   As you pay attention to the appropriate "match" of definitions and examples of vocabulary use in context, complete the following chart. In the second column, write the missing parts of speech (n. = noun; v. = verb; adj. = adjective; adv. = adverb). Write the missing explanations of meaning in the third column and correct examples of word use in the fourth, as in the filled-in sample answers. You can make up your definitions or examples or find and copy the appropriate information from a dictionary.

Word	Part of Speech	Definition (Explanation of Meaning)	Example of Appropriate Use in Context
1. radiation	n.	nuclear energy that is harmful to living things	Will <u>radiation</u> from electronic equipment negatively change or destroy the environment?
2. convicted	adj.	found or proven guilty in a court of law	
3. terminal	n.	a computer keyboard and screen connected to a computer somewhere else.	
4. electronically	adv.	in a manner related to the flow of electrons	
5. potential		possible; capable of happening or being true	
6. dial	v.		To "mail" information in electronic form, a computer first <u>dials</u> up a server.
7. delivery			With e-mail, <u>delivery</u> of a message is extra fast.
8. program			Computer chips make it possible for TV viewers to <u>program</u> their VCRs.
9. program			Do you ever record your favorite television <u>program</u> so you can can watch it again and again?
10. dish			Do you have cable or a satellite <u>dish</u> for your television reception?
11. microcomputer			
12. sonography			<u>Sonography</u> uses sound waves to "see" inside the body.

Do you want more vocabulary practice defining words according to their meanings and uses in context? Do you need to practice using words according to specific definitions of their meaning? Then choose some of the vocabulary items from this or previous chapters that have various meanings, such as *data, microwave, sensor, device, cable, scan, wave, beam, surgery, transplant, secret, detect, speed, performance, missing, case, court, suspect, wire, plant, creator,* and so on. Tell, write, or look up a specific definition for the item. Then use it in a phrase or sentence that clearly shows its use as that part of speech in that particular meaning. You can also make a vocabulary chart like the one in Exercise 3.

4   Real-Life Reading: Technology Instructions.   The computerized household and workplace of the present and future include many electronic devices and machines that come with instructions—either in printed form or online. The technical language of these instructions for use may not be easy to understand or follow.

Here are some simplified samples of instructions on how to use a VCR, with illustrations. First, underline the verbs of the instructions.

Which words are new or difficult for you? Circle them. In groups or in class, try to figure out the meanings of the circled words. For the numbered steps of the instructions (1–5 and 1–7), identify the verbs and their noun objects.

Finally, in your own words, answer this question: what are the basic steps in using the VCR that go with these instructions?

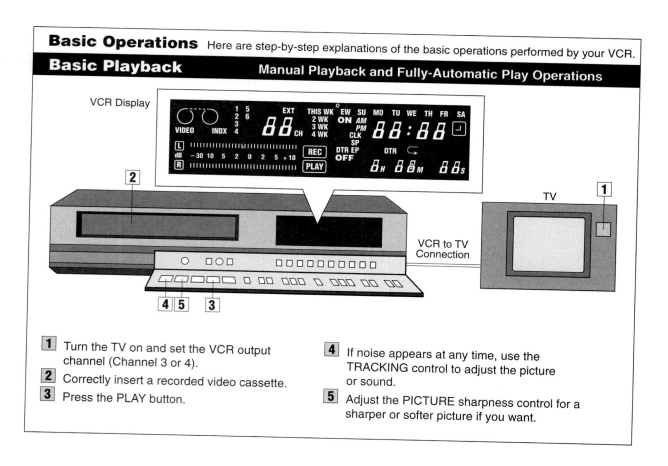

Basic Operations   Here are step-by-step explanations of the basic operations performed by your VCR.

Basic Playback   **Manual Playback and Fully-Automatic Play Operations**

1 Turn the TV on and set the VCR output channel (Channel 3 or 4).

2 Correctly insert a recorded video cassette.

3 Press the PLAY button.

4 If noise appears at any time, use the TRACKING control to adjust the picture or sound.

5 Adjust the PICTURE sharpness control for a sharper or softer picture if you want.

Basic Recording   Manual Recording

With the following procedure, you can record a TV program while watching it at the same time or record one program while watching another on your TV set. To watch the program you are recording, follow Steps 1 through 6. To watch a different program at the time of recording, follow Steps 1 through 7.

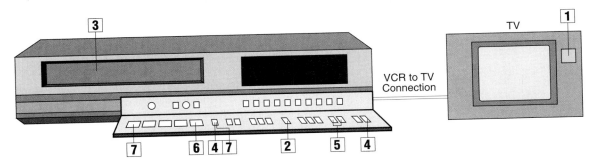

1 Turn the TV on and set the VCR output channel (Channel 3 or 4).

2 Push the VCR POWER on.

3 Insert a video cassette tape

4 Set the TV/VCR to VCR.

5 Press the CHANNEL select buttons to get the channel you want. Set the Tape Speed Selector to SP or EP.

6 Press the REC button.

7 Set the TV/VCR button to TV. The lamp will go off. To turn to the channel you want to watch, use the channel select buttons on your TV set.

Timer Recording   Manual Playback and Fully-Automatic Play Operations

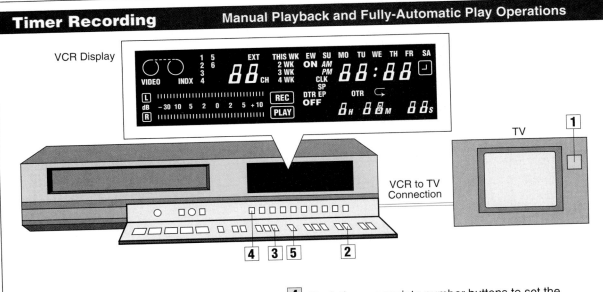

1 Make sure the power is ON. Set the TV set to the channel you want to record.

2 Set the tape speed to SP or EP.

3 Set the recorder timer to the time you want the the VCR to record.

4 Push the appropriate number buttons to set the amount of time that you want the VCR to record.

5 You can turn off the TV and the VCR. The machines will record your program for you while you are away.

5 **More Real-Life Reading.**   Here are some kinds of practical reading material on the topics of science and technology. Check (✔) the kinds available to you. Bring some examples to class, or copy some of the words from the materials. Write down the important vocabulary items with their meanings and phrase examples. Talk about the purpose and point of each piece of material. Summarize the important information.

- ■ _____ printed instructions for how to operate specific kinds of household or workplace devices, appliances, equipment, and machines

- ■ _____ online instructions for computer hardware or software programs

- ■ _____ general how-to instructions for doing practical things

- ■ _____ other _____

PART 4   # Personal Stories and Humor

1 Follow these steps for the two stories that tell experiences with high-tech equipment.

1. Read each story quickly and retell the main events.
2. Do you think each story is true? (Did it really happen?) Give reasons for your views.
3. What do you think the point of each story is? In your opinion, what is the attitude of each writer about science and technology?
4. Tell or write about your own experience with machines or technological devices or equipment.

The Trouble With Technology

[1]   I'm always reading ads for new products, such as computer parts and software, wireless speakers and headphones for sound systems, compact camcorders, color laser copiers, electronic book machines, and many others. Like millions

of other people, I'm interested in modern technological equipment and devices. Of course, I don't always understand how a product works, and I certainly don't know all the technological words in the ad, but somehow I'm fascinated, and I want that machine! Occasionally, I buy it. As soon as I bring my new "toy" home or to my office, I have trouble reading the long, complex manual or even the short booklet—the language just isn't clear or simple enough for me. When my children help, however, I can usually figure out how to set up the new equipment or device. But then something happens to cause a mechanical or electronic problem. Because I don't know how to fix it myself, I call the store where I bought it for advice. If the salesperson can't help, I bring the product to a repair shop. However, even after paying for new parts and a repairperson's time, I still can't get the product to work the same way it used to. Eventually, I lose interest in the machine or device—or in any technological products at all. I start to read again— books and newspapers and magazines. Soon I see ads for new technological products that fascinate me, so. . . . ■

[2]   I used to work as a customer support representative; my job was to talk on the telephone to users of the company's computer equipment so I could instruct callers on how to solve the problems. Here is a real call that I received on my last day at work.

Software support—customer service. How may I help you today?
 Yes, well, I'm having trouble with the Wordperfect program. It's not so perfect. . . .
 What kind of trouble?
 Well, I was just typing along, and all of a sudden the words went away. They just disappeared.
 Hmm . . . so what does your screen look like now?
 Nothing. It's blank. It won't accept anything I try to type into it.
 Are you still inside the word processing program, or did you get out?
 How do I tell?
 Never mind. Can you move the cursor around the screen?

There isn't any cursor. I told you: it won't accept anything I type on the keyboard.

Does your monitor have a power indicator?

What's a monitor?

It's the thing with a screen on it that looks like a TV. Does it have a little light that tells you when it's on?

I don't know.

Well, then look on the back of the monitor and find where the power cord goes into it. Can you see that?

Yes, I think so.

Great! Follow the cord to the plug, and tell me if it's plugged into the wall.

Yes, it is.

When you were behind the monitor, did you notice that there were two cables plugged into the back of it—not just one? You need to make sure they are both plugged securely into the back of your computer.

I can't reach it. It's not that anything is in the way or like that . . . it's just that it's too dark to see.

It's dark? Then turn on the light!

I can't. There's a power outage. There's no electricity in the building.

A power . . . outage? There's a power outage in the building?

I don't work at that job anymore. ■

The Humor of Science and Technology

2 A specific kind of "one-liner" (a very short joke) is a funny definition of a real or made-up word. Some of these include puns—that is, plays on words, humorous uses of words used in more than one way or words with different meanings that sound the same.

Page 249 contains some funny definitions of vocabulary items related to science and technology. The first half of the items were actual student answers on exams; the others were meant to bring laughter. Some explanations may follow the items in parentheses. Answer these questions about the one-liners.

1. What word or phrase is being defined? What is its real meaning?

2. Does the humorous definition include a pun, or play on words? If so, what is it?

3. Do you think the line is funny? Why or why not?

4. Can you think of other humorous one-line definitions of vocabulary related to science and technology? Tell your lines and see if you get a laugh.

planet: a body of earth surrounded by sky

Equator: a menagerie lion running around the Earth through Africa (menagerie = a collection of animals to entertain people)

the moon: a planet just like the earth, but even deader

H_2O: hot water. CO_2: cold water. (H_2O and CO_2 are combinations of chemical symbols. H = hydrogen; O = oxygen; C = carbon.)

water: a combination of two gins, oxygin and hydrogin. (gin = a strong alcoholic liquid)

respiration: inspiration and expiration (respiration = breathing; inspiration = getting creative ideas; expiration = coming to an end)

dew: what forms on the leaves of plants when the sun shines on them and makes them perspire

air travel: seeing less and less of more and more

microwave: a small greeting or goodbye (micro = very small)

faxident: facsimile machine paper jam (FAX = facsimile; -ident is part of the word accident.)

computer hardware: the parts of a computer you can kick

computer: a device designed to speed up and automate mistakes

a computer upgrade: a way of taking old bugs out and putting new bugs in (bugs = computer defects)

technological progress: a more efficient way of going backward

Video Activities: Sight for the Blind

Before You Watch. Discuss the following questions with your class or in a small group.

1. How can technology help physically challenged people? Give examples.
2. As a child, did you ever try to "pretend" you were blind (unable to see)? How did it feel?

Watch. Write answers to these questions.

1. Who is Jerry, and who is Craig? _____
2. How does the new technology help Jerry? _____
3. Jerry is _____ years old. He became blind _____ years ago.
4. Craig has been blind for _____ year(s).

Watch Again. Circle the correct answers.

1. Craig became blind

    a. at birth   b. in an accident   c. because of a disease

2. According to Craig, when people pretend to be blind, they always cheat. He means:

    a. They ask someone to help them.
    b. They never really close their eyes.
    c. They open their eyes just a little.

3. The new device that helps Jerry to see uses a

    a. camera   b. computer   c. transistor

4. Craig's biggest dream is to _____ again.

5. How does Craig feel about the future?

    a. sad   b. hopeful   c. worried

After You Watch. The underlined words and phrases on the left are from the video segment. Use the context to match them with their definitions on the right.

1. _____ George lost his <u>sight</u> four years ago.

    a. quickly

2. _____ You can become blind if you have a <u>disease</u> in your eye.

    b. safe

    c. connected

3. _____ It is hard to feel <u>secure</u> if you cannot see.

    d. a machine

4. _____ Doctors <u>hooked</u> the patient <u>up</u> to a machine.

    e. the ability to see

5. _____ A new <u>device</u> can help blind people to see.

    f. sickness

6. _____ Technology is advancing <u>at a torrid pace</u>. There are new inventions every day.

Chapter 12

The Global Consumer

IN THIS CHAPTER

Are you a smart consumer? The first reading selection, "The Advertising of a Product," talks about the influence that advertising has on what we buy and don't buy. The second selection, "Smart Shopping," gives advice on how to shop intelligently—in stores and over the Internet. In the final reading, "Big Business," you will find out about an interesting shopping experience.

| PART 1 | # The Advertising of a Product |

Before You Read

1 Discuss the picture in small groups.

1. Where is the person? What is he trying to do?
2. Why is he confused?
3. What kind of product is he looking at?
4. Do you think these products are similar to one another or different from one another?

2 Think about the answers to these questions. The reading selection answers them.

1. What influences us when we decide to buy one product instead of another?
2. What kind of information do we get from advertising?
3. What methods do advertisers use to sell products?
4. Who is not affected by advertising?

3 **Vocabulary Preview.** Here are some vocabulary items from the first reading selection. You can learn them now or come back to them later.

Nouns	Verbs	Adjectives	Phrases
a consumer	admit	shiny	laundry detergent
a brand	hide	advertised	the football team
soap		stupid	
commercials		unpopular	
shampoo			
toothpaste			
misinformation			
motive			
self-image			

Read

4 Read the following material quickly. Then read the explanations and do the exercises after the reading.

The Advertising of a Product

[A] A consumer walks into a store. He stands in front of hundreds of boxes of laundry detergent. He chooses one brand, pays for it, and leaves. Why does he pick that specific kind of soap? Is it truly better than the others? Probably not. These days, many products are nearly identical to one another in quality and price. If products are almost the same, what makes consumers buy one brand instead of another? Although we might not like to admit it, commercials on television and advertisements in magazines probably influence us much more than we think they do.

[B] Advertising informs consumers about new products available on the market. It gives us information about everything from shampoo to toothpaste to computers and cars. But there is one serious problem with this. The "information" is actually very often misinformation. It tells us the products' benefits but hides their disadvantages. Advertising not only leads us to buy things that we don't need and can't afford, but it also confuses our sense of reality. "Zoom toothpaste prevents cavities and gives you white teeth!" the advertisement tells us. But it doesn't tell us the complete truth: that a healthy diet and a good toothbrush will have the same effect.

[C] Advertisers use many methods to get us to buy their products. One of their most successful methods is to make us feel dissatisfied with ourselves and our imperfect lives. Advertisements show us who we aren't and what we don't have. Our teeth aren't white enough. Our hair isn't shiny enough. Our clothes aren't clean enough. Advertisements make us afraid that people won't like us if we don't use the advertised products. "Why don't I have any dates?" an attractive young woman sadly asks in a commercial. "Here," replies her roommate, "try Zoom toothpaste!" Of course she tries it, and immediately the whole football team falls in love with her. "That's a stupid commercial," we might say. But we still buy Zoom toothpaste out of fear of being unpopular and having no friends.

If fear is the negative motive for buying a product, then wanting a good self-image is the positive reason for choosing it. Each of us has a mental picture of the kind of person we would like to be. For example, a modern young woman might like to think that she looks like a beautiful movie star. A middle-aged man might want to see himself as a strong, attractive athlete. Advertisers know this. They write specific ads to make certain groups of people choose their product. Two people may choose different brands of toothpaste with the identical price, amount, and quality; each person believes that he or she is expressing his personality by choosing that brand.

[D]   Advertisers get psychologists to study the way consumers think and their reasons for choosing one brand instead of another. These experts tell advertisers about the motives of fear and self-image. They also inform them about recent studies with colors and words. Psychologists have found that certain colors on the package of an attractive product will cause people to reach out and take that package instead of buying an identical product with different colors. Also, certain words attract our attention. For example, the words "new," "improved," "natural," and "giant size" are very popular and seem to draw our eyes and hands toward the package.

[E]   Many people believe that advertising does not affect them. They feel that they have freedom of choice, and they like to think they make wise choices. Unfortunately, they probably don't realize the powerful effect of advertising. They may not clearly understand that advertisers spend billions of dollars each year in aggressive competition for our money, and they are extremely successful. Do you believe that ads don't influence your choice of products? Just look at the brands in your kitchen and bathroom.

After You Read

5 Outlining Points.   An outline that gives a picture of the organization of reading material can contain topics (words or phrases), statements of ideas (sentences), or a combination of the two. Although the form of the items may vary, the outline can have the same levels of detail after numbers like I, II, III, and IV, capital letters, numbers like 1, 2, 3, 4, and so on.

To outline the reading selection, write the main ideas in statement form on the appropriate lines after the numbers and capital letters. As clues to help you, the words in parentheses tell the topics of those parts of the material; the capital letters in parentheses at the end of lines refer to the lettered paragraphs of the reading. Some sample answers are given.

The Advertising of a Product

I.   (Introduction) _Commercials and advertising influence consumers._ (A)

   A. (Choice of brands) _Consumers choose certain brands._

   B. (Sameness of brands) _All the products are identical to one another in quality and price._

II. _Advertising give us the advantages only._ (B)

   A. (Benefits of products) _Advertising give us the benefits of product only._

   B. (Disadvantages) _" hides the products disadvantage._

   C. (Reality) _" makes us confuse of reality._

III.   (Methods of advertisers) _make us feel dissatisfied with ourselves and our imperfect lives._

    A.   (Fear) _____ (C)

    B.   (Self-image) _____ (D)

    C.   (Colors and words) _____ (E)

IV.   (Conclusion) _____

_____ (F)

On the lines, write the main idea of the whole reading selection.

_____

_____

6   **Understanding the Main Idea.**   In addition to stating information clearly and directly, the writer of a reading selection may imply or suggest certain facts or personal views. Readers infer, or figure out, what the writer wants to communicate on the basis of the information and context clues in the material.

    For which of the following statements does the reading selection "The Advertising of a Product" give or suggest information or views? On the lines before those items, write X. Write O beside those statements not given or suggested. Change the O sentences to make them statements of the information given or implied in the reading.

1.   __X__   Advertising influences us to buy one kind of product instead of another.

2.   __O__   Advertisements always provide us with important information about products.

3.   __X__   Wanting a good self-image is a powerful reason for choosing products.

4.   __X__   If you use Zoom toothpaste, there will be no more problems in your life.

5.   __O__   "The Psychology of Selling" is an important course in many business colleges.

7   **Recognizing Exaggeration of Details.**   To make a point in advertising, sometimes writers exaggerate. They make something seem more than it really is. The reader knows the information is not exactly true but understands the writer's reason for exaggerating.

Example:

Want your social life to take off? Zoom toothpaste will get it off the ground!

(The name _Zoom_ and the expressions _take off_ and _get it off the ground_ suggest speed and distance. They give the idea of results beyond the ordinary.)

For each of the following exaggerations, circle the letter of the best explanation of the advertiser's intended message. Explain your choice.

1. Snowflake laundry detergent makes clothes whiter than white!

   a. This product is only for clothes that are white.
   b. This product will get your laundry clean.
   c. This product will change the color of clothes.

2. Wake up to Heart & Soul breakfast cereal. It will warm you from the inside out.

   a. Cold breakfast foods produce more energy than hot cooked foods.
   b. If you eat this cereal in the evening, it will feel like morning.
   c. This cooked cereal is good for your heart, your spirit, and your energy.

3. When the pain is gone, life begins. Take Woebegone.

   a. Take this medication so you can forget about your pain and do other things.
   b. This pain reliever is good for growing plants and getting pregnant.
   c. The most important things in life come at the beginning. The pain comes later.

4. Think different from the rest. Buy Apex computers.

   a. To look good, computers should come in various colors. The colors should be bright and happy.
   b. You can rest and think better if your working environment is up to date.
   c. Only special and intelligent people buy our computers. You can be one of them.

5. Your mother wants you to fly on Comfort Airlines.

   a. Your mother owns stock in our company. Help her to make money.
   b. Our airplanes are safe and comfortable. We will take care of you like your mother does.
   c. A group of mothers owns our airlines. Therefore, we cook delicious meals for our passengers.

Now circle the letters of *all* the correct answers for each of the following blanks, according to the information and views expressed in the reading material.

1. Advertising _____.

   a. informs us about some products
   b. doesn't influence us very much
   c. misinforms us
   d. doesn't always tell us everything about a product

2. A person often buys a product because _____.

    ⓐ. he or she is dissatisfied with himself or herself

    b. of a need for a good self-image

    c. of the colors on the package

    d. of certain words on the package

3. Advertisers _____ to make us buy products

    a. offer very low prices

    b. get information from psychologists

    ⓒ. spend a lot of money

    d. need to use better detergent and shampoo

4. Psychologists tell advertisers _____.

    a. which brands of toothpaste to produce

    b. to stop influencing shoppers

    ⓒ. about people's motives for buying

    d. how much money to spend on television commercials

5. The words _____ on products are very popular and seem to attract our attention.

    a. "really cheap"

    b. "giant size"

    ⓒ. "new and improved"

    d. "good enough"

Now turn back to the Before You Read section on page 252 and answer the questions.

Discussing the Reading

8 In small groups, talk about your answers to the following questions.

1. What kinds of advertising attract your attention? Do you sometimes buy the products in the ads or commercials? For what reasons?

2. Do you think advertisements and commercials are similar or different in various cultures around the world. Give examples to support your answers.

3. Are there any rules or laws about advertising in your country? If so, what kinds of rules are they? If not, why not?

4. What image would you like to have for yourself? Do you envy or want to be like any of the people you see in television commercials or magazine ads?

5. What famous brands of products do you have in your home or workplace now? Why did you buy them?

PART 2   Smart Shopping

Before You Read

1   **Vocabulary Preview.**   Here are some vocabulary items from the next reading selection. You can learn them now or come back to them later.

Nouns	Verbs	Adjectives	Phrases
a manufacturer	examine	generic	a piece of advice
shoppers	advertise	plain	a grocery store
packaging		attractive	on sale
the bottom		reasonable	dressing rooms
a limit		defective	the small print
		misleading	

Read

2   **Reviewing Topics and Main Ideas.**   Here is a summary of the main points about reading for meaning presented in this reading skills book.

A paragraph of an informational reading usually gives information and ideas about one topic within the wider subject of the whole selection. If there is a paragraph title, it may tell or indicate the topic. Sometimes a paragraph contains a general topic sentence (a one-sentence statement of the main idea), but more often it simply suggests the main point or the writer's message—that is, it gives clues to what the writer wants to express. To read successfully for meaning, readers need to be able to recognize topics and to state the main ideas and important points about the topic.

After you read each of the following four paragraphs for basic meaning, think of a title that tells or indicates the topic; write it on the line above the material. After a more careful reading, think of one or two sentences that clearly state both the literal and suggested (implied) main idea or point of the reading; write it or them on the lines that follow. Finally, complete the exercises about the writer's viewpoint that follow the reading.

Smart Shopping

Title: _The most important point of shopping_

Most mothers have a good piece of advice: never go into a supermarket hungry! If you go shopping for food before lunchtime, you'll probably buy more than you plan to. Unfortunately, however, just this simple advice isn't enough for consumers these days. Modern shoppers need an education in how—and how not—to buy things at the grocery store. First, you should check out the weekly newspaper ads. Find out the items that are on sale and decide if you really need those things. In other words, don't buy anything just because it's cheaper than usual. Next, in the market, carefully read the information on the package, and don't let words like "New and Improved" or "All Natural" on the front of a package influence you. Instead, read the list of ingredients on the back. Third, compare prices; that is, you should examine the price both of different brands and different sizes of the same brand product.

Main Idea:

_____

_____

Title: How can you save your money when you make shopping

Another suggestion for consumers is to buy generic items instead of famous brands. Generic items in supermarkets come in plain packages. These products are cheaper because manufacturers don't spend much money on packaging or advertising. The quality, however, is usually identical to the quality of the well-known brands. In the same way, when buying clothes, you can often find high quality and low prices in brands that are not famous. Shopping in discount clothing stores can also help you save a lot of money. Although these stores aren't very attractive, and they usually do not have individual dressing rooms, the prices are low, and you can often find the same famous brands that you find in high-priced department stores.

Main Idea:

The generic items are cheaper than packaging items.
You can spend a less money when you whent buy chothes
If you buy chothes that have discount.

Title: Think pefor buy advertised product.

Wise consumers read magazine advertisements and watch TV commercials, but they do this with one advantage: knowledge of the psychology behind the ads. In other words, well-informed consumers watch for information and check for misinformation. They ask themselves questions: Is the advertiser hiding something in small print at the bottom of the page? Is there any real information in the commercial, or is the advertiser simply showing an attractive image? Is this product more expensive than it should be because it has a famous name? With the answers to these questions, consumers can make a wise choice.

Main Idea:

_____

_____

Title: _____

To protect consumers, there are many laws (usually state laws) about advertising. For instance, if a store advertises a special product at a certain price, the store must have a reasonable number of items to sell so that it doesn't run out of them right away. A sale ad may mention a limit on quantity, but if it doesn't, you have the right to buy as many of the items as you want. The product should not look much different from the picture in the ad. Also, an advertiser must tell you if a product is used or defective. In other words, false and misleading advertising is against the law.

Main Idea:

_____

_____

_____

After You Read

3   **Viewpoint.**   The author of the reading selection implies her point of view; that is, she doesn't state it directly. She gives suggestions about and clues to her opinion in the words she uses, the kinds of details she chooses, and other indirect ways. Complete the following sentence.

The writer's opinion of advertising is that _____

_____

_____

4   **Inferring the Meaning.**   Write an X on the lines in front of the ideas that the author clearly stated or implied. Put an O before the ideas that are not in the reading selection at all. Look back at the selection if necessary.

1. __X__ People who shop for groceries when they are hungry usually buy more than people who shop after eating.

2. __X__ Items on sale are cheaper than usual.

3. __X__ It's a good idea to read the ingredients on the back of a package.

4. _____ Sometimes it's better to buy one size of a product than another.

5. __O__ Generic items never say "New and Improved!" or "All Natural!"

6. __X__ Generic products are usually cheaper than famous brands.

7. __X__ To save money, you should buy clothes in discount stores rather than in expensive department stories.

8. __X__ An intelligent shopper knows something about the psychology of selling.

9. __X__ It is illegal to try to mislead consumers through false advertising.

10. __X O__ If a store has too few advertised items, limits quantity, or doesn't tell buyers that the products are used or defective, consumers may sue.

5 **Learning to Summarize.** You can summarize better if you are aware of the purpose of a reading selection. For instance, if the main purpose is to give advice—as in the reading selection "Smart Shopping"—a good summary might consist of a list of the pieces of advice.

The four paragraphs in the reading selection "Smart Shopping" answer the question "How can a consumer be a smart shopper?" Work in groups of four. Each student chooses a different paragraph from the reading. Write (in paragraph or list form) all the advice in your paragraph. Then take turns sharing your advice with your group. Finally, combine your points to make one summary.

Discussing the Reading

6 In small groups, talk about your answers to the following questions.

1. Has anyone ever given you advice about shopping? If so, who was it, and what was the advice?

2. Do you buy generic items? Why or why not?

3. Do you think consumer-protection laws are the same or different in various cultures around the world? Give examples to support your answer.

4. How is shopping similar in different countries, cities, and other areas? How is it different?

5. What advice can you give a visitor who wants to go shopping in your country?

Talk It Over

To market their products more successfully, manufacturers and companies advertise in the print and broadcast media, on billboards (big highway signs), and so on. The purpose of much of this advertising is "name recognition"—that is to say, advertisers want consumers to notice and remember the names of what they are trying to sell. Slogans (clever or memorable short phrases, repeated over and over again) are a large part of the marketing effort.

Following on page 262 are some old and new slogans for products that are well known worldwide. Even if you don't recognize the lines, can you figure out what they were or are designed to sell? To match the slogan on the left with the products on the right, write the letters on the lines. Give the reasons for your decisions. Then for each slogan, discuss your answers to these questions.

1. What image does the slogan create of the product (e.g., an image of fun, of reliability, of attractiveness, or youth, or what?)

2. Do you think the slogan was or is effective in helping to sell the product? Why or why not?

3. Have you heard a version (or an attempted translation) of the slogan in another language or culture? Did it give the same message or create the same impression of the product? Why or why not?

Slogan	Product
1. _____ Just for the taste of it.	a. Maxwell House Coffee
2. _____ Finger lickin' good	b. Visa Card (a credit card company)
3. _____ Melts in your mouth, not in your hands.	c. M & Ms (small pieces of candy with chocolate inside)
4. _____ Squeezably soft	d. United Airlines
5. _____ Good to the last drop	e. Kentucky Fried Chicken (a fast-food chain)
6. _____ Don't leave home without it.	f. the yellow pages of telephone books (containing business addresses and ads)
7. _____ Fly the friendly skies.	g. Vidal Sassoon (shampoo)
8. _____ If you don't look good, we don't look good.	h. Dove (complexion bars with moisturizing lotion)
9. _____ Let your fingers do the walking.	i. Charmin Bathroom Tissue (toilet paper)
10. _____ Doesn't dry like soap.	j. Diet Coke (a soft drink)
11. _____ We bring good things to life.	k Gold Medal Flour (baking ingredient)
12. _____ 100 years of baking success	l. General Electric (manufacturer of a large variety of electrical and mechanical items)

PART 3   Vocabulary and Language Learning Skills

1   Reviewing Vocabulary-Learning Methods.   Here is a summary of the main points about vocabulary learning presented in this reading skills book.

There are three important things to know about every new vocabulary item: (1) its part of speech—if it is a noun, a verb, an adjective, or an adverb; (2) its definition—an explanation of its meaning in a phrase that does not include the item itself; and (3) its correct and appropriate use in the context of meaningful sentences. Readers can often guess or figure out the approximate meanings of new items from context clues—words with similar or opposite meanings, examples of the item, and other words in the same meaning category—within the same sentence or other sentences in the reading material. A systematic way to learn new vocabulary is to compare related words—that is to say, words of the same or different parts of speech that have the same stem or base but different prefixes (added beginnings) and suffixes (added endings).

In the box there are some sentences on the topic of this chapter. Following are some questions about the underlined vocabulary—the most important words of the material. If there is a choice of answers inside brackets [ ], circle the correct one. If there is a blank line, write the answer. The first item is done as a sample.

Advertising informs consumers about new products available on the market. But advertising sometimes leads us to buy things that we don't need and can't afford.

---

1. What is the prefix of the word *advertising?* __ad-__ What is its suffix? __-ing__
    What part of speech is it? _____noun_____ How do you know? _____
    It's the sentence subject and has a noun ending.

    Which definition is most appropriate for the word use in the context?
    [(ads and commercials) / public notices / a business]
    What are some related words and their parts of speech?
    advertise (v.), advertisement (n.), advertiser (n.)

    Write a sentence that uses the word in the same way:
    There is advertising everywhere in the print and broadcast media.

2. What is the prefix of the word *informs?* _____ What part of speech is it?
    _____ How do you know? _____

    _____

    Which definition is most appropriate for the context?
    [gives out secrets / tells / knowledge]
    What are some related words and their parts of speech?

    _____

    Write a sentence in which the word has about the same meaning:

    _____

3. What is the prefix of the word *consumers?* _____ What is the suffix? _____
    What part of speech is it? _____ How do you know? _____

    _____

    Finish this definition of the word: people that _____

    _____.

    What are some related words and their parts of speech?

    _____

    Write a sentence that uses the word in the same way:

    _____

4. What is the prefix of the word *products?* _____ What part of speech is it?
_____ How do you know? _____
_____.

What does the word name? [people / places / things] Which definition is
most appropriate for the context? Which verb is related to the word?
[prod / produce / pride]
What are some related words and their parts of speech?

_____

Write a sentence that uses the word with the same meaning:

_____

5. What is the suffix of the word *available?* _____ What part of speech is it?
_____ How do you know? _____
_____

Which definition is most appropriate for the word in this context?
[single and looking / free; not busy / in good supply; obtainable]
What word is the opposite of *available?* _____
Write a sentence that uses the word with the same meaning:

_____

6. Which definition is most appropriate for the phrase *on the market?*
[in a grocery store / available for buying; for sale / favorable to sellers]
Write another sentence that illustrates the meaning of the phrase:

_____

7. What part of speech is the word *leads?* _____ How do you know? _____
_____

Which other word has the most similar meaning in this context?
[to show the way / to be first / to influence]
Which phrase has the opposite meaning of the phrase *leads us to buy?*
[makes us buy / keeps us from buying / follows our purchases]
Write a sentence that uses the word *lead* in the same way:

_____

8. What explanation is most appropriate for the phrase *can't afford?*
[don't have enough money for / find insulting / are able to buy]
Write another sentence that illustrates the meaning of the phrase:

_____

As you review to the vocabulary information in each row of the following chart, write the missing information in the empty boxes. (An X indicates that there is probably no information for that box.)

Vocabulary Item	Part of Speech	Definition or Words with Similar Meanings	Examples of Use in Context	Words with Opposite Meanings	Related Words
1. consume	v.	eat or drink; take in	How many calories do you <u>consume</u> in a typical day?	X	consumer (n.), consumerism (n.), consumption (n.)
2. brand	n.	a particular kind or make of product		X	brand (v.)
3. laundry	n.	clothes to wash		X	launder (v.), laundromat (n.)
4. admit		to confess or agree reluctantly that something is right		reject; deny	
5. sense		a physical or unclear emotional feeling		X	
6. attractive			Will advertised products make us more <u>attractive</u> to the opposite sex?		
7. stupid			Commercials often seem <u>stupid</u> to educated viewers.		
8. compete			Advertisers <u>compete</u> for customers to buy their products	X	
9. aggressively			Companies with big advertising budgets <u>aggressively</u> market their products.		
10. exaggerate				understate	exaggerated (adj.), exaggeration (n.)

Do you want more practice learning new vocabulary in systematic ways? Choose some of the vocabulary items from this or previous chapters that are especially important or useful, such as *controversial, brand, advice, examine, generic, plain, quality, discount, commercial, attractive, image, wise, product, mention, defective,* and so on. Make a chart like the one in this exercise. Write new vocabulary items in Column 1 and the appropriate information about each word or phrase in the other columns. You can put the same item into the chart more than once—with different meanings and perhaps as different parts of speech. As you read more and more, you will find the same words in various contexts and forms; you will begin using them correctly and appropriately in your own speech and writing.

2   **Real-Life Reading: Surveys and Questionnaires.**   Surveys and questionnaires are a major part of consumerism—in printed form, on the telephone, on the Internet, and so on. For instance, to market their products more successfully, manufacturers and advertisers create various kinds of customer surveys. These lists of questions, often with multiple-choice answers to choose from, are designed to collect information about consumer preferences and shopping habits. Following on page 267 is a simplified marketing questionnaire, containing typical sample questions.

Which words are new or difficult for you? Circle them and try to figure out their general or specific meanings. Then take the survey. (You can give real or made-up answers.) For each item, mark your preferences with Xs in the appropriate boxes. As you compare your answers to those of your classmates, explain the reasons for your choices.

3   **More Real-Life Reading.**   Here are some kinds of consumer-related reading material. Check (✔) the kinds available to you. Bring some examples to class, or copy some of the words from the materials. Write down the important vocabulary items with their meanings and phrase examples. Talk about the purpose and point of each piece of material. Summarize the important information.

- ■ _____ consumer or customer surveys—included with products, sent through the mail, or online

- ■ _____ supermarket ads—in newspapers or on fliers, with special offers and coupons

- ■ _____ newspaper ads for department store and other large store sales

- ■ _____ magazine ads

- ■ _____ other _____

For the magazine ads in particular, here are some questions to answer: What product or service does each ad advertise? What kind of consumer (teenage, adult, senior, rich, middle-income, etc.) is the ad directed at? What image of the product or service does the advertiser want to create? How do you know? (Which words lead you to this conclusion?) Do you find the ad effective in attracting attention? Why or why not? Would you buy this product or service on the basis of the ad? Why or why not?

Questionnaire

Please help our company better serve its customers. Answer the following questions by putting an X in the boxes of all the answers that apply.

1. How do you most often shop for groceries?
- ☐ I walk to small neighborhood stores.
- ☐ I go to open-air markets.
- ☐ I do my shopping in supermarkets.
- ☐ I buy from large discount warehouses with large-size packaging.
- ☐ I order groceries over the telephone or computer for home delivery.

2. Where do you get most of your other consumer items?
- ☐ In small neighborhood stores or downtown areas
- ☐ In indoor or outdoor shopping malls
- ☐ In large discount stores
- ☐ From mail-order companies
- ☐ From the Internet

3. Which of these large appliances do you have in your household?
- ☐ A freezer (not attached to the refrigerator)
- ☐ A dishwasher
- ☐ A washing machine and dryer, or a washer-dryer combination
- ☐ A microwave oven or convection oven
- ☐ Other _____

4. Which of these kinds of home entertainment do you own?
- ☐ Large-screen television
- ☐ Video recording and/or playback equipment (VCR, DVD, etc.)
- ☐ Digital still camera or video camera (camcorder)
- ☐ Stereo equipment: CD player, tape player, tuner, radio, and so on
- ☐ Video game players

5. Which of these kinds of office or business equipment do you own?
- ☐ Personal computer or Web TV
- ☐ Photocopier
- ☐ Fax (facsimile) machine
- ☐ Cordless phones, answering system
- ☐ Electronic adding machines, calculator

6. Which of these products do the members of your household use regularly?
- ☐ Over-the-counter health remedies
- ☐ Vitamins, food supplements, and nutritional products
- ☐ Skin and facial care products
- ☐ Shampoos and conditioners
- ☐ Toothpaste, mouthwash, or other oral hygiene products

7. How many people are there in your household? Circle the appropriate numbers.
- ☐ One adult only: under 30, 30–40, 40–50, 50–60, 60–70, over 70
- ☐ Adult couple only: under 30, 30–40, 40–50, 50–60, 60–70, over 70
- ☐ One or more adults with children ages 1–12: How many children? 1, 2, 3, 4, 5, 6 or more
- ☐ One or more adults with teenagers up to age 20: How many? 1, 2, 3, 4, 5, 6 or more
- ☐ Unrelated adults (members of more than one nuclear family): How many? 2, 3, 4, 5, 6 or more

8. What is your yearly family or household income?
- ☐ Under $20,000
- ☐ $20,000–$40,000
- ☐ $40,000–$75,000
- ☐ $75,000–$100,000
- ☐ Over $100,000

9. What are your living conditions or arrangements?
- ☐ We rent an apartment.
- ☐ We live in a mobile home park or have a motor home.
- ☐ We own a condominium or townhouse.
- ☐ We own a house or farm with land.
- ☐ I live in a dormitory or rent a room.

10. For which interests do you purchase the most products or services?
- ☐ Food and cooking, in-home entertaining
- ☐ Home education, reading, learning
- ☐ Sports, outdoor activities
- ☐ Home decorating
- ☐ Gardening, plant growing

PART 4   **Personal Stories and Humor**

1   Follow these steps for the two stories that give experiences and attitudes related to consumerism.

1.   Read each story quickly and retell the main events.

2.   Do you think each story is true? (Did it really happen?) Give reasons for your views.

3.   What do you think the point of each story is? In your opinion, what is the attitude of each writer about selling and buying or advertising in marketing?

4.   Tell or write about your own consumer experience—either as a seller or a shopper.

Big Business

[1]   Back in my country, when I was a child, I used to go to "market day" with my mother. One day each week, farmers used to bring their fruit and vegetables into the city. They closed one street to all cars, and the farmers set up tables for their produce. This outdoor market was a great place to shop. Everything was fresher than produce in grocery stores because the farmers brought it in immediately after the harvest. My mother and I always got there early in the morning to get the freshest produce.

The outdoor market was a wonderful adventure for a small child. It was like a festival—full of colors and sounds. There were red tomatoes, yellow lemons, green lettuce, peppers, grapes, onions. The farmers did their own advertising. They all shouted loudly for customers to buy their produce. "Come and buy my beautiful oranges! They're juicy and delicious and full of vitamins to make your children healthy and strong!"

Everyone used to argue with the farmers over the price of their produce. It was like a wonderful drama in a theater; the buyers and sellers were the "actors" in this drama. My mother was an expert at this. First, she picked the freshest, most attractive tomatoes, for example. Then she asked the price. The seller told her.

"What?" she said. She looked very surprised. "So expensive?"

The seller looked terribly hurt. "My dear lady!" he replied. "I am a poor, honest farmer. These are the cheapest tomatoes on the market!"

They always argued for several minutes before agreeing on a price. My mother took her tomatoes and left. Both buyer and seller were satisfied. The drama was over. ■

[2]   With my high-paying, high-pressure position in international marketing, I spend most of my time deciding about advertising, product image, slogans, and the like—and being unsure and nervous about my decisions. I want the products we represent to sell, of course, because I want to keep my job and be successful in it. So I need to learn from other company's mistakes. Here are some typical ones:

When Kentucky Fried Chicken entered the Chinese market, to their horror they discovered that their slogan "finger lickin' good" came out in Chinese characters as "eat your fingers off."

When Pepsi Cola tried to compete with Coca-Cola in China, the translation "Pepsi brings you back to life" was understood literally. In the Chinese language, it meant "Pepsi brings your ancestors back from the grave."

The Gerber Company is famous for selling baby food with a picture of a cute baby on the label. But then they found out that in parts of Africa where many people can't read, customers expect to see a picture of the contents of containers on the labels.

When Parker Pen Company marketed a ballpoint pen in Mexico, its ads were supposed to say "It won't leak in your pocket and embarrass you." However, because of a misunderstanding of the Spanish word "embarazar," the ads said, "It won't leak in your pocket and make you pregnant."

I love big business around the globe! ■

The Humor of Advertising

2 Advertising, in both print and broadcast form, is designed to attract attention. One way to get people to notice it is to make it funny. The humor may not appeal to all consumers, but it will get them to remember the ad or commercial—and therefore the product or service that the company wants to sell.

One of the most successful sales ideas in U.S. history was advertising for Burma-Shave, a brushless shaving cream, from 1927 to 1963. In a series of from four to six white-on-red highway signs—much smaller than billboards—there were many different funny little poems (pieces of writing in short lines that rhymed) related to the product in some way—or something else, like safe driving. While driving in their cars, people read the lines one by one. Following are a few of them. For each piece of humorous verse, answer these questions.

A.

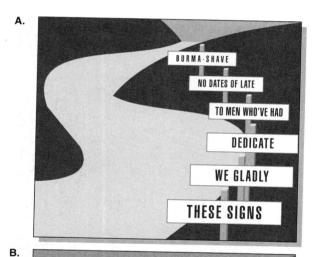

B.

C.

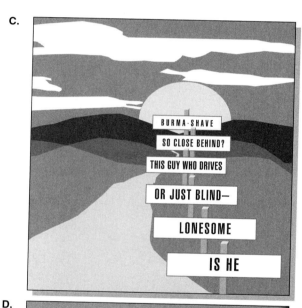

D.

1. Which two words rhyme? (Read the lines aloud in the appropriate rhythm to find out.)

2. What does the poem really mean literally—that is, what is its basic meaning?

3. Do you think the verse is funny? Why or why not?

4. Do you think the verse is good advertising—in other words, how might it help to sell the product?

5. Can you think of any funny short poems about products or kinds of products? If so—and if you get a laugh—perhaps you ought to go into advertising!

E.

F.

G.

H.

Video Activities: Spoiled Kids

Before You Watch. Discuss these questions in a group.

When you were a child:

1. How often did you receive gifts from your parents and relatives?
2. Was it hard for your parents to say "no" to you?
3. Did you have to work in the house?
4. Did you receive money from your parents?

Watch. Write answers to these questions.

1. What are some of the toys and things that Bret (the boy) and Jessica (the girl) have in their rooms? _____

2. How did Bret and Jessica get their things? _____

3. What is Jane Annunziata's profession? _____

4. Why do some American parents give their children so much? _____

_____

Watch Again. Match the opinions on the left with the speakers on the right.

1. _____ It's OK to have a lot of things if you appreciate what you have.

2. _____ People have a lot of money and they love their children, so they buy them toys.

3. _____ If parents have only one child, it's easy to give that child too much.

4. _____ Children who always get everything they want may have problems with their friends.

5. _____ It's easier to say yes to children than to say no.

6. _____ What children really want is time with their parents, not just a lot of stuff.

a. Psychologist
b. Jessica's mother
c. Bret
d. Toy store owner

After You Watch. In the video, the announcer says: "Psychologist Jane Annunziata helps kids and parents cope with a fairly new problem—*affluenza*—having too much and giving your child everything he wants."

You will not find the word *affluenza* in your dictionary. The psychologist created it out of two real words, affluence + influenza. Look up these words in your dictionary. What do they mean?

affluence: _____

influenza: _____

Now write a definition of affluenza: _____

_____

Photo Credits